A CONSTITUTIONALIST APPROACH TO THE EUROPEAN CONVENTION ON HUMAN RIGHTS

This book presents a new constitutional argument for the legitimacy of evolutive interpretation of the ECHR. It constructs a model, in which evolutive and static constitutional principles are balanced with each other.

The author argues that there are three possible interpretive approaches in timesensitive interpretations of the ECHR, but that only one of them is justifiable by reference to the constitutional principles of the ECHR in every single case.

The ECHR's constitutional principles either require an evolutive or static interpretation or they do not establish a preference relation at all, which leads to a margin of appreciation of the member states in the interpretation of the Convention. The balancing model requires the determination of the weights of the competing evolutive and static constitutional principles. For this purpose, the author defines weighting factors for determining the importance of evolutive or static interpretation in a concrete case.

Hart Studies in Constitutional Theory: Volume 3

Hart Studies in Constitutional Theory

Series Editors
Charles Barzun, University of Virginia, USA
Maartje De Visser, Singapore Management University
Matthias Klatt, University of Graz, Austria

The *Hart Studies in Constitutional Theory* series publishes thought-provoking works of scholarship addressing diverse aspects of constitutional theory in a concise and crystalline manner. Authors writing for this series cover a wide range of perspectives, methods, and regions, to enhance our understanding of constitutions as central institutions of modern public life. Taken together, the books in this series aim to challenge established wisdom and advance original ideas.

This series is a natural home for books interrogating the concepts and structures of constitutions on the national, the supranational and the international level. Its guiding philosophy is that the task of constitutional theory is not only to delineate the basic structures of government and to protect human rights, but also more broadly to offer methods for grappling with the social, political, and economic problems societies face today.

The series is open to theoretical, normative, analytical, empirical and comparative approaches, stemming from legal studies as well as from political philosophy and political science. In its ambition to become a global forum for debate about constitutional theory, the series editors welcome submissions for monographs as well as edited volumes from all parts of the world.

Recent titles in this series:

Proportionality and Facts in Constitutional Adjudication
by Anne Carter

The Methodology of Constitutional Theory
edited by Dimitrios Kyritsis and Stuart Lakin

A Constitutionalist Approach to the European Convention on Human Rights: The Legitimacy of Evolutive and Static Interpretation
by Lisa Sonnleitner

A Constitutionalist Approach to the European Convention on Human Rights

The Legitimacy of Evolutive and Static Interpretation

Lisa Sonnleitner

•HART•
OXFORD • LONDON • NEW YORK • NEW DELHI • SYDNEY

HART PUBLISHING

Bloomsbury Publishing Plc

Kemp House, Chawley Park, Cumnor Hill, Oxford, OX2 9PH, UK

1385 Broadway, New York, NY 10018, USA

29 Earlsfort Terrace, Dublin 2, Ireland

HART PUBLISHING, the Hart/Stag logo, BLOOMSBURY and the Diana logo are trademarks of Bloomsbury Publishing Plc

First published in Great Britain 2022

A catalogue record for this book is available from the British Library.

A catalogue record for this book is available from the Library of Congress.

Library of Congress Control Number: 2021055611

ISBN: HB: 978-1-50994-687-7
ePDF: 978-1-50994-689-1
ePub: 978-1-50994-688-4

Typeset by Compuscript Ltd, Shannon

Foreword

In our times of ever-growing constitutionalisation, constitutional structures are no longer limited to the legal province of the nation-state. They also exist in international and supranational spheres. The European Convention on Human Rights, on which the present monograph focusses, is one good example. Despite differences in both structure and detail, the European Union and the various regional systems for protecting human rights around the world also display characteristics of constitutional arenas. The discipline of constitutional theory accordingly has acute relevance in relation to these realms.

We are delighted that Dr Sonnleitner's book allows us to signal this international scope of our series early on. Theoretical analyses of constitutional structures beyond the state are at the heart of our series just as much as research on the classical canon of state-centred constitutions.

This book provides an illuminating discussion of one of the most controversial interpretive techniques deployed by the European Court of Human Rights, viz. evolutive interpretation. At its core, it queries to what extent the interpretation of rights is either open or resilient to societal change. To answer this question, the author develops a sophisticated theoretical argument that integrates evolutive interpretation and its counterpart, static interpretation. By engaging with the temporal dimension of rights interpretation, this monograph is exemplary in bridging constitutional theory with international law and the theory of legal argumentation.

In its ambition to provide normative guidance, Dr Sonnleitner's book reflects our series' intention of illuminating the practical impact of constitutional theory. It does not merely provide a theoretical analysis, but also draws conclusions as to the practical consequences thereof. Dr Sonnleitner's book is, just as we hope this series in its entirety will prove to be, built upon the insight that legitimate constitutional practices, which are not just incidentally legitimate, must be guided by a deeper understanding of the relations between norms, decisions, institutions, and methods. We are dependent upon this valuable function of theoretical research to provide systematic orientation, all the more in our modern times that are characterised by chronic information overload. Only in this way will we be able to in overcome the dictate of mere routines, the reign of unreflected day-to-day practices, and the fumbling around based on trial and error. There is nothing so practical as a good theory.

Maartje de Visser
Charles Barzun
Matthias Klatt
Singapore/Charlottesville/Graz, January 2022

Contents

PART III
BALANCED LEGITIMACY MODEL

PART IV
THE BALANCED LEGITIMACY MODEL APPLIED

List of Abbreviations

Art	Article
CETS, ETS	Council of Europe Treaty Series
CJEU	Court of Justice of the European Union
CM, Committee	Committee of Ministers (of the Council of Europe)
CoE	Council of Europe
ECHR, Convention	Convention for the Protection of Human Rights and Fundamental Freedoms/European Convention on Human Rights
EComHR, Commission	European Commission of Human Rights
ECtHR, Court	European Court of Human Rights
GC	Grand Chamber of the European Court of Human Rights
HUDOC	Database for the case law of the European Court of Human Rights and the former European Commission of Human Rights
ICJ	International Court of Justice
ILC	International Law Commission
MND	motor neurone disease
PACE	Parliamentary Assembly of the Council of Europe
UDHR	Universal Declaration of Human Rights
UN	United Nations
UNTS	United Nations Treaty Series
VCLT	Vienna Convention on the Law of Treaties

Table of Cases

Legal Documents and Reports

CDL-AD(2016)007, Study No 711/2013, Rule of Law Checklist 18 March 2016 (European Commission for Democracy Through Law).

CM(2008)170, The Council of Europe and the Rule of Law – An overview 21 November 2008 (Committee of Ministers of the Council of Europe).

Convention for the Protection of Human Rights and Fundamental Freedoms (Rome, 4 November 1950) (Council of Europe).

Doc 8560, Future action to be taken by the Council of Europe in the field of environmental protection, Report, 5 October 1999 (Council of Europe Parliamentary Assembly).

Doc 9791, Environment and human rights, Report, 16 April 2003 (Council of Europe Parliamentary Assembly).

Document A/6309/Rev.1: Reports of the International Law Commission on the second part of its seventeenth session and on its eighteenth session 1966 (International Law Commission).

High Level Conference on the Future of the European Court of Human Rights, Brighton Declaration (Brighton, 2012, Council of Europe).

Protocol No 6 to the Convention for the Protection of Human Rights and Fundamental Freedoms concerning the Abolition of the Death Penalty (Strasbourg, 28 April 1983) ETS No 114.

Protocol No 7 to the Convention for the Protection of Human Rights and Fundamental Freedoms (Strasbourg, 22 November 1984) ETS No 117.

Protocol No 11 to the Convention for the Protection of Human Rights and Fundamental Freedoms, restructuring the control machinery established thereby (Strasbourg, 11 May 1994) ETS No 155.

Protocol No 13 to the Convention for the Protection of Human Rights and Fundamental Freedoms concerning the Abolition of the Death Penalty in all circumstances (Strasbourg, 3 May 2003) ETS No 187.

Protocol No 15 amending the Convention for the Protection of Human Rights and Fundamental Freedoms (Strasbourg, 24 June 2013) CETS No 213.

Protocol to the Convention for the Protection of Human Rights and Fundamental Freedoms (Strasbourg, 20 March 1953) ETS No 009.

Report (A/61/10) of the International Law Commission on its 58th session (2006) (United Nations General Assembly).

Report (A/73/10) of the International Law Commission (Seventieth Session (30 April–1 June and 2 July 2018) International Law Commission).

Report at the fourth International Colloquy about the European Convention on Human Rights (Rome, 5–8 November 1975) H/Coll (75)2.

Resolution 800 (1983), Principles of Democracy (Council of Europe Parliamentary Assembly).

Resolution 1594 (2007), The principle of the Rule of Law 2007 (Council of Europe Parliamentary Assembly).

Resolution 1746 (2010), Democracy in Europe: Crisis and Perspectives (Council of Europe Parliamentary Assembly).

Statute of the Council of Europe (London, 5 May 1949) ETS No 1.

Third Report on the Law of Treaties Document A/CN.4/167, Vol II (1964) (Humphrey Waldock, Special Rapporteur, International Law Commission).

Third Summit of Heads of State and Government of the Council of Europe, Warsaw Declaration (Warsaw, 2005, Council of Europe).

UN General Assembly Resolution 217 A (III) Universal Declaration of Human Rights (Paris, 10 December 1948).

Vienna Convention on the Law of Treaties (Vienna, 23 May 1969) UNTS Vol 1155.

Introduction

SOCIETIES, MORAL CONCEPTS and ideas about what human rights people should have change in the course of time. The term 'family life' in Article 8 of the European Convention on Human Rights (ECHR, 'the Convention') illustrates the diverse ways in which modern society tests the practicability of human rights norms. In 1950 the drafters of the Convention probably did not think of applicants claiming to grant equal legal status to children born in and out of wedlock,[1] to facilitate change of gender in the birth register[2] or to recognise homosexual couples as families.[3] Yet, these matters have become pressing legal questions in many families since the entry into force of the ECHR. Such societal developments pose a particular challenge to the interpretation of human rights treaties such as the ECHR, which were negotiated decades ago as a bulwark against totalitarianism.[4] Should the ECHR be responsive to those changes in order to maintain an effective level of human rights protection? And if so, is it for the European Court of Human Rights (ECtHR) to determine the pace of this adaptation process through its interpretation of the Convention text? These are the central questions that triggered this investigation.

How the ECtHR should approach the interpretation of the ECHR was an open question from the entry into force of the Convention.[5] Although Article 32 ECHR transfers all authority in interpretive matters to the ECtHR, the text remains silent on the concrete interpretive approach that the Court should follow.[6] There is no reference to specific interpretive methods or to the methods of treaty interpretation in international law as established by the Vienna Convention on the Law of Treaties (VCLT).[7]

It took the Court until 1975 to clarify that it perceived itself to be bound by the interpretive rules of Articles 31–33 VCLT.[8] At about the same time, Max Sørensen, former President of the European Commission of Human Rights,

[1] *Marckx v Belgium* Series A no 31 (1979).

[2] *Christine Goodwin v UK* [GC] EHRR 2002-VI.

[3] *Schalk und Kopf v Austria* EHRR 2010-IV 409.

[4] Ed Bates, *The Evolution of the European Convention on Human Rights: From Its Inception to the Creation of a Permanent Court of Human Rights* (Oxford, Oxford University Press, 2010) 3 and 360.

[5] ibid 304ff.

[6] Art 32 ECHR extends the Court's jurisdiction 'to all matters concerning the interpretation and application of the Convention' but does not determine the interpretive methods that should be applied. See Convention for the Protection of Human Rights and Fundamental Freedoms (Rome, 4 November 1950) (Council of Europe).

[7] Arts 31–33 Vienna Convention on the Law of Treaties (Vienna, 23 May 1969) UNTS Vol 1155.

[8] *Golder v UK* Series A no 18 (1975) para 29.

in his report at the fourth International Colloquy about the ECHR in Rome 1975, for the first time in the ECHR context labelled the Convention a 'living legal instrument'.[9] What he meant by this was that the Convention should be interpreted in a more flexible manner in order to keep the rights in pace with the changing European society.[10] His main concerns for the necessity of a more evolutive reading of the Convention were the open-textured formulation of the rights on the one hand, and the enhanced political difficulty in amending the treaty on the other.[11] According to Sørensen, evolutive interpretation would be in full accordance with the core ideals behind the ECHR, being 'humanity, the rule of law and freedoms'.[12]

Three years later, in the case of *Tyrer v UK*, the ECtHR took up this label by Sørensen and called the Convention 'a living instrument ... which must be interpreted in the light of present-day conditions'.[13]

The case touched upon the question whether judicial corporal punishment by means of birching, as prescribed by the penal code at the Isle of Man, could be classified as degrading and thus be in breach of Article 3 ECHR.[14] Whereas these kinds of penal practices had been accepted by some member states at the time of the drafting of the Convention and continued to be publicly accepted on the Isle of Man, the penal systems of most member states had abandoned corporal punishment by the time of the *Tyrer* case.[15] A legislative development had thus taken place among the majority of European societies to refrain from any form of corporal punishment on behalf of the state at the time when *Tyrer* was decided. This development paved the way for the first explicit use of the 'living instrument' doctrine by the ECtHR. For more than 40 years now, the ECtHR has practised and further developed its evolutive interpretation of the ECHR. It has resulted in some of the most important – and controversial – decisions of the ECtHR and has contributed to a 'fine-tuning' of the rights and obligations under the Convention.[16] Many of those cases touched upon issues of discrimination[17] or on positive obligations of states to effectively protect people from criminal offences,[18] but in more general terms, evolutive interpretation has led to an up-to-date interpretation of most of the Convention rights.[19]

[9] Report at the fourth International Colloquy about the European Convention on Human Rights, (Rome, 5–8 November 1975) H/Coll (75)2 22.

[10] ibid 5–6.

[11] ibid 4–5.

[12] ibid 22.

[13] *Tyrer v UK* Series A no 26 (1978) para 31.

[14] ibid paras 28–30.

[15] ibid para 31.

[16] Luzius Wildhaber, 'Rethinking the European Court of Human Rights' in Jonas Christoffersen and Mikael R Madsen (eds), *The European Court of Human Rights between Law and Politics* (Oxford, Oxford University Press, 2011) 210.

[17] See, eg, *Marckx v Belgium* (n 1) on 'illegitimate children'; *Christine Goodwin v UK* [GC] (n 2) on the right of transsexuals; *Hirst v UK (No 2)* [GC] EHRR 2005-IX on prisoner voting rights.

[18] See, eg, *Opuz v Turkey* EHRR 2009-III on criminal prosecution of domestic violence against women; *M.C. v Bulgaria* EHRR 2003-XII on criminal prosecution of rape.

[19] See, eg, *Selmouni v France* [GC] (1999) EHRR 1999-V on the definition of torture regarding police custody (Art 3); *Schalk und Kopf v Austria* (n 3) on the definition of family life with regard

From the very beginning, evolutive interpretation has been accompanied by criticism from within the Court and outside. Evolutive interpretation is deemed to be one of the most contentious tools of the ECtHR.[20] The most famous opponent within the Court was the former British judge Sir Gerald Fitzmaurice, who sat on the bench of the Court in the 1970s, when it decided the first cases of evolutive interpretation such as *Tyrer v UK* or *Golder v UK*. The British judge dissented in both,[21] claiming that the ECHR was an instrument to protect Europe against the most serious breaches of human rights and not an instrument that should be used for indirect political reforms.[22] Opposition against the Court's practice of evolutive interpretation was also formed outside the Court, in the political as well as in the academic realm. The Court's evolutive approach to interpretation was a point of intense discussion at the High Level Conference in Brighton in 2012, a political reform meeting on the future of the ECHR. There, the member states of the Council of Europe (CoE) agreed on Additional Protocol No 15 amending the ECHR.[23] It amends the Preamble of the Convention in a way which leaves us with a question mark regarding the legitimacy of evolutive interpretation. The new Protocol adds a final paragraph to the Preamble of the Convention, which reads:

> Affirming that the High Contracting Parties, in accordance with the principle of subsidiarity, have the primary responsibility to secure the rights and freedoms defined in this Convention and the Protocols thereto, and that in doing so they enjoy a margin of appreciation, subject to the supervisory jurisdiction of the European Court of Human Rights established by this Convention.[24]

The new paragraph indirectly affects evolutive interpretation through its emphasis on the principles of subsidiarity and margin of appreciation. The principle of subsidiarity expresses the Court's function as a mere control mechanism for whether the member states, as the primary guardians of the Convention rights, have complied with their obligations.[25] The margin of appreciation doctrine is an approach developed by the ECtHR, which leaves the member states a certain room for manoeuvre in the application and implementation of the Convention rights.[26] The reference to these two principles in the new Preamble touches the

to homosexual couples; *Bayatyan v Armenia* [GC] EHRR 2011-IV on the right to conscientious objection (Arts 9 and 4); *Magyar Helsinki Bizottsag v Hungary* [GC] EHRR 2016 on the right of access to state-held information (Art 10); *Young, James and Webster v UK* Series A no 44 (1982) on the negative right not to be part of an association (Art 11).

[20] Björnstjern Baade, *Der EGMR als Diskurswächter* (Berlin, Springer, 2016) 157.

[21] Bates (n 4) 361f.

[22] *Tyrer v UK* (n 13) dissenting opinion of Judge Fitzmaurice, para 14.

[23] Protocol No 15 amending the Convention for the Protection of Human Rights and Fundamental Freedoms (Strasbourg, 24 June 2013) CETS No 213. Entry into force 1 August 2021.

[24] ibid Art 1.

[25] Janneke H Gerards, *General Principles of the European Convention on Human Rights* (Cambridge, Cambridge University Press, 2019) 5.

[26] ibid 168.

legitimacy sphere of evolutive interpretation for several reasons. First, while no other doctrine for the application of the Convention is mentioned in the Convention text, the margin of appreciation is the only one to which the text explicitly refers.[27] It seems as though the member states are seeking to push the ECtHR to be more deferential to national conceptions of human rights. Critics of the amendment have labelled this an illegitimate interference with the Court's autonomy to interpret the Convention.[28] Second, it is the first amendment to the Preamble since the drafting of the ECHR. Given that from a general point of view preambles are declarations specifying the identity of a legal system,[29] an amendment to the Preamble of the ECHR implies that the member states are aiming to redesign the identity of the CoE system.[30] It seems that the member states are trying to shape the Court's approach to interpretation in such a way that it should leave any evolution of the Convention rights to the member states.[31] A particular example of the critical reception of evolutive interpretation in the member states is the reluctance of the United Kingdom to implement judgments of the ECtHR concerning the evolutive interpretation of prisoners' voting rights.[32] This case even gave rise to a political discussion in the United Kingdom about leaving the Convention system.[33] There is also a lively academic debate on the illegitimacy of evolutive interpretation, which points to its democratic illegitimacy[34] or the risk of human rights inflation.[35] Consequently, the evolutive interpretation by the ECtHR has been appreciated as well as criticised in politics and academia. Yet, the question whether it is legitimate, and whether it leads to decisions with authoritative character, remains unanswered. This is the central question to which this book provides an answer.

The aim of this book is to determine the conditions of legitimate evolution of the interpretation of the ECHR in reaction to new factual or moral developments in society. The investigation also includes the contrasting quest for the

[27] Lisa Sonnleitner, 'The Democratic Legitimacy of Evolutive Interpretation by the European Court of Human Rights' (2019) 33(2) *Temple International & Comparative Law Journal* 279, 281.

[28] Amnesty International, 'Joint NGO input to the ongoing negotiations on the draft Brighton Declaration on the Future of the European Court of Human Rights, 20 March 2012' (2012) 3, www.amnesty.org/en/documents/IOR61/005/2012/en/.

[29] Mark Tushnet, 'The Possibilities of Comparative Constitutional Law' (1999) 108(6) *Yale Law Journal* 1225, 1271f; Vicki C Jackson, 'Comparative Constitutional Law: Methodologies' in Michel Rosenfeld (ed), *The Oxford Handbook of Comparative Constitutional Law* (Oxford, Oxford University Press, 2012) 71.

[30] Sonnleitner (n 27) 281.

[31] ibid 280–81.

[32] See, eg, *Hirst v UK (No 2)* [GC] (n 17).

[33] Alice Donald and Philip Leach, *Parliaments and the European Court of Human Rights* (Oxford, Oxford University Press, 2016) 6–7.

[34] Lord Sumption, 27th Sultan Azlan Shah Lecture: The Limits of Law, 20 November 2013, Kuala Lumpur, published in: Lord Sumption, 'The Limits of Law' in NW Barber, Richard Ekins and Paul Yowell (eds), *Lord Sumption and the Limits of the Law* (Oxford, Hart Publishing, 2016).

[35] Alfred WB Simpson, 'Hersch Lauterpacht and the Genesis of the Age of Human Rights' (2004) 120 *Law Quarterly Review* 49, 78.

conditions of legitimate stagnation in the Convention's interpretation by means of static interpretation. Static interpretation means that the ECtHR does not further develop the interpretation of the Convention but leaves these issues to the member states of the CoE. It needs to be settled from the outset that this book does not aim to provide a descriptive analysis of the ECtHR's practice of evolutive interpretation. Rather, the research will determine the legitimate role of evolutive and static interpretation in a more abstract manner while still being embedded in the concrete context of interpretation of the ECHR. This book presents a normative theory for the legitimacy of evolutive and static interpretation of the ECHR.

What do I mean by legitimacy? Legitimacy is intrinsically connected with the concept of 'authority'. A court may use a theory of interpretation only if it has authority to do so.[36] Hence, whenever the ECtHR interprets evolutively, it raises a claim to the authority of its decision. The crucial question is whether cases of evolutive interpretation have authoritative character, hence, whether they must be obeyed by the member states to the Convention. This is a question of legitimacy. One can distinguish between normative and descriptive accounts of legitimacy.[37] The latter requires that people have faith in the authority of an institution or decision in order for it to be legitimate. This descriptive account of legitimacy was fundamentally shaped by Max Weber and his notion of 'Legitimitätsglaube'.[38] Contrary to that, I will use the term legitimacy in a normative sense, which requires that the claimed authority is justifiable.[39] For example, Raz's account of the legitimacy of a political authority is a normative account, which is linked to the justification of this authority.[40] Only if an authority fulfils a certain threshold of justifiability is there a moral obligation to obey it.[41] I follow the idea that justifiability is key for the legitimacy of evolutive and static interpretation. Yet, how do we pass the threshold of good justification? I argue that the justification of the Convention's interpretation must conform to the constitutional commands of the ECHR. Consequently, this book constructs a justification model, which draws the legitimacy of evolutive and static interpretation from the constitutional principles of the ECHR.

The second theme that drives this investigation is the debate on absolute or relative legitimacy of evolutive interpretation. Absolute legitimacy means

[36] Arguing in the context of American constitutional interpretation: Robert Post, 'Theories of Constitutional Interpretation' (1990) 30 *Representations* 13, 19.

[37] Fabienne Peter, 'Political Legitimacy' in Edward N Zalta (ed), *The Stanford Encyclopedia of Philosophy*, 2017, https://plato.stanford.edu/archives/sum2017/entries/legitimacy/.

[38] Max Weber, *Wirtschaft und Gesellschaft: Grundriss der verstehenden Soziologie* (5th edn, Tübingen, Mohr-Siebeck, 2009) 122.

[39] Peter (n 37).

[40] Joseph Raz, *The Morality of Freedom* (Oxford, Clarendon Press, 2010) chapters 2 and 3; Joseph Raz, *Between Authority and Interpretation: On the Theory of Law and Practical Reason* (Oxford, Oxford University Press, 2009) chapter 13, especially pp 353f on constitutional interpretation.

[41] Peter (n 37).

that it is legitimate in any case concerning the interpretation of the ECHR, whereas relative legitimacy means that the legitimacy depends on the fulfilment of further requirements that are relative to the specific circumstances of the case. Most legitimacy theories in the academic discourse about evolutive interpretation build on arguments that legitimise the use of evolutive interpretation in all cases.[42] Alternatively, there are theories that dismiss the legitimacy of evolutive interpretation in any case while arguing in favour of an exclusive legitimacy of static interpretation. These absolute theories imply that once the normative source of evolutive or static interpretation is identified *in abstracto*, a court no longer needs further justification for applying the interpretive argument in a concrete case. This book proves absolute theories wrong. Instead, it defends a relative legitimacy theory for static and evolutive interpretation, according to which they are justified in principle, while their concrete legitimacy must be justified case by case. The theory builds on the argument that the constitutional system of the ECHR protects competing constitutional principles. Chapter 7 identifies the principles of human rights, democracy and the rule of law as the constitutional core of the Convention. There is an innate dichotomy in these three principles between more formal and more substantive aspects. This dichotomy creates tension within the constitutional core. This tension is not problematic, however. It reflects the dual nature of law, which has a real and an ideal dimension. While the real dimension requires static interpretation, the ideal dimension requires evolutive interpretation. This is the reason why there can be no absolute answer to the question of legitimacy of evolutive or static interpretation. The dual nature of law requires a relative legitimacy, which depends on a case-sensitive consideration of the Convention's constitutional principles in the justification process. Consequently, I argue that the tension between the competing constitutional principles can be resolved by means of balancing. In this book I construct a balancing model for determining the legitimacy of evolutive and static interpretation of the ECHR.

Why is it relevant to study the legitimacy of evolutive and static interpretation in the concrete context of the ECHR? Evolutive interpretation is not an exclusive practice of the ECtHR. National constitutional courts and other international courts make use of evolutive interpretation as well. The debate on matters of 'intertemporal interpretation' is not new to scholars of international and constitutional law either.[43] The ECtHR's picture of the Convention as a living instrument connects to older debates in constitutional law on the idea of a 'living constitution', which refers to 'judicial development of constitutional law'.[44] Kavanagh has demonstrated that many national supreme courts or

[42] This will be demonstrated by means of the analysis of the current legitimacy arguments in Chapter 3.

[43] TO Elias, 'The Doctrine of Intertemporal Law' (1980) 74(2) *American Journal of International Law* 285.

[44] Aileen Kavanagh, 'The Idea of a "Living Constitution"' (2003) 16(1) *Canadian Journal of Law and Jurisprudence* 55, 56.

constitutional courts, such as the courts in Canada, Ireland or the United States, do use evolutionary approaches to interpretation.[45] The idea of static interpretation connects to the debate on originalism, which claims that a legal norm needs to be interpreted in line with the intentions of the original drafters or the original meaning of the text.[46] There is still a lively debate on originalism and dynamism in interpretation, mostly among American scholars.[47] Yet, 'the legitimacy-dilemma of intertemporal interpretation is no less acute in international law than in other fields of law'.[48] The International Court of Justice (ICJ), in its *Report on the Legal Consequences for States of the continued presence of South Africa in Namibia*, dating from 1971, stated that 'certain concepts are not static, but were by definition evolutionary'.[49] In the more recent case of *Dispute regarding Navigational and Related Rights (Costa Rica v Nicaragua)*, the ICJ stated that the use of generic terms in treaties implies that the contracting parties have agreed on an evolutive interpretation of these terms.[50] Since evolutive interpretation is thus an approach to interpretation that is also practised by other courts, the choice of studying the ECHR rather than any other legal system requires further justification. I argue that the legitimacy of evolutive interpretation is contextual. Although the legitimacy model, which I present in this book, has a sufficient level of abstraction to be transferable to other legal systems, concrete legitimacy can only be established on the basis of the constitutionalist principles in a specific legal system. The practicability of the theory can thus only be demonstrated by means of a concrete example. Therefore, it is necessary to investigate the topic with focus on a specific legal system. Additionally, the ECHR is one of the most advanced and progressive systems for the protection of human rights on a global level.[51] Chapter 6 demonstrates the advanced level of constitutionalisation in the ECHR in more detail. Lastly, the fact that the ECtHR is the focus of attention of the international debate on the legitimacy of evolutive interpretation renders the study of this specific human rights protection system particularly relevant. It has the potential to make a vital contribution to the most controversial debate on evolutive interpretation in international law by developing a convincing legitimacy model.

[45] ibid 55.

[46] Jack M Balkin, *Living Originalism* (Cambridge, MA, Belknap Press of Harvard University Press, 2011) 3, 6f.

[47] See, eg, David A Strauss, *The Living Constitution* (Oxford, Oxford University Press 2010); Amy Gutmann and Antonin Scalia (eds), *A matter of Interpretation: Federal Courts and the Law* (Princeton, NJ, Princeton University Press, 1997); Balkin (n 46).

[48] Christopher A Ford, 'Judicial Discretion in International Jurisprudence: Article 38(1)(C) and "General Principles of Law"' (1994) 5 *Duke Journal of Comparative and International Law* 35, 36.

[49] *Legal Consequences for States of the continued presence of South Africa in Namibia (South West Africa) notwithstanding Security Council Resolution 276* Advisory Opinion, ICJ Reports 1971 para 53.

[50] *Dispute regarding navigational and related rights (Costa Rica v Nicaragua)* Judgment, ICJ Reports 2009 para 66.

[51] Bates (n 4) 4.

This book is divided into four parts and 13 chapters, preceded by an introduction and followed by a conclusion. Part I sets up the fundaments of the theory presented in this book. As my argument builds on Alexy's idea of the dual nature of law, Chapter 1 explores this concept of law, which also informs the concept of human rights. I have already pointed out that this book does not aim to provide a descriptive analysis of the ECtHR's interpretive practice in intertemporal interpretation. Therefore, Chapter 2 introduces a new concept of evolutive and static interpretation, which places the two interpretive approaches in the time dimension of interpretation. It highlights why the study of the legitimacy of evolutive interpretation is intimately connected to the study of static interpretation.

Many scholars have discussed the legitimacy of evolutive interpretation of the ECHR, and they have introduced a variety of argumentative paths for proving or disproving its legitimacy.[52] I will demonstrate in Chapter 3 that so far these efforts have remained unfruitful. The debate is dominated by three main approaches, which either ground the legitimacy of evolutive interpretation in one of the canons of interpretation of Articles 31–33 VCLT,[53] or in particular principles of international law,[54] or which build legitimacy on a factual basis by tying its justification to the existence of a consensus among the member states of the CoE.[55] One of the major weaknesses of these arguments is that they represent absolute legitimacy arguments that either neglect or overstate the role of static interpretation. Those which overstate the role of static interpretation mostly do so because they criticise evolutive interpretation for infringing principles such as sovereignty, democracy and the rule of law. Chapter 4 addresses these critical views and reinforces the argument that both evolutive and static interpretation assume a legitimate role in the interpretation of the ECHR if they pass the threshold of justifiability.

In this book I advance the argument that the constitutional principles of the ECHR determine this threshold of justifiability. Part II of the book constructs

[52] See, eg, George Letsas, 'The ECHR as a Living Instrument: Its Meaning and Legitimacy' in Andreas Føllesdal, Birgit Peters and Geir Ulfstein (eds), *Constituting Europe: The European Court of Human Rights in a National, European, and Global Context* (Cambridge, Cambridge University Press, 2013); Kanstantsin Dzehtsiarou, *European Consensus and the Legitimacy of the European Court of Human Rights* (Cambridge, Cambridge University Press, 2015); Steven Greer, *The European Convention on Human Rights: Achievements, Problems and Prospects* (Cambridge, Cambridge University Press, 2008); Eirik Bjorge, *The Evolutionary Interpretation of Treaties* (Oxford, Oxford University Press, 2014).

[53] See, eg, Bjorge (n 52); Rudolph Bernhardt, 'Evolutive Treaty Interpretation, Especially of the European Convention on Human Rights' (1999) 42 *German Yearbook of International Law* 11; Soren C Prebensen, 'Evolutive Interpretation of the ECHR' in Paul Mahoney, F Matscher, H Petzold and L Wildhaber (eds), *Protecting Human Rights: The European Perspective: Studies in Memory of Rolv Ryssdal* (Cologne, Heymanns, 2000); for a more detailed discussion of these approaches see Chapter 3.

[54] These arguments are particularly common in the ECtHR's justifications of evolutive interpretations, as Chapter 3 will demonstrate.

[55] Dzehtsiarou (n 52).

the constitutional framework for the legitimacy of intertemporal interpretation of the ECHR. Given the fact that the object of analysis is an international human rights treaty the constitutional nature of which is disputable, Chapter 5 introduces the arguments of cosmopolitan constitutionalism and deliberative constitutionalism, which will then be applied to determine the constitutional status of the ECHR in Chapter 6. In Chapter 7 I argue that the three principles of human rights, democracy and the rule of law constitute the main body of the Convention's constitution. These principles display formal and substantive sides, which are constantly in tension. This innate duality of the Convention's constitution is key for understanding that, in principle, evolutive and static interpretation are both justifiable by normative constitutional principles.

The finding that the Convention's constitutional core protects competing principles serves as a starting point for the legitimacy model, which I construct in Part III of the book. Chapter 8 introduces the idea of balancing principles, which is usually applied to resolve conflicts between colliding fundamental rights,[56] to the debate on the legitimacy of intertemporal interpretation. I will strongly defend the argument that the balancing of the Convention's constitutional principles for determining the legitimacy of the interpretive approach is preferable to other arguments for establishing a ranking between interpretive methods. Chapter 9 then constructs the balancing model in detail, while also reflecting on criticism of the use of balancing in human rights adjudication. Chapter 10 deals with one of the most difficult issues arising in the use of balancing: the external justification of the weights accorded to the relevant constitutional principles. I present evolutive and static weighting rules, which help to determine the concrete weights of the principles in a case.

Part IV illustrates the practicability of the theoretical model by applying it to selected cases of the ECtHR. Chapters 11, 12 and 13 discuss the subject matters of the right to divorce, the right to assisted suicide and the right to preservation of the environment, which currently pose challenges to the interpretation of the ECHR. The practical application of the theory to these cases reveals that the balancing model leads to reasonable outcomes in intertemporal interpretation. The balancing of the Convention's constitutional principles enables us to identify clearly whether evolutive interpretation or static interpretation is the legitimate interpretive approach to a case, and whether the member states enjoy a margin of appreciation in their interpretation of the Convention rights.

By the end of the book, we will know that the ECHR rests on a very sound constitutional footing. Reflecting the ideal and real dimension of law, the constitutional core protects static as well as evolutive constitutional principles. Paradoxically as it may seem, the study of this book demonstrates ambivalent behaviour by the member states of the CoE, which have contributed

[56] For the major work on the theory of balancing, see Robert Alexy, *A Theory of Constitutional Rights* (Julian Rivers trans, Oxford, Oxford University Press, 2010 (repr)).

tremendously to the fostering of evolutive constitutional principles since the entry into force of the Convention, while criticising the ECtHR for its evolutive interpretation. Recent efforts to strengthen the Court's subsidiary role or its respect for the state's margin of appreciation through the amendment of the Convention's Preamble are redundant. These values already form an essential part of the Convention's constitutional core. From the innate tension within the Convention's constitution, it follows that both evolutive and static interpretation are justifiable in principle. The key to the concrete legitimacy of evolutive or static interpretation lies in the Court's justification, which must strike a reasonable balance between evolutive and static constitutional principles.

Part I

Fundamentals

THE ECTHR DECLARED in various judgments that it would interpret the ECHR evolutively. Yet, what exactly is this interpretive approach we are talking about? How should we conceive of evolutive interpretation? And should we accept this practice as being legitimate? This chapter will explore these fundamental questions. It will not accept that due to the manifold use of this interpretive doctrine, 'the ECtHR is allowed to "play" the "living instrument"'.[1]

Chapter 1 will elucidate the theoretical framework of analysis. It presents the underlying concept of law, and particularly of human rights, which informs this study. Chapter 2 will then construct a new concept for evolutive interpretation, which goes beyond the Court's practice. Chapter 3 investigates academic theories and the Court's justifications for the legitimacy of evolutive interpretation. Finally, Chapter 4 analyses critical voices arguing against the legitimacy of evolutive interpretation.

Part I of this book will demonstrate that the key to the legitimacy problem lies in a theory that is not only case sensitive, but which also shows due respect to static as well as evolutive elements. This is exactly what is missing in existing legitimacy theories.

[1] Christian Djeffal, 'Dynamic and Evolutive Interpretation of the ECHR by Domestic Courts? An Inquiry into the Judicial Architecture of Europe' in Helmut P Aust and Georg Nolte (eds), *The Interpretation of International Law by Domestic Courts: Uniformity, Diversity, Convergence* (Oxford, Oxford University Press, 2016) 177.

1

On the Concepts of Law and Human Rights

As I WILL delve deeply into the interpretation of human rights, I first need to clarify the concept not only of human rights, but of law in general. Böckenförde has rightly stated that there is an intrinsic connection between the constitutional interpretation and the underlying theory of constitutional rights.[1] Taking this observation to hold true for the realm of human rights interpretation as well, my concepts of law and human rights will be presented briefly in the following. I will start by recapitulating a particular theory for the concept of law by Alexy, the 'dual nature of law' (Section I), and will then continue with a delineation of the underlying concept of human rights (Section II). While I am fully aware that these concepts of law and human rights are prone to criticism in some respect, I am convinced that these are the most persuasive theories we currently have. I will thus not go into detail about alternative theories but will simply introduce them so that readers can follow my subsequent argument.

I. THE DUAL NATURE OF LAW

While the main subject of this study is international human rights as a specific category of law, and their interpretation, I follow an underlying concept of law, which informs the analytical framework for my analysis of human rights interpretation. This is a non-positivist concept of law. It has implications not only for the more specific concept of human rights, but also for the interpretation of human rights.

Following a suggestion by Alexy, law has a dual nature.[2] It combines a real dimension, which embraces authoritative issuance and social acceptance, and an ideal dimension, which stands for the law's claim to correctness. This claim is a claim to moral correctness, which could also be called a claim to truth or objectivity.[3] Consequently, law has a legal and moral character.

[1] Ernst-Wolfgang Böckenförde, 'Grundrechtstheorie und Grundrechtsinterpretation' in Ralf Dreier (ed), *Probleme der Verfassungsinterpretation: Dokumentation einer Kontroverse* (Baden-Baden, Nomos, 1976) 266–67.

[2] Robert Alexy, 'The Dual Nature of Law' (2010) 23(2) *Ratio Juris* 167, 167.

[3] ibid 167, 170.

The connection between the claim to correctness and morality has been criticised for being irrational as it is prone to moral subjectivity or relativism.[4] In reaction to this criticism, the dual-nature theory adheres to discourse theory, which provides a procedure of rational practical discourse and which helps to achieve outcomes that are as correct as possible.[5] A rational practical discourse empowers everyone to participate equally in a discourse that takes place under certain conditions, which enhance the rationality of the discourse.[6]

Law's claim to correctness is twofold. Although the primary claim to correctness aims at justice, the dual-nature thesis accepts that the real or positivised dimension of law also serves valuable principles such as legal certainty. Therefore, according to Alexy, the claim to correctness has a second level, which looks not only at the ideal dimension, but also at the real dimension, and thus at legal certainty.[7] This second level is relevant because on its first, purely ideal level, the claim to correctness might end up in legitimate moral disagreement, that is to say a situation in which rational discourse leads to several morally equally acceptable outcomes.[8] In this case, the correctness follows from the real dimension of law, hence from positive law as established in a democratic procedure. However, the second level, as indicated above, actually combines the real and the ideal dimension in order to ensure that the democratically achieved outcomes are in conformity with law's claim to correctness.[9] From this it follows that the dual-nature concept of law grants not only 'ideal correctness' in the sense of justice, but also 'real correctness' in the sense of legal certainty. Hence, both dimensions of law are indispensable for legal practice.[10]

Yet, naturally the ideal and real dimension of law often compete in practice, which requires that both are balanced.[11] According to this concept of law, justice and legal certainty thus constantly need to be put in the correct proportion. This balance is inherent in the concept of law itself.[12]

II. THE CONCEPT OF HUMAN RIGHTS

The ECHR, as an international human rights treaty, sets up a list of rights that can be classified as legal human rights.[13] Yet, it is important to distinguish

[4] ibid 171–72.

[5] ibid 171–72.

[6] ibid 172. For further information on the conditions of the discourse, see Robert Alexy, *A Theory of Legal Argumentation: The Theory of Rational Discourse as Theory of Legal Justification* (Ruth Adler and Neil MacCormick trans, Oxford, Oxford University Press, 2011).

[7] Alexy, 'The Dual Nature of Law' (n 2) 174.

[8] ibid 173.

[9] ibid.

[10] ibid 174.

[11] ibid.

[12] ibid.

[13] Samantha Besson, 'Justifications' in Daniel Moeckli, Sangeeta Shah and Sandesh Sivakumaran (eds), *International Human Rights Law* (3rd edn, Oxford, Oxford University Press, 2018) 28, arguing in the context international human rights treaties in general.

whether one follows a conception of human rights as legal rights or as legal and moral rights. While the first conception assumes that human rights are 'created by law',[14] the latter assumes that human rights are moral rights that are 'recognized by law'.[15] This distinction between human rights as legal or moral rights can be connected with Alexy's terminology of the real and ideal dimension of law, which I have discussed in the previous section. Legal rights can be accorded to the real dimension of law, eg because they have been issued by a competent authority, while human rights as moral rights would belong to the ideal dimension of law.[16] If human rights become positivised in a human rights catalogue, the real and ideal dimension of human rights are connected.[17] Conceiving of human rights as legal rights implies that they may or may not correspond to moral rights.[18] Conceptualising human rights as legal and moral rights implies that a legal human right, implicitly or explicitly, seeks to give effect to a more abstract, pre-existing moral right.[19] Arguably, legal human rights may also create moral rights 'in recognition of certain fundamental moral interests'.[20] I take the conception of human rights as legal and moral rights as the basis of my study.

The way in which we conceptualise human rights has implications for the way in which we may justify their authority.[21] While purely legal justifications suffice for human rights as legal rights, human rights conceptions, which entail moral rights are in need of a further moral justification.[22] Whereas most theories for the justification of human rights strive for moral justifications in the fashion of a '"top-down" derivation of human rights'[23] from moral justifications, it seems more reasonable not to lose track of legal human rights practice in the justification of human rights.[24] This is achieved by 'bottom-up'[25] approaches, which stress the relevance of legal reasoning for the normative justification of human rights.[26]

I will thus follow a bottom-up concept for the justification of human rights, which is best expressed in Forst's 'constructivist conception of human rights'.[27] It is based on the central idea that every human being has the

[14] Joseph Raz, 'Human Rights in the Emerging World Order' (2010) 1(1) *Transnational Legal Theory* 31, 34.
[15] ibid.
[16] Alexy, 'The Dual Nature of Law' (n 2) 178.
[17] ibid.
[18] Raz (n 14) 34.
[19] ibid.
[20] Besson (n 13) 28.
[21] ibid 27.
[22] ibid 29.
[23] ibid.
[24] Buchanan stresses that the justification of human rights should not focus exclusively on moral justifications: Allen E Buchanan, *The Heart of Human Rights* (Oxford, Oxford University Press, 2014) chapter 2, especially at 82; Besson (n 13) 29.
[25] Besson (n 13) 29.
[26] ibid.
[27] Rainer Forst, *The Right to Justification: Elements of a Constructivist Theory of Justice* (Jeffrey Flynn trans, New York, Columbia University Press, 2012) 203.

basic right to justification.[28] It expresses the claim of every individual to be respected as a moral person who has the right to be given reasons for the way he or she is treated.[29] This leads to a conception of human rights that is thoroughly constructivist, as the claim for providing reasons leads to an ongoing process of justification of rights which is never concluded.[30] The constructivist conception of human rights is fully compatible with the conception of human rights followed by Alexy.[31] According to Alexy, the moral justification of human rights lies in their rational justifiability.[32] Furthermore, the justification of a concrete human right must be constructed in a concrete context due to the abstractness of positivised human rights.[33] Forst's conception of human rights is universal as it only institutionalises a 'central morality', which makes the concrete justification of rights and institutions as well as the set of legitimate reasons for their justification dependent on the concrete context of the right.[34] The only condition for a right to be a human right then is its justifiability by means of rational arguments that cannot be rejected by a reasonable person.[35] Whereas this justificatory core of human rights is universal as it cannot reasonably be denied by any culture, the concrete set of reasons may vary between different cultures.[36] Consequently, the model provided by Forst also amounts to a discursive concept of human rights, which connects to discourse theory.[37]

Exactly because of its inherent focus on legal reasoning, Forst's theory is particularly appealing for studies of human rights interpretation. Given the interpretive character of human rights, it appears that they are dynamic to a certain extent. Yet, is evolutive interpretation a legitimate way to do justice to this dynamic feature? In order to answer this fundamental question, we need to be sure what exactly we understand by evolutive interpretation. The following chapter constructs a concept of evolutive interpretation.

[28] ibid 205.
[29] ibid 209–10.
[30] ibid 211–12.
[31] Robert Alexy, 'Die Institutionalisierung der Menschenrechte im demokratischen Verfassungsstaat' in Stefan Gosepath and Georg Lohmann (eds), *Philosophie der Menschenrechte* (Frankfurt am Main, Suhrkamp, 2007) 246–54.
[32] ibid 249–50.
[33] ibid 253–54.
[34] Forst (n 27) 212.
[35] ibid 213, but then he argues more precisely at 215 that the reasons provided must meet the requirements of reciprocity and generality.
[36] ibid 215.
[37] ibid 217.

2

A New Concept of Evolutive and Static Interpretation

IN STUDYING THE legitimacy of evolutive interpretation, it strikes one that the debate actually turns on a doctrine without a concept. There is no clear-cut definition of evolutive interpretation. In its case law, the ECtHR usually confines itself to the phrase as established in *Tyrer*, which states that the ECHR is a 'living instrument … which must be interpreted in the light of present-day conditions'.[1]

However, instead of defining evolutive interpretation, this is rather a statement that the ECHR should be interpreted in an evolutive manner. It remains unclear what exactly the Court means by the terms 'living instrument' or 'present-day conditions'. This results in the fact that scholars, judges and practitioners have different concepts in mind when talking about evolutive interpretation.

Additionally, authors use different labels such as 'dynamic interpretation', 'living instrument doctrine' and 'evolutive interpretation'.[2] I perceive the three of them to refer to the same phenomenon in the interpretation of the Convention, but I stick to the latter label in this book. This is because the use of the term 'living instrument' would create the wrong impression that my concept of evolutive interpretation is based on the Court's practice of evolutive interpretation. The term 'dynamic interpretation' is less frequently used in the academic debate than the term 'evolutive interpretation'. It has even been argued that the term evolutive interpretation expresses its connection to societal development in a better way than the term dynamic interpretation.[3]

This chapter introduces a comprehensive, normative concept of evolutive interpretation which is not confined to the analysis of conceptual elements

[1] *Tyrer v UK* Series A no 26 (1978) para 31.

[2] See, eg, Kanstantsin Dzehtsiarou, 'European Consensus and the Evolutive Interpretation of the European Convention on Human Rights' (2011) 12(10) *German Law Journal* 1730; George Letsas, 'The ECHR as a Living Instrument: Its Meaning and Legitimacy' in Andreas Føllesdal, Birgit Peters and Geir Ulfstein (eds), *Constituting Europe: The European Court of Human Rights in a National, European, and Global Context* (Cambridge, Cambridge University Press, 2013) Malgosia Fitzmaurice, 'Dynamic (Evolutive) Interpretation of Treaties' (2009) 22 *Hague Yearbook on International Law* 3.

[3] Rudolph Bernhardt, 'Evolutive Treaty Interpretation, Especially of the European Convention on Human Rights' (1999) 42 *German Yearbook of International Law* 11, 12, fn 3.

based on the Court's practice. No one so far has provided a similar comprehensive account of evolutive interpretation.[4] The suggested model embraces three elements. First, evolutive interpretation is not an interpretive method itself, but forms part of a normative theory of interpretation which is located on a meta-level of interpretive methods. Second, evolutive interpretation may unfold in all methods of interpretation as an element of their time dimension. Third, the point of reference for evolution as opposed to stagnation is the state of established interpretations of rights and obligations as established in the Court's case law or by the drafters of the ECHR. This is to say that the conceptualisation of evolutive interpretation necessarily demands a conceptualisation of static interpretation as well. In the following, these three elements will be presented in more detail.

I. EVOLUTIVE INTERPRETATION WITHIN A NORMATIVE THEORY OF INTERPRETATION

The first element concerns the very nature of evolutive interpretation as an interpretive approach. The academic discourse about evolutive interpretation oscillates between categorising it as an interpretive method or an interpretive principle.[5] The qualification as a method implies that like other interpretive methods such as literal or systematic interpretation, evolutive interpretation is a means to identify the meaning of a term.

It is maintained here that evolutive interpretation forms part of a normative theory of intertemporal interpretation. It is certainly not an interpretive method that adds up to the other classic canons as set forth in the VCLT in the substantive interpretation of a right.[6] As Senden states, 'Qualifying evolutive interpretation as a method of interpretation, thus, wrongly implies that a judge with the help of this principle alone can interpret a specific provision'.[7]

Evolutive interpretation tells us something about how to approach an interpretation, but it provides no semantic information about a right. In order to identify an evolution in the meaning of a norm, evolutive interpretation needs to be informed by other arguments, be it a comparative analysis or a purposive interpretation or any other canon of interpretation. Consequently, one cannot

[4] I have outlined an embryonic version of this concept in my article: Lisa Sonnleitner, 'The Democratic Legitimacy of Evolutive Interpretation by the European Court of Human Rights' (2019) 33(2) *Temple International & Comparative Law Journal* 279, 285–87.

[5] Steven Greer, *The European Convention on Human Rights: Achievements, Problems and Prospects* (Cambridge, Cambridge University Press, 2008) 193–94. Greer is one of the few exceptions who speaks of interpretive principles. He does not clarify the implications of this qualification however. For a good overview of the 'chaos' in the literature, see Hanneke Senden, *Interpretation of Fundamental Rights in a Multilevel Legal System: An Analysis of the European Court of Human Rights and the Court of Justice of the European Union* (Cambridge, Intersentia, 2011) 71.

[6] Senden (n 5) 145–46.

[7] ibid 72.

identify the meaning of a norm by means of evolutive interpretation. This evaluation is shared by Djeffal, who defines evolutive interpretation as the 'result' of interpretation,[8] and Senden, who categorises it as a principle of interpretation which realises the 'general objective' to interpret a treaty in a dynamic instead of a static fashion.[9] The qualification as an interpretive principle remains quite diverse and obscure however. Greer, for example, does not explain what exactly he means by interpretive principle,[10] but from his use of the term it seems that he refers to all doctrines of interpretation that are used in the Court's practice, and which go beyond the methods listed in Articles 31–33 VCLT.

Chirardis argues that there are 'tools' for realising evolutive interpretation. According to his understanding, some interpretive tools of the ECtHR, such as the living instrument doctrine, autonomous concepts, or practical and effective rights, serve the function of implementing evolutive interpretation.[11] This seems to imply that he perceives evolutive interpretation as an interpretive goal that may be realised by tools of interpretation, but which is not a tool itself.

To me, evolutive interpretation has a guiding function whenever the use of interpretive methods leads to a variety of interpretive outcomes.[12] It will often be the case that interpretive arguments will lead to different, equally possible interpretations of a norm.[13] For example, an intentionalist argument might reveal an intended meaning that differs from the meaning following a purposive argument, which asks for the rational purpose of a norm. As the general rule of interpretation in Article 31 VCLT also institutionalises more than one interpretive method, international courts such as the ECtHR, which apply these methods, will often arrive at a variety of interpretations.[14] A court naturally needs to take a decision between these possible meanings. It has to justify that one of these meanings is the accurate understanding of the norm.[15]

Put differently,

> [g]iven the existence of a plurality of arguments and types of argument relevant to interpretation, there necessarily exist possibilities of conflict between rival readings

[8] Christian Djeffal, *Static and Evolutive Treaty Interpretation: A Functional Reconstruction* (Cambridge, Cambridge University Press, 2016) 22. Djeffal also rejects the conceptualisation of evolutive interpretation as a 'means of interpretation' and describes it as 'a class of results of interpretations'.

[9] Senden (n 5) 72.

[10] Greer (n 5) 194, where he introduces the term 'interpretive principles'.

[11] Vassilis Chirardis, 'The Limits of Interpretation of the Strasbourg Court and the Principle of Non-regression' in Dean Spielmann (ed), *La Convention européenne des droits de l'homme, un instrument vivant: Mélanges en l'honneur de Christos L. Rozakis, The European Convention on Human Rights, a Living Instrument* (Brussels, Bruylant, 2011) 97.

[12] Wróblewski uses the terminology of second-level 'directives of preference' in interpretation which guide the choice between different meanings achieved by means of 'first-level directives of interpretation': Jerzy Wróblewski, *Judicial Application of Law* (Dordrecht, Springer, 1992) 91.

[13] ibid 92–93.

[14] See also Sonnleitner (n 4) 286.

[15] Wróblewski (n 12) 93.

> or interpretations of a statutory text, ... This implies that the most urgent task for a theory of interpretative justification relates to the resolution of such conflicts.[16]

Wróblewski provides a convincing theory of interpretation, which will be used in the following to determine the nature of evolutive interpretation. He suggests that the resolution of conflicts between rival interpretations could be guided by what he calls 'second-order directives'[17] and ultimately by 'normative theories of interpretation'.[18] To Wróblewski, those guiding factors act on a different level from the identification of possible meanings itself. Wróblewski differentiates between 'first level directives' such as linguistic, systemic and functional directives, and 'second level directives',[19] among which only the 'second level directives of preference' are of interest here. First-level directives are the primary source for determining the meaning of a norm in the interpretive process.[20] They thus amount to the classic methods of interpretation. 'Second level directives of preference' only need to be used if one cannot satisfyingly determine the meaning of a norm by means of the first-level directives.[21] In this case, Wróblewski argues, 'The court has to make a choice declaring that one of them is "the true meaning" or the "proper meaning". This is made with the aid of second level directives of preference.'[22]

Second-level directives form part of normative theories of interpretation, which 'fix the values which the interpretation ought to implement'.[23] A complete normative theory of interpretation would be an ideal of interpretation in which all difficulties in interpretation could be answered by reference to some second-level directive of interpretation.[24] By reference to such directives and to the values they seek to achieve, the interpreter provides a justification for an interpretation.[25] For Wróblewski, evolutive interpretation amounts to such a normative theory of interpretation.[26] As such, it determines dynamic second-level directives, which guide the interpreter in arguing for dynamic interpretations of a norm.[27] Wróblewski's differentiation draws a convincing picture of the interpretive process, in which interpretive canons or methods interact with further guiding factors of interpretation. If we reconstructed the evolutive interpretation of the ECHR in Wróblewski's terms, it would thus amount to

[16] Jerzy Wróblewski and Neil MacCormick, 'On Justification and Interpretation' (1994) 53 *ARSP Beiheft* 255, 261.
[17] Wróblewski (n 12) 92f.
[18] ibid 108f.
[19] ibid 91.
[20] ibid 92.
[21] ibid.
[22] ibid 93.
[23] ibid 96.
[24] ibid 108.
[25] ibid.
[26] ibid 109.
[27] ibid.

a normative theory of interpretation consisting of a set of second-level directives, which can be used to justify the choice of an evolutive interpretation. Yet, I think that Wróblewski's picture needs to be slightly reconstructed in the sense that evolutive interpretation is not 'the' normative theory of interpretation itself but forms part of a normative theory of interpretation. Evolutive interpretation has the function to satisfy those values of the theory of interpretation that are of dynamic character. To stay with Wróblewski's terminology, this aim would be achieved by evolutive second-level directives. As such, evolutive interpretation is not a method of interpretation but part of a theory of interpretation. It provides guidance in cases in which no clear interpretive outcome can be achieved using interpretive methods such as literal, systematic or teleological interpretation. As such, it forces the interpreter to take the dynamic normative values of the Convention's legal system into consideration. Following the above considerations, I thus categorise evolutive interpretation as an integral part of a normative theory of interpretation, which guides the ECtHR in interpreting the Convention.

II. EVOLUTIVE INTERPRETATION AS AN ELEMENT OF THE TIME DIMENSION OF INTERPRETATION

The second feature of evolutive interpretation is that in its guiding function it may be displayed in all methods of interpretation. It is shown in what may be called the 'time dimension' of interpretive methods. In constitutional theory there is a model which categorises interpretive results as belonging to dimensions of interpretation. Mennicken has introduced a model with two spectrums, which represent two dimensions of interpretation. Any interpretation can be mapped in these two spectrums.[28] The first spectrum refers to the material dimension of interpretation, which maps subjective and objective meanings on a scale. The second spectrum refers to the time dimension of interpretation, which maps historical and contemporary meanings on a scale.[29] It is the latter dimension which is of interest for defining the space in which evolutive interpretation operates. If we stick to Wróblewski's wording, which I have discussed in the previous section, each end of a spectrum seeks to accomplish different values of a wider normative theory of interpretation. In Mennicken's time dimension, the contemporary meaning would stand for evolutive interpretation, whereas the historical meaning would stand for static interpretation. Evolutive interpretation is thus one of two poles in the time dimension of interpretation. This is an important observation, which leads to some further insights about the nature of

[28] Axel Mennicken, *Das Ziel der Gesetzesauslegung: Eine Untersuchung zur subjektiven und objektiven Auslegungstheorie* (Bad Homburg, Verlag Gehlen, 1970).

[29] ibid 17–18.

evolutive interpretation. First, it shows very clearly that evolutive interpretation is not attached to a specific method of interpretation. This is a perspective missing in the discussion on evolutive interpretation of the ECtHR hitherto. Most authors connect evolutive interpretation to a specific method of interpretation.[30] It is important to note that this also holds true for Wróblewski's understanding of 'dynamic theories' of interpretation, which allocates them to teleological interpretation.[31] One exception is the argument of Senden, who characterises evolutive interpretation as being an integral part of various methods of interpretation.[32] Yet, this is also imprecise, as I argue that evolutive interpretation is displayed in all commonly known methods of interpretation. Admittedly, the evolutive dimension is more obvious in some methods, such as teleological interpretation, than in others, such as historical interpretation. Yet, even a historical interpretation could change in the course of time if, for example, new facts about the legislative intentions or the drafting process of a legal document were revealed. Contrary to the discourse on evolutive interpretation, the fact that any method of interpretation has a time dimension is acknowledged in the discourse on constitutional interpretation.[33] Häberle, for example, argues that all interpretive methods bear a static and dynamic time dimension.[34]

There is another important lesson that we can learn from the second feature of evolutive interpretation. It demonstrates very clearly that evolutive interpretation only covers interpretive results, which are located at one end of the time dimension of interpretation, the evolutive end. There are thus other interpretive results, which can be mapped at the static end of the time dimension of interpretation. Consequently, evolutive interpretations are in potential conflict with interpretations located at the static end of the spectrum. A theory for the legitimacy of evolutive interpretation thus has to provide a solution for the conflict within the time dimension of interpretation. The resolution of this conflict must be in line with the normative commands of the underlying theory of interpretation. The conflict in the time dimension of interpretation must not be confused with a conflict between different methods of interpretation. It is rather a conflict between interpretive directives, which are supposed to guide us in case of conflict between different interpretations resulting from the previous application of interpretive methods.

If we picture evolutive interpretation as part of the time dimension, we can also see more clearly the first feature which I have identified above, namely that

[30] See, eg, Wróblewski (n 12) 105; Malgosia Fitzmaurice, 'Interpretation of Human Rights Treaties' in Dinah Shelton (ed), *The Oxford Handbook of International Human Rights Law* (Oxford, Oxford University Press, 2013) 751.

[31] Wróblewski (n 12) 105.

[32] Senden (n 5) 146.

[33] Peter Häberle, 'Zeit und Verfassung' in Ralf Dreier (ed), *Probleme der Verfassungsinterpretation: Dokumentation einer Kontroverse* (Baden-Baden, Nomos, 1976) 306.

[34] ibid 316–17.

it forms part of a normative theory of interpretation. It provides guidance for the choice among a plurality of interpretive results in the time dimension. When transferred to the language of human rights interpretation, the time dimension of interpretation displays interpretive results, of which some are closer to the human rights conceptions at the time of enactment (static) and others are closer to the conceptions at the time of the interpretation (evolutive). It needs to be specified, though, that in the course of time, 'static' conceptions do not solely refer to the time of enactment anymore, but also to later developments, such as established case law of the Court. Whenever a court such as the ECtHR opts for an interpretation which can be mapped at the end of evolutive interpretation in the time dimension spectrum, it decides to choose this end of the time dimension over the other. This choice requires justification.

Picturing evolutive interpretation on the time dimension of interpretation thus leaves us no choice but to study evolutive interpretation in connection with static interpretation. This correlation must not be confused with other static–dynamic dichotomies in the literature, such as the theory of static and dynamic natural law by Verdross. He sees static natural law as a set of universal moral principles which may be concretised in specific contexts as secondary or dynamic natural law, eg through positive law.[35] This leads to a hierarchical structure between the two set of norms, in which the principles of the dynamic natural law flow from the principles of static natural law. While the former are subject to constant change, the latter remain stable.[36] This stands in contrast to the static–dynamic dichotomy in the time dimension of interpretation, in which there is no hierarchy between static and dynamic interpretations, but only in relation to the normative interpretive theory in which they are embedded.

III. STATIC INTERPRETATION AS THE PARAMETER FOR EVOLUTIVE INTERPRETATION

The third element is probably the most challenging element of the concept. It is clear by now that evolutive interpretation amounts to a change in interpretation over the course of time. However, it remains unclear which parameter applies to measure this 'change'.

If we look at a conceptualisation of evolutive interpretation by Jean-Paul Costa, former president of the ECtHR, it appears that multiple categories of 'change' are taken into account by evolutive interpretation: 'The text should be interpreted … by adapting it to the changes that have taken place over time – to changes in society, in morals, in mentalities, in laws, but also to technological

[35] Alfred Verdross, *Statisches und dynamisches Naturrecht* (Freiburg im Breisgau, Rombach, 1971) 113.

[36] ibid 116.

innovations and scientific progress'.[37] This has led some authors to differentiate between different intensities of evolutive interpretations depending on the category of change the interpretation refers to.[38] They argue for a lower degree of intensity of evolutive interpretation if it just takes into account new 'social facts'. New social facts in this conception amount to technological or scientific developments.[39] This would be the case if one applied the right to freedom of expression to the context of the internet, a new technology which was not yet known at the time of enactment.[40] This form of evolutive interpretation is usually not deemed to constitute a genuine change of meaning and is thus widely accepted.[41] These authors argue for a higher intensity of evolutive interpretation if it refers to an evolution in 'moral values'.[42] This form of evolutive interpretation is more contentious in the academic debate. This is considered to amount to a genuine departure from the intended meaning of a norm.[43] The ECtHR's reasoning regarding the equal treatment of children born in or out of wedlock serves as an example.[44] Consequently, developments in social facts and developments in moral values constitute the two poles of an intensity scale of evolutive interpretation, reaching from narrow to broad.[45] Whether this differentiation in intensities between changes in social facts and moral values is meaningful is questionable,[46] but more importantly, it still leaves us with the question how we can distinguish between evolutive and static interpretations.

Bridging this question to my previously identified features of evolutive interpretation, I can rephrase the question: how are we to map an interpretation as static or evolutive in the time dimension? To tell whether an interpretation departs from static interpretation and can be characterised as evolutive, we need to define static interpretation first.[47] Therefore, evolutive interpretation must

[37] Jean-Paul Costa, 'Introductory Remarks' in European Court of Human Rights (ed), *Dialogue Between Judges: What Are the Limits to the Evolutive Interpretation of the Convention?* (Strasbourg, Council of Europe Publishing, 2011) 5.

[38] These differentiations are visible in the 'living constitution' debate: Mark D Greenberg and Harry Litman, 'The Meaning of Original Meaning' (1998) 86 *Georgia Law Journal* 568, 598f. See also Senden (n 5) 148.

[39] Aileen Kavanagh, 'The Idea of a "Living Constitution"' (2003) 16(1) *Canadian Journal of Law and Jurisprudence* 55, 80.

[40] In the American debate, Antonin Scalia also draws a distinction between these two poles, although not as analytically clear: Antonin Scalia, 'Common-Law Courts in a Civil-Law System: The Role of United States Federal Courts in Interpreting the Constitution and Laws' in Amy Gutmann and Antonin Scalia (eds), *A Matter of Interpretation: Federal Courts and the Law* (Princeton, NJ, Princeton University Press, 1997) 45.

[41] Kavanagh (n 39) 82.

[42] ibid 80–81; Scalia (n 40) 45. For Scalia, only the high-intensity pole seems to refer to the concept of a 'living Constitution' or evolutive interpretation.

[43] Senden (n 5) 147–48, summarising contributions of Scalia, Kavanagh and Roosevelt.

[44] *Marckx v Belgium* Series A no 31 (1979).

[45] Greenberg and Litman (n 38) 603f. See also Kavanagh (n 39) 80.

[46] See also Kavanagh (n 39) 82.

[47] I want to thank George Letsas for raising this point with me.

not be analysed alone, but always with an eye to the opposing end in the time dimension of interpretation, being static interpretation.[48]

Letsas provides further insights on what this parameter for differentiating between static and evolutive interpretation could be: 'The use of present-day developments and standards in the Council of Europe as a counterweight to the moral climate prevailing in the respondent state is the central feature of evolutive interpretation as applied by the old Court'.[49] According to this understanding, it is thus the 'moral climate in the respondent state', which is measured against the moral climate in the CoE. 'Static' in this conception is thus the moral state of the art in the member state, which lags behind the European moral development. The underlying premise is that the human rights in the ECHR as moral rights are not able to develop further as they only evolve towards the objective core of human rights as moral rights.[50] According to Letsas, therefore, the yardstick for development needs to be 'external' to the Convention system, hence in the legal systems of the member states of the CoE.

I think, however, that this is only one side of the coin. Although I agree with the concept of human rights as moral and legal rights,[51] I do see room for evolution within the rights set forth in the Convention. The starting point of this consideration is the highly interpretive character of law in general, and human rights in particular. As Barak rightly states, law cannot be applied without interpretation.[52] Human rights treaties are an attempt to transfer moral rights into positive law, and as such they remain highly abstract.[53] Given the high level of abstraction of human rights norms such as those proclaimed in the Convention, the judiciary is urged not only to specify the meaning of these abstract rights, but first and foremost to specify the corresponding duties in specific contexts.[54] The specification of human rights duties is a crucial aspect of international human rights adjudication, which necessitates a law-making function of international human rights courts.[55] The concrete obligations corresponding to human rights

[48] Compare Robert Post's identification of a 'symmetry' and 'structural similarity' between what he calls 'historical interpretation' and 'responsive interpretation': Robert Post, 'Theories of Constitutional Interpretation' (1990) 30 *Representations* 13, 28–29.

[49] Letsas, 'The ECHR as a Living Instrument' (n 2) 112.

[50] George Letsas, 'Strasbourg's Interpretive Ethic: Lessons for the International Lawyer' (2010) 21(3) *European Journal of International Law* 509, 530f.

[51] For a more thorough discussion of the concept of human rights followed in this book, see Chapter 1.

[52] Aharon Barak, *The Judge in a Democracy* (Princeton, NJ, Princeton University Press, 2006) 17.

[53] Robert Alexy, 'Menschenrechte ohne Metaphysik' (2004) 52(1) *Deutsche Zeitschrift für Philosophie* 15, 16.

[54] Samantha Besson, 'Legal Philosophical Issues of International Adjudication: Getting Over the Amour Impossible between International Law and Adjudication' in Cesare Romano, Karen J Alter and Yuval Shani (eds), *The Oxford Handbook of International Adjudication* (Oxford, Oxford University Press, 2014) 423.

[55] ibid.

can never be predefined, but can only be specified in a concrete situation.[56] This corresponds to Alexy's characterisation of human rights as abstract rights which are in need of further concretisation in concrete contexts.[57] Consequently, the justification of human rights always precedes the justification of the obligations which come with this right.[58] As Beitz and Goodin have put it in discussing Shue's theory of basic rights:

> [W]e might say that 'standard threats' are those 'ordinary and serious but remediable' potential interferences that can reasonably be expected to arise in the normal circumstances of human social life. … what counts as an 'ordinary and serious' potential interference to any particular type of action may be different in one society or at one historical moment rather than another. As a result, basic rights have different institutional requirements in different social contexts.[59]

Beitz and Goodin thus perceive human rights to give rise to different obligations in different contexts. Forst arrives at the same result when arguing that his constructivist conception of human rights distinguishes between 'moral constructivism', which defines rights abstractly, and 'political constructivism', which puts rights into their historical and social context.[60] He argues that

> [t]he main reason why moral constructivism must be accompanied by and integrated with political constructivism is that, since moral construction can only lead to a very general list of rights for which we can assume that no normatively acceptable reasons count against their validity, these rights can only be *concretely* justified, interpreted, institutionalized, and *realized* in social contexts, that is to say, only within a legally constituted political order.[61]

Consequently, human rights, and especially their corresponding duties, must primarily be justified in concrete social contexts and not in abstract terms.[62] Given the context dependence of concrete human rights obligations, they are thus dynamic by nature.[63]

These considerations lead to my argument that the yardstick for measuring change goes beyond Letsas' proposal of the moral views in the member states.

[56] Samantha Besson, 'Justifications' in Daniel Moeckli, Sangeeta Shah and Sandesh Sivakumaran and others (eds), *International Human Rights Law* (3rd edn, Oxford, Oxford University Press, 2018) 29.

[57] Robert Alexy, 'Die Institutionalisierung der Menschenrechte im demokratischen Verfassungsstaat' in Stefan Gosepath and Georg Lohmann (eds), *Philosophie der Menschenrechte* (Frankfurt am Main, Suhrkamp, 2007) 253–54.

[58] Neil MacCormick, 'Rights in Legislation' in Peter MS Hacker (ed), *Law, Morality, and Society: Essays in Honour of H. L. A. Hart* (Oxford, Clarendon Press, 1977) 201.

[59] Charles R Beitz and Robert E Goodin (eds), *Global Basic Rights* (Oxford, Oxford University Press, 2011) 10.

[60] Rainer Forst, *The Right to Justification: Elements of a Constructivist Theory of Justice* (Jeffrey Flynn trans, New York, Columbia University Press, 2012) 213.

[61] ibid 218.

[62] ibid.

[63] Besson, 'Justifications' (n 56) 29.

Static according to this understanding refers to the 'stock' of interpretations of the rights and duties which have been acknowledged by the drafters of the Convention or in the Court's case law so far. On the other hand, an interpretation is evolutive if it departs from this established 'stock' in reaction to a new context such as developments of a moral, scientific or societal nature. It needs to be added that an evolutive interpretation itself turns into a static interpretation in the course of time.[64] Making use of Dworkin's picture of a judge as one author among others in a 'chain novel',[65] Barak captures this phenomenon when saying that 'The chapters that we are writing become, after they are written, chapters from the past'.[66] More precisely, one and the same interpretation cannot be evolutive in two subsequent cases. Consequently, I adopt a broad definition of 'static', which bears in itself a dynamic feature. The inherent dynamism in the concept of human rights as well as in their interpretation spotlights the role of justification for attaining the best possible interpretation.

The three conceptual elements elaborated in this chapter will serve as points of reference for the subsequent analysis of attempts to legitimise or invalidate the evolutive interpretation of the ECHR.

[64] Häberle described this phenomenon in the context of constitutional interpretation as the abolition of the subjective–objective dichotomy alongside the time axis: Häberle (n 33) 311. See also, in the context of American constitutional interpretation, Post (n 48) 28.

[65] Ronald Dworkin, *Law's Empire* (Cambridge, MA, Belknap Press of Harvard University Press, 1986) 229ff.

[66] Barak (n 52) 13.

3

The Legitimacy of Evolutive Interpretation Revisited

BOTH CASE LAW of the ECtHR and literature research reveal a variety of arguments for legitimising evolutive interpretation. This chapter constitutes the first attempt in the literature to discuss the range of arguments in a systematic and comparative way. By this means, I will be able to point out the major problems of the existing legitimacy theories, to which my theory needs to be responsive.

The multitude of existing legitimacy arguments may be divided into two categories. First, there are arguments that take the specific regional human rights system of the ECHR as a starting point (consensus, moral truth, state's commitment, rights principle). Second, there are arguments that take an existing principle in general international law as their starting point (effectiveness, party's intentions, object and purpose, other rules of international law, human dignity, *pro persona*). Within the second category of arguments a further subdivision into two categories of arguments is possible. On the one hand, there are arguments that stem from the general rule of interpretation in Article 31 VCLT (party's intentions, object and purpose, other rules of international law, effectiveness). These arguments will be discussed in Section II. On the other hand, I have identified arguments in the Court's case law that refer to general principles of international law theory (human dignity, *pro persona*, objectivity of human rights). These arguments will be discussed in Section III.

As will be demonstrated in this chapter, none of the two categories of arguments turns out to be better in principle. Whereas ECHR-specific approaches tend to take greater account of specificities of the Convention, the international law approaches can rely on a better theoretical fundament due to the number and depth of academic contributions concerning the various arguments. Both accounts equally display weaknesses. As this chapter will demonstrate, the existing attempts to legitimise evolutive interpretation all suffer from major deficiencies. Also these deficiencies may be grouped into three categories.

The first deficiency is rooted in the lack of distinction between the static and evolutive dimension of interpretation. The theories hitherto have suffered from a neutrality towards a static or evolutive approach, although a legitimising theory for evolutive interpretation naturally must be supportive of an evolutive interpretive approach. This holds particularly true if an argument seeks to legitimise evolutive interpretation exclusively while excluding static interpretation. Such an approach creates a one-sided perspective on the legitimacy problem, which ignores the aspect of the dual nature of law. Therefore, the current literature provides no theory that seeks to combine static and evolutive elements in the interpretation of the ECHR.

Second, the debate lacks conceptual clarity as to whether evolutive interpretation is considered to be a method of interpretation or something distinct from a method. As I have clearly demonstrated in Chapter 2, evolutive interpretation does not help to identify the substantive content of a norm. This has repercussions for the approach towards legitimising evolutive interpretation. Any theory which links the legitimacy of evolutive interpretation to an interpretive method such as purposive interpretation or intentionalist interpretation must be rejected from the outset. This is because evolutive interpretation is an inherent element in all canons of interpretation.

Third, many legitimising arguments lack thoroughness. This holds particularly true for the legitimacy approaches of the ECtHR, which may be illustrated by two examples. On the one hand, the problem is evident in the typical introductory phrase for evolutive interpretations in the Court's judgments. The argument of the ECtHR says that the Convention is a living instrument, which must be interpreted in the light of present-day conditions. However, this phrase is certainly not an argument for the legitimacy of evolutive interpretation as it merely states that the Convention is a living instrument, while giving no justification for why this is so. Hence, it is an argument which already presupposes the legitimacy of the evolutive approach within the Convention system rather than establishing it. On the other hand, the Court often lists several cursory arguments for justifying the evolutive approach instead of elaborating its argumentation in depth. The case of *Christine Goodwin v UK* provides a good example of this typical approach:

> However, since the Convention is first and foremost a system for the protection of human rights, the Court must have regard to the changing conditions within the respondent State and within Contracting States generally and respond, for example, to any evolving convergence as to the standards to be achieved … It is of crucial importance that the Convention is interpreted and applied in a manner which renders its rights practical and effective, not theoretical and illusory. A failure by the Court to maintain a dynamic and evolutive approach would risk rendering it a bar to reform or improvement.[1]

The argument begins with the special nature of the Convention as a human rights treaty, then continues with a European consensus argument and ends with an effectiveness argument. It is not clear which of those arguments the Court considers particularly decisive for the legitimacy of its evolutive approach. The

[1] *Christine Goodwin v UK* [GC] EHRR 2002-VI para 74.

same scheme of reasoning can be found in various other judgments.[2] This argumentation lacks a profound case-related justification of the evolutive approach to interpretation.

The following analysis will critically reflect upon existing attempts to legitimise evolutive interpretation. It will proceed by examining the three identified categories of arguments listed above.

I. EVOLUTIVE INTERPRETATION AND THE ECHR

The first category of arguments refers to those theories which deal with the legitimacy of evolutive interpretation from the specific perspective of the regional human rights mechanism of the ECHR. These are the argument of European consensus (A), Letsas' arguments of moral reading and state's commitment (B), and Greer's rights principle (C).

A. European Consensus

The existence of a European consensus on a specific legal question is one of the most important arguments for justifying evolutive interpretation in the case law of the ECtHR.[3] However, it must be noted at the outset that the consensus argument may not only lead to an evolutive interpretation, but also to a static interpretation of the Court. The consensus argument takes into consideration the current legislative reality in the member states of the CoE. By this means, an interpretation of a right which was not envisaged in the drafting process of the ECHR can be read into the Convention if this evolutive interpretation mirrors today's legislative practice of the majority of the member states. This is a positive consensus in the sense that if there is consensus on a new legal matter, the Court will follow this trend in the interpretation of the Convention.[4] The other side of the coin is that, in its examination of the legislative reality, the ECtHR might also conclude that there exists no consensus on a new legal question. This negative consensus would then guide the Court to follow a static interpretive approach in this matter.[5]

[2] *Magyar Helsinki Bizottsag v Hungary* [GC] EHRR 2016 68–69. In their concurring opinion, Judges Sicilianos and Raimondi present three different lines of reasoning in three subsequent paragraphs to justify evolutive interpretation, but none of these arguments is elaborated in depth.

[3] Compare *A, B and C v Ireland* [GC] EHRR 2010-VI para 234, where the ECtHR explicitly points to this established connection between consensus and evolutive interpretation.

[4] Kanstantsin Dzehtsiarou, *European Consensus and the Legitimacy of the European Court of Human Rights* (Cambridge, Cambridge University Press, 2015) 12.

[5] George Letsas, 'The ECHR as a Living Instrument: Its Meaning and Legitimacy' in Andreas Føllesdal, Birgit Peters and Geir Ulfstein (eds), *Constituting Europe: The European Court of Human Rights in a National, European, and Global Context* (Cambridge, Cambridge University Press, 2013) 114.

The three cases of *Rees v UK*,[6] *Cossey v UK*[7] and *Sheffield and Horsham v UK*[8] on the rights of transsexuals build the perfect example for the ECtHR's approach to the negative consensus argument. In these cases, the Court had to deal with the right of transsexual people to change their gender in official documents after gender reassignment surgery. The applicants claimed that their rights under Article 8(1) ECHR were violated by maintaining the birth gender in official documents which must be presented in diverse contexts, eg to future employees or state authorities.[9] By this practice, the gender reassignment becomes obvious to everyone receiving these documents.[10] In all three cases the Court argued that there was no consensus among the Convention states on how to deal with transsexual people in general, and with legal questions arising after gender reassignment surgeries in particular.[11] Consequently, the ECtHR did not interpret Article 8 ECHR evolutively and dismissed the applicants' claims. Due to this line of reasoning, Letsas even labels the Court's approach to consensus the 'Sheffield and Horsham-test'.[12]

Apart from positive and negative consensus mentioned above, three other variations of the consensus argument may be identified in the Court's case law. First, the Court sometimes refers to an emerging rather than an established European consensus. In *Soering v UK* the Court accepted the existence of an emerging consensus among Western European states on abolishing the death penalty even though capital punishment was at that time still an explicit exception of the right to life in Article 2 ECHR. However, the Court justified its evolutive approach by the fact that the member states had already decided on the adoption of Additional Protocol No 6 to the ECHR concerning the Abolition of the Death Penalty,[13] which was not yet in force but open for ratification at the time of the decision in *Soering*.[14] Second, in cases such as *Marckx v Belgium* and *Christine Goodwin v UK* the Court referred to an international instead of a European consensus. The ECtHR considered the signature rate and the ratification process of international treaties in order to identify an international consensus on a legal matter.[15] Third, in its reasoning in *Bayatyan v Armenia*

[6] *Rees v UK* Series A no 106 (1986).

[7] *Cossey v UK* (1990) Series A no 184 (1990).

[8] *Sheffield and Horsham v UK* [GC] (1998) EHRR 1998-V.

[9] See, eg, *Cossey v UK* (n 7) para 13, in which the applicant was unable to marry because her birth certificate still displayed the birth gender; *Rees v UK* (n 6) para 17, where the name of the applicant was not changed in the passport because his birth certificate still referred to the birth gender.

[10] See, eg, *Sheffield and Horsham v UK* [GC] (n 8) para 16.

[11] *Rees v UK* (n 6) para 47, in which the Court stated that any further development of the rights of transsexuals would be dependent on further developments in the contracting states; *Cossey v UK* (n 7) para 40; *Sheffield and Horsham v UK* [GC] (n 8) paras 56–58.

[12] Letsas, 'The ECHR as a Living Instrument' (n 5) 114–15.

[13] Protocol No 6 to the Convention for the Protection of Human Rights and Fundamental Freedoms concerning the Abolition of the Death Penalty (Strasbourg, 28 April 1983) ETS No 114.

[14] *Soering v UK* Series A no 161 (1989) 102.

[15] *Marckx v Belgium* Series A no 31 (1979) 41; *Christine Goodwin v UK* [GC] (n 1) 85.

the Court elevated the consensus criterion to a more abstract sphere in arguing that 'the Convention is a living instrument which must be interpreted in the light of present-day conditions and of the ideas prevailing in the democratic States today'.[16] Although the final argument in *Bayatyan* did refer to a concrete legislative reality in the member states,[17] the quoted phrase draws a connection between evolutive interpretation and an abstract global consensus on the necessary guarantees of a democratic state.[18]

The Court's departure from an established consensus is seen critically in academia. Dzehtsiarou argues that evolutive interpretation is only legitimate in those legal questions on which an established European consensus exists, whereas it is not legitimate in cases of lacking consensus.[19] Dzehtsiarou stresses that the consensus doctrine serves the fundamental principle of legal certainty and avoids any subjectivity in legal reasoning.[20] On the one hand, consensus provides for the contextualisation of the evolutive argument within European legal concepts. On the other, it enhances legal certainty in the ECtHR's jurisprudence.[21] In its first function, consensus ensures that evolutive interpretation is in accordance with today's substantive conception of the Convention rights in the contracting states.[22] In the latter function, consensus serves as an objective element for predicting an evolutive interpretation in a legal matter.[23] By raising the predictability of the interpretive outcome, European consensus thus enhances the 'process legitimacy' of evolutive interpretation.[24] Dzehtsiarou argues that consensus is the only reasonable argument for justifying evolutive interpretation because it avoids mere subjective judgments.[25] He sees support for his theory in the Court's established practice, which – as a standard rule – justifies evolutive arguments by reference to a consensus argument.[26]

Proponents of consensus see another advantage of the consensus argument in its ability to equip evolutive interpretations with democratic legitimacy. For Prebensen, 'democratic legitimacy could be seen as a linchpin of the doctrine of evolutive interpretation'.[27] He argues that the consideration of domestic

[16] *Bayatyan v Armenia* [GC] EHRR 2011-IV para 102.

[17] ibid para 108.

[18] Letsas, 'The ECHR as a Living Instrument' (n 5) 122, who does not refer to the case of *Bayatyan* but argues more generally that the Court has developed a tendency to refer to 'common values' in international law.

[19] Dzehtsiarou (n 4) 138.

[20] ibid.

[21] ibid 132.

[22] ibid 140.

[23] ibid 138.

[24] ibid 139. In fn 115 Dzehtsiarou defines process legitimacy as predictability, legal certainty, and foreseeability.

[25] ibid 140.

[26] ibid.

[27] Soren C Prebensen, 'Evolutive Interpretation of the ECHR' in Paul Mahoney, Franz Matscher, Herbert Petzold and Luzius Wildhaber (eds), *Protecting Human Rights: The European Perspective: Studies in Memory of Rolv Ryssdal* (2000) 1127.

legal developments in the jurisprudence of the ECtHR may contribute to the democratic legitimacy of an evolutive argument. This is because these domestic developments emerge from a democratic process at the national level.[28] The democratic legitimacy of an evolutive interpretation of the ECHR is conditional, however. The evolutive argument needs to find support in a 'common ground among the great majority of the domestic systems'[29] in order to meet the requirements of democratic legitimacy.

Although this approach has experienced widespread support in practice, I argue that consensus cannot be the determining argument for the legitimacy of evolutive interpretation *in abstracto*. However, Chapter 10 will demonstrate that it can serve as a supporting argument for an evolutive interpretation in a concrete case.

Dzehtsiarou praises the objectivity of the consensus argument because it is indifferent to the substantive content of the consensus. According to him, it helps to avoid subjective ad hoc decisions which rest on moral arguments.[30] The objectivity of empirical data cannot be denied. The factual unity among the majority of member states on the interpretation of a legal concept is a vulnerable argument, however. It has no normative power, or, put differently, 'Consensus does not generate validity'.[31] From the fact that something 'is' never follows that something 'ought to be'.[32] These are two different, although related, concepts, which is why we need more than an empirical report on the legislative realities of member states in order to legitimise the normative statement of an evolutive interpretation. Human rights cases demand substantial reasoning.[33] They require more than simply following a majoritarian view, which bears the risk of being no more than a 'passing trend'.[34]

The problems caused by a purely factual legitimacy fundament may also be demonstrated by means of a concrete scenario. If an evolutive interpretation is legitimised solely by a contingent harmony of concepts among a certain territory at a certain time, this legitimising footing crumbles as soon as these concepts change again. This problem does not appear as long as the level of human rights protection within the member states is above the level of the ECHR system because the Court could simply follow the legislative achievements of

[28] ibid.

[29] ibid.

[30] Dzehtsiarou (n 4) 139–40.

[31] Maeve Cooke, 'Contingency and Objectivity in Critical Social Theory: Horkheimer and Habermas' in Giancarlo Marchetti and Sarin Marchetti (eds), *Facts and Values: The Ethics and Metaphysics of Normativity* (New York, Routledge, 2018) 75.

[32] Hans Kelsen, *Pure Theory of Law* (trans Max Knight, Berkeley, CA, University of California Press, 2005 (repr)) 6.

[33] Hanneke Senden, *Interpretation of Fundamental Rights in a Multilevel Legal System: An Analysis of the European Court of Human Rights and the Court of Justice of the European Union* (Cambridge, Intersentia, 2011) 165.

[34] Aharon Barak, *The Judge in a Democracy* (Princeton, NJ, Princeton University Press, 2006) 133.

the member states. It rather occurs in the opposite scenario, if member states start to revoke their previous achievements and end up with a lower protection level, as has already happened in reaction to challenges such as terrorism or increasing migration flows.[35] The Court cannot simply follow domestic legislation in these situations by going one step back in human rights protection and by departing from previous case law in the negative sense.[36] This is usually perceived to run counter to the purpose of the Convention to protect individual rights.[37] Chirardis even argues that a regression in human rights protection is prohibited.[38] In this scenario, the Court's interpretation would lose its legitimacy and could not re-establish it as long as the member states decided not to live up to their (previous) human rights standards again. This example demonstrates the risk of an interpretive approach that is guided by mere empirical facts without any further consideration of substantive principles.

The example of a development backwards is of course an extreme one, but it only shows in more clarity the general problem with consensus, which is already visible in some deadlocked policy issues concerning vulnerable groups. Case law analysis shows that mostly in equality cases the Court struggles with this gap between principled requirements for human rights protection and the lack of consensus within the member states on these requirements. The extensive use of the consensus argument in the Court's case law in the past seems to make consensus a precondition for an evolutive interpretation. Consequently, the Court faces problems in justifying an interpretation which is at odds with an obvious negative European consensus. In *I v UK* the Court had to address the question of the legal recognition of gender reassignment surgery in the birth certificate of the applicant.[39] The Court argued that the principle of human dignity, which the Convention generally serves, demands the granting of that right.[40] However, there was no consensus in Europe on this question, which is why the Court embarked on a very awkward argument. It started by recalling that in several earlier cases the Court had granted the member states a wide margin of appreciation on this specific question, exactly because of the lack of European consensus.[41] The Court then admitted that this very practice has set

[35] Paul Mahoney, 'Judicial Activism and Judicial Self-restraint' (1990) 11(1–2) *Human Rights Law Journal* 57, 67–68. Senden made a similar discovery when discussing the possibility of an evolution downwards: Senden (n 33) 168.

[36] *Hassan v UK* [GC] EHRR 2014-VI, partly dissenting opinion of Judge Spanos, joined by Judges Nicolaou, Bianku and Kalaydjieva, paras 13, 15.

[37] Mahoney (n 35) 67.

[38] Vassilis Chirardis, 'The Limits of Interpretation of the Strasbourg Court and the Principle of Non-regression' in Dean Spielmann (ed), *La Convention européenne des droits de l'homme, un instrument vivant: Mélanges en l'honneur de Christos L. Rozakis, The European Convention on Human Rights, a Living Instrument* (Brussels, Bruylant, 2011) 105.

[39] *I v UK* [GC] (2002) no 25680/94.

[40] ibid 70.

[41] eg *Sheffield and Horsham v UK* [GC] (n 8).

up a hurdle for the development of a European consensus.[42] It then concluded that the principled argument of human dignity was needed to overcome this hurdle.[43] Although this principled approach to justification is noteworthy, its strength is also diminished by the argument which is put forward to avoid the relevance of consensus. An accurate, principled reasoning from the outset would render the Court's approach more convincing.

B. Moral Reading and States' Commitment

George Letsas has developed a more comprehensive theory of interpretation of the ECHR, in which evolutive interpretation plays a vital role.[44] Letsas conceptualises evolutive interpretation as serving the function of developing an interpretation that is independent from the 'moralistic views' at the time of the drafting process. According to Letsas, these 'moralistic views' could refer to any minority or vulnerable group deemed to be less equal and thus deprived of Convention rights.[45] In order to overcome these views, the Court needs to apply a 'moral reading' to the Convention.[46] It is for the Court to identify the normative propositions of human rights.[47] Letsas defines three characteristic features of this moral reading: first, there is an objective core of a substantive right; second, this right can only evolve towards this core value; third, the correctness of the interpretation is not dependent on any established European consensus.[48] In applying the Convention to a new situation, the Court needs to employ the standard of a reasonable third person.[49]

The legitimising source for evolutive interpretation in Letsas' theory lies in the purpose states pursued in agreeing on a human rights treaty.[50] The specific purpose of any international human rights treaty is to 'make states accountable for the violation of some fundamental moral rights which individuals have against their government'.[51]

They did not aim to set up a list of new obligations, they rather aimed to hold states accountable for violations of obligations they already had due to the

[42] *I v UK* [GC] (n 39) para 65.

[43] ibid para 70.

[44] George Letsas, *A Theory of Interpretation of the European Convention on Human Rights* (Oxford, Oxford University Press, 2009) 58ff (chapter 3).

[45] George Letsas, 'Strasbourg's Interpretive Ethic: Lessons for the International Lawyer' (2010) 21(3) *European Journal of International Law* 509, 527.

[46] ibid 527; see already in Letsas, *A Theory of Interpretation of the European Convention on Human Rights* (n 44) 79.

[47] Letsas, 'Strasbourg's Interpretive Ethic' (n 45) 535.

[48] ibid 531.

[49] ibid.

[50] ibid 540.

[51] ibid.

intrinsic connection of human rights to moral obligations.[52] Letsas thus perceives human rights as moral rights. The Court's role is to figure out the concrete concept of these moral obligations through reasonable, moral arguments.[53] Its evolutive interpretation can thus be construed as a 'discovery' process and not a further development of the substance of human rights.[54] It is an investigation into what Letsas calls 'the moral foundations of human rights'.[55]

According to Letsas, the ECtHR already employs the standard of moral reading in numerous cases and merely complements it with considerations about common European standards.[56] He refers to the example of the *Marckx*[57] case, in which the Court argued that the right to private and family life in Article 8 ECHR as such does not distinguish between legitimate and illegitimate families.[58] The Court's reasoning in *Marckx* resulted in what Letsas would call a discovery that 'the complained-of behaviour has always constituted a violation, even when it was not considered to be so'.[59]

In later writings, Letsas has further developed his legitimacy theory of moral truth towards a stronger, 'commitment-based legitimacy' theory.[60] It does not replace the moral truth theory but accomplishes it by expanding it to a theory for the Court's legitimacy to interpret evolutively.[61] This further development of his theory had been triggered by the Court's changing practice of evolutive interpretation.[62] In early cases of evolutive interpretation, the ECtHR had referred either to present-day conditions or to a strict consensus among the contracting states. In its more recent case law, however, it has changed its perspective to common values in international law or an emerging consensus.[63] This practice involves a tendency to elevate the level of human rights protection above the European average.[64] As this new practice had provoked ongoing debate about the legitimacy of the ECtHR, Letsas has adapted his legitimacy approach in order to react to this debate.[65]

The starting point of his later argument is that the member states have committed themselves to a uniform enforcement procedure by means of a common human rights court.[66] Article 46 ECHR even explicitly stipulates this

[52] ibid.
[53] ibid.
[54] Letsas, 'The ECHR as a Living Instrument' (n 5) 125.
[55] ibid 123.
[56] Letsas, 'Strasbourg's Interpretive Ethic' (n 45) 531.
[57] *Marckx v Belgium* (n 15).
[58] Letsas, 'Strasbourg's Interpretive Ethic' (n 45) 530; *Marckx v Belgium* (n 15) 31.
[59] Letsas, 'Strasbourg's Interpretive Ethic' (n 45) 530.
[60] Letsas, 'The ECHR as a Living Instrument' (n 5) 106–41.
[61] ibid 125.
[62] ibid 124.
[63] ibid 119; in cases such as *Christine Goodwin v UK* [GC] (n 1).
[64] Letsas, 'The ECHR as a Living Instrument' (n 5) 122.
[65] ibid 124–25.
[66] ibid 138.

commitment to accept the decisions of the Court as binding.[67] This being only a procedural rule to legitimise the imposition of the Court's decisions on the contracting states, Letsas goes on to elaborate on the more specific question, whether the further substantive development of the Convention rights through evolutive interpretation is covered by this commitment.[68] Letsas argues that the commitment to evolutive interpretation becomes obvious in two aims, which the contracting states have expressed in the Preamble to the ECHR: 'the achievement of greater unity'[69] among the contracting states on the one hand, and the 'collective enforcement'[70] of human rights on the other.[71] Furthermore, they have given the mandate for achieving these aims to one central institution, the ECtHR. Thus, the Court has the mandate to define the nature of these Convention rights and not to replicate domestic conceptions of the rights enshrined therein.[72] Letsas argues that in order to comply with its mandate, the Court cannot but apply evolutive interpretation.[73] However, this does not amount to arbitrary interpretive power, as the ECtHR needs to justify its interpretations reasonably and coherently.[74] Letsas finishes by arguing not only that evolutive interpretation is legitimate, but also that its use 'becomes essential to the Court's legitimacy'[75] because it helps to achieve coherence in its adjudication. It does so by developing rights with reference to the same fundamental set of principles which guide the Convention and the jurisprudence of the Court.[76]

Letsas' argument transfers the Dworkinian theory of moral reading[77] to the concrete context of the ECHR. While I support his holistic perspective on the whole interpretive methodology to which evolutive interpretation belongs, this claim for generality also constitutes the weak spot in the argument. It is too little nuanced to meet the requirements of the various interpretive approaches and particularly of evolutive interpretation. Letsas builds the fundament of his interpretive theory on the purpose of the ECHR as an instrument to hold states accountable for human rights obligations they already had regarding the moral core of these rights. This argument lacks the purely dynamic stance, which is necessary for any foundational argument of evolutive interpretation, and which is itself purely dynamic by nature. Letsas' argument may as well support static

[67] ibid.
[68] ibid.
[69] Convention for the Protection of Human Rights and Fundamental Freedoms (Rome, 4 November 1950) (Council of Europe) Preamble, recital 3.
[70] ibid Preamble para 5.
[71] Letsas, 'The ECHR as a Living Instrument' (n 5) 139.
[72] ibid 139.
[73] ibid.
[74] ibid 140.
[75] ibid.
[76] ibid.
[77] See Ronald Dworkin, *Freedom's Law: The Moral Reading of the American Constitution* (Cambridge, MA, Harvard University Press 1996), where Dworkin argues for a moral reading of the American Constitution.

interpretations as long as they respect the objective core of the interpreted right. This would not be problematic if Letsas provided a further theoretical fundament on how to choose between static and evolutive interpretations in a concrete case. So far, his theory does not, which is why his argument does not fit properly as a legitimacy theory for evolutive interpretation and lacks clarity in detail.

The argument suffers from a further weakness. Letsas seems to presuppose a non-consensual character of the ECHR, without justifying why this is so. He supposes that the obligations arising from the Convention do not depend on state consent but are somehow objective. This presupposition becomes obvious in his conception of evolutive interpretation, which he describes as the Court's task to identify the objective moral values of the Convention rights. He puts these objective values in contrast to the moral views of the drafters, the member states or the judges. This, of course, contrasts with the traditionally supported principle of sovereignty in international law, which accords the role of setting up duties primarily to the nation states.[78] Following this principle, international treaties thus have a consensual character and depend on states' consent. Any theory which departs from this fundamental principle needs to come up with a profound argument for why it accords this non-consensual character to an international treaty, in order to be steadfast against criticism. This is exactly what is missing in Letsas' theory.

Letsas' theory of states' commitment also lacks the necessary dynamic stance as far as the substance of the right is concerned. Letsas mentions two purposes of the ECHR which express states' commitment to evolutive interpretation: the achievement of greater unity and the collective enforcement of human rights through the ECtHR. These two objectives obviously aim at harmonisation, which by itself does not require any dynamism in interpretation. It could simply amount to a harmonisation of the minimum standards in the Convention. If one leaves aside Letsas' previous argument for a moral reading of the Convention, the state's commitment approach could even be understood as merely supporting a consensus interpretation. Implementing a European consensus interpretation would also contribute to greater unity among the contracting states and it would constitute an act of collective enforcement. The unifying mandate of the ECtHR, according to this aim in the Preamble, could also be limited to identifying common ground in the human rights conceptions of the member states and to applying this common understanding consistently. This undertaking is not necessarily evolutive. From these considerations it follows that there is a missing link in Letsas' argument. He does not clarify why the commitment to these two purposes implies a mandate of the Court to inquire into 'whatever human rights people in fact have, and not what human rights domestic authorities or public opinion think people have'.[79]

[78] Michel Troper, 'Sovereignty' in Michel Rosenfeld (ed), *The Oxford Handbook of Comparative Constitutional Law* (Oxford, Oxford University Press, 2012) 359.

[79] Letsas, 'The ECHR as a Living Instrument' (n 5) 139.

C. Rights Principle

According to Steven Greer, the legitimacy of any interpretive method of the ECtHR depends on the constitutional structure of the ECHR.[80] Greer suggests a constitutional theory of the ECHR in which he subdivides the Convention into a hierarchical order of primary and secondary constitutional principles.[81] Greer argues that within this scheme, evolutive interpretation needs to be put in its place in order to identify its source of legitimacy.

In Greer's constitutional framework, the ECHR builds on one core principle, which is the teleological principle.[82] The constitutional status of all other principles then depends on how closely they are connected to this fundamental teleological principle.[83] He defines it as the purpose of the Convention to protect individual rights in the context of democracy and the rule of law, being the two main objectives of the CoE.[84] Then he goes on to outline the shape of the subordinate constitutional scheme.

In a first step Greer distinguishes three primary constitutional principles, to which all interpretive principles are subordinate.[85] The 'rights principle', the 'democracy principle' and the 'priority-to-rights principle'.[86] In the hierarchy of Greer's ECHR constitutional system, each primary principle establishes a group of subordinate secondary principles.[87] In a second step, Greer identifies evolutive interpretation as a subordinate principle of the 'rights principle', joined by other principles such as the 'commonality principle' and the principle of 'autonomous interpretation'.[88] The 'rights principle' states 'that in a democratic society Convention rights should be protected by national courts and by the European Court of Human Rights through the medium of law'.[89]

It is an abstract concept, the shape of which is formed by concrete interpretive principles such as the principle of effectiveness or the principle of implied rights and implied limitations.[90] The principle of effectiveness guides the Court in its decisions and leads to more practical instead of abstract rights.[91] The principle of implied rights can support the Court's argument to interpret a Convention right more extensively.[92] Therefore, Greer argues, the 'rights principle' supports

[80] Steven Greer, *The European Convention on Human Rights: Achievements, Problems and Prospects* (Cambridge, Cambridge University Press, 2008) 228.
[81] ibid 193–230.
[82] ibid 195.
[83] ibid 194.
[84] ibid 195.
[85] ibid 196.
[86] ibid.
[87] ibid 213.
[88] ibid.
[89] ibid 196.
[90] ibid 197.
[91] ibid.
[92] ibid 198.

an evolutive interpretation of the ECHR and thus serves as the primary source for evolutive interpretation.[93] Conversely, evolutive interpretation, in its function as a secondary constitutional principle, supports the realisation of the 'rights principle' and serves as a mediator.[94] The practical implication of this function is that an evolutive interpretation can have priority over other means of interpretation in order to give effect to the superior principle.[95] Thus, evolutive interpretation of the ECHR is legitimised through its purpose to fulfil the primary constitutional principle of rights, which accords the principal responsibility for protecting the Convention rights to the national courts and the ECtHR.

Greer's theory sheds light on the big picture of the Convention by defining the complex interactions between the dominant principles therein. I agree that a comprehensive, constitutionalist approach is crucial for determining the legitimacy of evolutive interpretation. The detailed legitimacy chain in Greer's theory is puzzling, however. This will be demonstrated by shedding light on the two possible legitimacy sources for evolutive interpretation offered in his theory.

First, in Greer's account, the principle of evolutive interpretation as a secondary constitutional principle is subordinate to the primary constitutional principle of 'rights'.[96] This principle states that it is for the national courts and the ECtHR to protect the rights of the ECHR. Yet, it is obvious that this procedural principle alone is not sufficient to introduce a dynamic element into the adjudicative process. Adjudication according to the 'rights principle' would be neutral to a static or dynamic theory of interpretation. Hence, it is not appropriate to legitimise evolutive interpretation on its own. However, in his discussion on the shape of the rights principle, Greer establishes a close connection between the principle of effectiveness and the rights principle. Maybe this added feature is able to provide the missing dynamic stance of the primary principle. At least, Greer stresses the relevance of the effectiveness principle for evolutive interpretation as he maintains that the latter, in particular, serves the principle of effective protection of rights.[97] However, even the basic relations in this triangle of principles remain nebulous in Greer's theory. On the one hand, Greer creates this hierarchical constitutional structure with primary and secondary principles, in which he does not accord a specific position to the effectiveness principle. On the other, Greer seems to equate the rights principle to the principle of effectiveness as he does not clearly distinguish between the two of them.[98] But then what exactly is the place of effectiveness in Greer's constitutional system? If it were tantamount to the rights principle, it would become a primary constitutional principle. However, from a substantive point of view it is hard to maintain

[93] ibid.
[94] ibid 214.
[95] ibid.
[96] ibid 213.
[97] ibid 214.
[98] ibid 197f.

that the rights principle and the principle of effectiveness are synonymous. The principle of effectiveness is not a procedural but an interpretive principle with a 'dual aspect',[99] namely practical effectiveness (*ut res magis valeat quam pereat*) and purposive effectiveness.[100] Greer obviously shares this account of effectiveness when he defines it as guiding the interpreter to a more practical, reality-oriented interpretation of the Convention rights.[101] Thus defined, it is arguably not his intention to equate the two principles of 'effectiveness' and 'rights'. If this is the case, the only alternative position of the principle of effectiveness is a subordinate position to the rights principle. Still, it would be hierarchically superior to evolutive interpretation, according to Greer's theory. Would it then be at the second level of constitutional principles, putting evolutive interpretation on a kind of third level of this constitutional hierarchy? Or would it introduce an intermediate level into Greer's theory? As long as the correlation between the 'rights principle' and the principle of effectiveness remains unclear, the quality of the rights principle for legitimising evolutive interpretation is questionable in Greer's theory.

The second source for the principle of evolutive interpretation in Greer's theory could be found in the teleological principle. It must be noted that Greer's teleological principle is not equivalent to the argument of purposive or teleological interpretation. Greer identifies the teleological principle as the cardinal principle of the Convention, which is hierarchically superior to all other adjudicative principles.[102] Therefore, one could interpret his theory as legitimising evolutive interpretation by reference to the teleological principle. However, according to Greer's definition, the teleological principle serves the two primary objectives of the CoE: rule of law and democracy. Thus defined, it may support both a more evolutive and a more static approach to interpretation: evolutive, since material rule-of-law considerations, such as the protection of individual rights, may demand a strong role for the Court; static, since democracy usually requires the Court to show deference to the decisions of the nation states. This must inevitably lead to tensions between the two objectives. Greer's theory provides no guidelines on how to decide which objective should be followed in an individual case. Hence, the teleological principle in his theory is too vague to serve as an appropriate source of legitimacy of evolutive interpretation.

II. EVOLUTIVE INTERPRETATION AND THE VIENNA CONVENTION ON THE LAW OF TREATIES

The second category of arguments deals with legitimacy theories, which build on an established principle of interpretation in international law. They thus

[99] Richard K Gardiner, *Treaty Interpretation* (Oxford, Oxford University Press, 2010) 160.
[100] For further details see Section IID on the principle of effectiveness.
[101] Greer, *The European Convention on Human Rights* (n 80) 197.
[102] ibid 194.

all refer to interpretive arguments of Articles 31 and 32 VCLT. More precisely, this section will deal with the arguments of party's intentions (1), object and purpose (2), other rules of international law applicable in the relations between the parties to a treaty (3), and the argument of effectiveness (4).

A. Parties' Intentions

Bjorge suggests a theory of parties' intentions, which is supportive of evolutive interpretation.[103] This seems to be at odds with the widespread narrow conception of drafters' intentions, which is committed to a more textualist and originalist approach to interpretation. However, Bjorge even argues that 'evolutionary interpretation is nothing if not tied to the intention of the parties'.[104] He sees an ultimate connection between evolutive interpretation and the VCLT.[105] Evolutive interpretation is thus the result of applying the general rule of interpretation as established in Article 31 VCLT.[106] More precisely, it is the result of employing the object and purpose interpretation, which is part of the general rule of interpretation. The fact that the VCLT does not explicitly mention the drafters' intentions in the general rule of interpretation is a sign that the interpretation of the intentions is not a method but the overarching aim of interpretation.[107] Hence, according to Bjorge, a teleological interpretation ultimately leads to an interpretation of the intentions of the parties. This is because 'the object and purpose of a treaty are the essential elements of the intention of the parties'.[108] Whether evolutive interpretation is legitimate needs to be clarified for every treaty system individually. Applied to the European context, the Court objectivises the intentions when it is investigating the object and purpose of the ECHR.[109] The Preamble of the ECHR speaks of 'the maintenance and further realisation of human rights' as its aim. According to Bjorge, this reflects the intention of the parties that the Convention should be open to an evolutive interpretation.[110]

In his theory of parties' intentions, Bjorge also refers to another vital aspect of his legitimacy argument, namely the principle of good faith.[111] Although it is a distinct principle of treaty interpretation according to the VCLT, it is in Bjorge's theory closely connected to the intentions of the parties. In Bjorge's

[103] Eirik Bjorge, *The Evolutionary Interpretation of Treaties* (Oxford, Oxford University Press, 2014) see especially Chapter 3.
[104] ibid 120.
[105] ibid 139.
[106] ibid 140.
[107] ibid 89.
[108] ibid 114.
[109] ibid.
[110] ibid 85.
[111] ibid 63–75.

argument, interpretation in good faith is the overarching principle of international treaty interpretation, which serves as the nexus for all other interpretive canons.[112] Hence, he assumes that also evolutive interpretation must be linked to the principle of good faith.[113] The focal point of interest for Bjorge lies in the connection of the good faith principle to the 'legitimate expectations engendered by promises which the parties made in the treaty'.[114] Thus understood, good faith requires an interpretation which is not at odds with these legitimate expectations.[115] Bjorge stresses that this version of good faith, though it might have a static bias,[116] is supportive of evolutive interpretation. This is so if the drafters of a treaty had in mind to create a dynamic treaty.[117] Moreover, if the parties intended to allow for the further development of the treaty, this constitutes a legitimate expectation for an evolutive interpretive approach, which must be respected due to the principle of good faith.[118] Bjorge does not clarify whether the legitimising power of the good faith principle is thus ultimately dependent on the intentions of the parties, or the other way round. However, in combination with his elaboration on the parties' intentions theory, this conclusion may be assumed.

The discussion on the connection between evolutive interpretation and the two vital components of Bjorge's theory, drafters' intentions, and good faith, is also led beyond the European context in general international law. Contrary to their inferior role in Article 31 VCLT, the intentions of the parties have traditionally been the primary source for treaty interpretation in international law and have continued to play a vital role.[119] These intentions are considered to be identified in the historical context, being the time of the drafting of the treaty.[120] Although this approach seems to be rather static and incompatible with evolutive interpretation, this is not necessarily so. The cardinal question is whether the intentions of the parties are perceived as giving a definite meaning to the legal concepts used in the treaty or as allowing an evolution of the meaning.[121] The latter alternative has been acknowledged on some occasions by the ICJ. In the case of the *Namibia Opinion*[122] the ICJ held that the terms used by the parties were by definition evolutive concepts: 'the parties … must consequently

[112] ibid 63.
[113] ibid 64.
[114] ibid.
[115] ibid 71, 73.
[116] ibid 73.
[117] ibid 74.
[118] ibid.
[119] Humphrey Waldock, 'The Evolution of Human Rights Concepts and the Application of the European Convention of Human Rights' in Paul Reuter (ed), *Mélanges offerts à Paul Reuter: le droit international: unité et diversité* (Paris, Pedone, 1981) 536.
[120] ibid.
[121] ibid 538.
[122] *Legal Consequences for States of the continued presence of South Africa in Namibia (South West Africa) notwithstanding Security Council Resolution* 276 Advisory Opinion, ICJ Reports 1971.

be deemed to have accepted them as such'.[123] Similarly, in the *Aegean Sea Continental Shelf*[124] case, the ICJ concluded that the use of generic terms in treaties indicates the tendency of the parties to accept an evolving meaning, orienting itself towards the current developments in international law.[125] This inference from the use of generic terms to the intentions of the parties is particularly relevant for the interpretation of human rights treaties, which are usually written in a very open-textured way.[126] At the CoE level, these developments towards evolutive interpretations of imprecise concepts were acknowledged at a very early stage. As early as in 1975, a report on the ECHR concluded that an evolutive interpretation is in conformity with international methods of treaty interpretation as it does not conflict with the presumed intentions of the parties.[127] The connection of evolutive interpretation with the intentions of the parties to a treaty was also upheld by the International Law Commission (ILC) in its recent report on the relevance of subsequent agreements and subsequent practice for the interpretation of treaties.[128] There, the ILC emphasised that subsequent agreements provide guidance for determining whether the parties to a treaty intended to convey an evolutive meaning to a term.[129]

Unlike Bjorge's conception, the discussion in general international law about the good faith principle is not connected to the intentions of the parties. However, there is literature which highlights its connection with evolutive interpretation. For example, the ILC considers the temporal aspect of treaty interpretation to be effectuated by the principle of interpretation in good faith.[130] This is particularly interesting for the European context because good faith is one of the few principles which enjoys universal recognition. This universality is stressed in recital 3 of the Preamble to the VCLT, which reads: 'Noting that the principles of free consent and of good faith and the pacta sunt servanda rule are universally recognized'.[131]

Furthermore, the principle is also part of the general rule of interpretation according to Article 31 VCLT. Although its concrete repercussions on the interpretive process are still nebulous,[132] the following characteristic features are

[123] ibid para 53.

[124] *Aegean Sea Continental Shelf, Judgment* (1978) ICJ Reports 1978.

[125] ibid para 77.

[126] Waldock (n 119) 542.

[127] Report at the fourth International Colloquy about the European Convention on Human Rights, (Rome, 5–8 November 1975) H/Coll (75)2 4.

[128] Conclusion 8 of the draft conclusions on subsequent agreements and subsequent practice in relation to the interpretation of treaties, International Law Commission, 'Report of the International Law Commission (A/73/10)' (Seventieth Session (30 April–1 June and 2 July 2018)) para 51.

[129] ibid para 51, Conclusion 8.

[130] Document A/6309/Rev.1: Reports of the International Law Commission on the second part of its seventeenth session and on its eighteenth session 1966, 222; see also Waldock (n 119) 535.

[131] Vienna Convention on the Law of Treaties (Vienna, 23 May 1969) UNTS Vol 1155 recital 3 of the Preamble.

[132] Gardiner, *Treaty Interpretation* (n 99) 148.

attributed to it. First, it is a principle which accompanies every stage of the interpretive process.[133] Second, it demands an effective interpretation of treaties, which is why the effectiveness principle is also considered to form part of the good faith principle.[134] This particular aspect of good faith is held to open any good faith interpretation to the evolution of concepts beyond the original wording.[135] Third, the principle of good faith asks for a reasonable interpretation when establishing the ordinary meaning of a term, which also opens it up to a more evolutive interpretation.[136] Fourth, any extensive interpretation in good faith finds its limits in the creation of new obligations, which surpass the intentions of the parties.[137] Hence, it has been discovered that good faith may serve as a source of legitimacy for evolutive interpretations, but no comprehensive research so far has been dedicated to this question.

Intentionalist arguments typically face certain innate problems. First, the subjective intentions of the parties are difficult to reproduce after a longer period of time as the primary source for identifying the intentions, the *travaux préparatoires*, are not conducted without gaps.[138] Second, they are exclusive or not representative in the sense that intentions refer to the thoughts and expectations of the original drafters of a treaty but do not take into account the intentions of parties that have joined a treaty later on.[139] Third, the relevance of parties' intentions in international treaty interpretation is questionable as the general rule of treaty interpretation does not even mention the role of intentions.[140] Bjorge's argument on parties' intentions is different, however. Instead of arguing that the Court needs to consider the intentions in order to find out whether they support a dynamic or static approach to interpretation, he already offers an account of how to understand the intentions of drafters of the ECHR and concludes that they were open for evolution. Still, his theory is not convincing.

The most fundamental point of criticism, which addresses any intentionalist theory, is the question why the intentions may confer legitimacy. If we assume that evolutive interpretation is legitimate because the parties so intended, we also need to ask further: why are the intentions relevant at all? If they are not,

[133] ibid; see also Oliver Dörr, 'Interpretation of Treaties' in Oliver Dörr and Kirsten Schmalenbach (eds), *Vienna Convention on the Law of Treaties: A Commentary* (Berlin, Springer, 2012) 548, mn 60.

[134] Gardiner, *Treaty Interpretation* (n 99) 148.

[135] Steven Reinhold, 'Good Faith in International Law' (2013) 2(1) *UCL Journal of Law and Jurisprudence* 40, 61.

[136] Gardiner, *Treaty Interpretation* (n 99) 151; Dörr (n 133) 548, mn 61.

[137] Reinhold (n 135) 61–62.

[138] Rudolph Bernhardt, 'Evolutive Treaty Interpretation, Especially of the European Convention on Human Rights' (1999) 42 *German Yearbook of International Law* 11, 14.

[139] ibid.

[140] For a good discussion on the tension between the principle of reciprocity in international law and the non-reciprocity of human rights obligations, see Malgosia Fitzmaurice, 'Interpretation of Human Rights Treaties' in Dinah Shelton (ed), *The Oxford Handbook of International Human Rights Law* (Oxford, Oxford University Press, 2013) 579f. Intentions only have a secondary role in international treaty interpretation according to Art 32 VCLT (n 131).

the legitimacy of evolutive interpretation also falls apart. Addressing this question is further relevant for avoiding a hidden circularity in the argument, which would be the case if the relevance of the intentions was also based on the argument that this corresponds to what the parties intended in drafting human rights treaties. For Bjorge, the identification of the parties' intentions is the overarching aim of the general rule of interpretation in Article 31 VCLT. We thus need to consider the intentions because the general rule of interpretation leads us to it. However, this seems to be a far-fetched argument. The fact that Article 31 VCLT remains silent on the role of intentions and that Article 32 VCLT dedicates only a secondary role to the views expressed in the *travaux préparatoires* conveys a completely different picture.[141] His argument could be seen as being a subjective-teleological argument, which focuses on the intentions of the historical drafters,[142] as he argues that the investigation into the objectives reveals the intentions of the drafters. Yet, he does not make this point clear and merely stresses the necessary connection between evolutive interpretation and the intentions. Furthermore, it remains unclear what exactly is meant by his analysis that the Court objectivises the intentions of the parties in following a purposive argument.

The second element of Bjorge's argument, the good faith principle, seems promising in the sense that good faith is a strongly developed and universally recognised principle of international law. The ECtHR has never explicitly legitimised an evolutive interpretation by reference to the principle of good faith. Bjorge's theory fills this research gap but deals with it from a very narrow angle as the focus of his interest lies on the role played by the intention of the parties to a treaty. The conception of interpretation in good faith in Bjorge's analysis is strongly connected to his theory of parties' intentions. For him, the good faith principle ensures that an interpretation does not go beyond the legitimate expectations of the parties. Hence, it rather serves as a mediator for the ultimate source of legitimacy, being the intentions of the parties. As I have already mentioned, the appropriateness of the drafters' intentions for the interpretation of a human rights treaty is highly questionable. The intention-focused dimension of good faith, as supported in Bjorge's argument, is thus not convincing as a source of legitimacy.

It remains to be seen whether the other identified features of the good faith principle, effectiveness and reasonableness, are more suitable legitimacy sources for evolutive interpretation. So far, no one has elucidated the appropriateness of reasonableness for legitimising evolutive interpretation. Reasonableness is about establishing an interpretation, which does not amount to an absurd meaning

[141] VCLT (n 131).

[142] On subjective-teleological arguments in legal argumentation, see Robert Alexy, *A Theory of Legal Argumentation: The Theory of Rational Discourse as Theory of Legal Justification* (Ruth Adler and Neil MacCormick trans, Oxford, Oxford University Press, 2011) 236.

of the term.[143] Aust gives an example of what that means, saying that the reference in the Russian Constitution to the 'Union of Soviet Socialist Republics' must today be reasonably understood as referring to the Russian Federation.[144] It thus seems to be open to support an evolving meaning as long as it is above the threshold of reasonableness. However, without constructing a profound argument behind it and without shedding more light on the point of reference for the threshold of reasonableness, the appropriateness of this aspect of good faith cannot be answered conclusively for now.

B. Object and Purpose

It is a recurring argument in the debate about evolutive interpretation that the object and purpose of human rights treaties legitimise enhanced dynamism. In international law, purposive or teleological interpretation is part of the general rule of interpretation according to Article 31(1) VCLT.[145] However, the notion of 'object and purpose' is controversial. Considering the authentic version of the French words *objet* and *but*, the concepts of object and purpose can be separated as having two slightly different meanings. Object in this sense is the concrete right enshrined in a treaty and purpose is the reason why a right is protected by a treaty.[146] This is a distinction that is not often followed in practice, however.[147] There is the more common argument that separating these two concepts is not advisable as it might lead to different standards within one treaty, which could support contradicting interpretations.[148] Thus understood, teleological interpretation should be guided by one overarching purpose of a treaty, even if every right therein follows a distinct purpose.[149]

There are two different strategies for approaching a teleological justification for evolutive interpretation of human rights: first, to establish a purposive argument based on the purpose of human rights treaties more generally; and second, to examine specific purposes of the ECHR. Some argue that it is possible to identify an overarching purpose of a group of international treaties, such as

[143] Dörr (n 133) 548, mn 61.

[144] Anthony Aust, *Handbook of International Law* (2nd edn, Cambridge, Cambridge University Press, 2014) 84.

[145] VCLT (n 131); Michael Waibel, 'Principles of Treaty Interpretation: Developed for and Applied by National Courts?' in Helmut P Aust and Georg Nolte (eds), *The Interpretation of International Law by Domestic Courts: Uniformity, Diversity, Convergence* (Oxford, Oxford University Press, 2016) 11.

[146] Gardiner, *Treaty Interpretation* (n 99) 191.

[147] Jan Klabbers, 'Treaties, Object and Purpose' in Oxford Public International Law (ed), *Max Planck Encyclopedia of Public International Law (MPEPIL)* (Oxford, Oxford University Press, 2008) para 8.

[148] ibid.

[149] ibid paras 6–7, 23.

human rights treaties. The purpose of a human rights treaty is different from that of other treaties of international law because it focuses on the safeguarding of individual rights rather than those of states.[150] From this it follows that also the ECHR pursues the overarching purpose of shielding individuals against the misuse of rights by nation states and thus supports evolutive interpretation.[151] Bernhardt argues that this special character as a human rights treaty demands a dynamic element in interpretation, which takes into consideration the subsequent practice of the parties to a treaty.[152] From this it follows that evolutive interpretation is legitimate in the ECHR due to its character as a human rights treaty.[153] In Bernhardt's account, evolutive interpretation is any interpretation which follows the changing practices of member states.[154] For the case of human rights treaties, he adds that developments within the legal systems of the member states build the basis of evolutive interpretation.[155] To the contrary, legal developments on the international level can only serve as a supportive, but not decisive, argument for an evolutive interpretation.[156] Others see justification for evolutive interpretation only in those treaties the purpose of which is to establish a permanent legal relationship, as long-lasting treaties need to be more flexible in terms of changing circumstances.[157] Consequently, the purpose of permanence may legitimise evolutive interpretation.[158]

The argument of subsequent practice as well as the argument of permanence face the problem of being purely subjective, while shutting out objective-teleological arguments. While the subjective–objective dichotomy in teleological interpretation certainly is controversial, it provides a helpful framework of analysis for purposive arguments. It starts with the idea that teleological arguments may be divided into objective and subjective arguments. A subjective-teleological argument identifies the purposes which the party to a treaty intended to promote, and thus actually belongs to the category of genetic or historical interpretive arguments.[159] The intentions referred to may be those of the drafter or of a contemporary party.[160] I have discussed this subjective dimension already in the section on parties' intentions and have rejected it due to several weaknesses.[161] In its objective dimension, the teleological argument seeks to identify

[150] George Letsas, 'Intentionalism and the Interpretation of the ECHR' in Malgosia Fitzmaurice and OA Elias (eds), *Treaty Interpretation and the Vienna Convention on the Law of Treaties: 30 Years On* (Leiden, Martinus Nijhoff, 2010) 272.

[151] ibid 257, 272.

[152] Bernhardt (n 138) 17, 21.

[153] ibid 23–24.

[154] ibid 21.

[155] ibid.

[156] ibid.

[157] Bjorge (n 103) 119.

[158] ibid.

[159] Alexy (n 142) 236.

[160] ibid 241.

[161] For further discussion see Section IIA above.

the rational aims of a rule. These are aims that are objectively determined by the legal order of which the rule is part.[162] One could also express it as the 'purpose of the rule itself'.[163] In international law doctrine this distinction is not clearly drawn. It has even been said that the objective dimension does not exist in international law.[164] It is true that international law literature traditionally follows a categorisation of three interpretive canons as listed by Sir Humphrey Waldock in his report on the law of treaties: 'textual, subjective and teleological'.[165] The 'subjective' category herein refers to the intentions of the parties only[166] and is thus equal to the above-mentioned category of genetic interpretation.[167] The 'teleological' category, however, is defined as '(c) the declared or apparent objects and purposes of the treaty'[168] and later in that report as 'interpretations of the text which go beyond, or even diverge from, the original intentions of the parties'.[169] It thus combines the subjective dimension, 'declared purposes', and the objective dimension, 'apparent purposes'. From this it follows that also the objective dimension of teleological interpretation has been part of international law methodology for a long time, even though the terminological distinction from the subjective-teleological dimension is not as clearly promoted. The support of a more objective approach to teleological interpretation is all the more visible when it comes to literature about human rights interpretation. There, the intentions of the parties have become less salient in judicial reasoning.[170] It is argued that the 'normative nature' of human rights treaties allows for a more objective-teleological interpretation.[171] Since the very nature of human rights is to protect human beings from intrusions by state authorities, it would be rather absurd to limit the interpretation of human rights to the will of exactly this authority.[172]

In the context of evolutive interpretation, both teleological arguments may support a dynamic interpretive stance. Whereas the objective dimension is generally open to dynamism, the subjective dimension can be static or dynamic. It is static if the purpose is established according to the intentions of the past legislator (originalist). It is dynamic if it refers to the purpose promoted by a 'contemporary law-maker'.[173]

[162] Alexy (n 142) 241.

[163] Jerzy Wróblewski, *Judicial Application of Law* (Dordrecht, Springer, 1992) 105.

[164] Ulf Linderfalk, *On the Interpretation of Treaties: The Modern International Law as Expressed in the 1969 Vienna Convention on the Law of Treaties* (Dordrecht, Springer, 2010) 205.

[165] Humphrey Waldock, Third Report on the Law of Treaties Document A/CN.4/167, Vol II (1964) (Special Rapporteur, International Law Commission) 54.

[166] ibid 53, stating '(b) the intentions of the parties as a subjective element distinctive from the text'.

[167] Alexy (n 142) 236.

[168] Humphrey Waldock, Third Report on the Law of Treaties Document A/CN.4/167, Vol II (1964) (n 165) 53.

[169] ibid 54.

[170] Martti Koskenniemi, *From Apology to Utopia: The Structure of International Legal Argument* (New York, Cambridge University Press, 2009) 336.

[171] Fitzmaurice (n 140) 754.

[172] Letsas, 'Intentionalism and the Interpretation of the ECHR' (n 150) 272.

[173] Wróblewski (n 163) 105. Wróblewski only focuses on the distinction between static and dynamic teleological arguments but does not distinguish between objective- and subjective-teleological arguments.

Bernhardt's account of the purposive argument seems to follow the latter, subjective-dynamic dimension, when he argues that evolutive interpretation means taking into account the subsequent practice of the member states. However, it is problematic to equalise evolutive interpretation with the mere reception of state practice. This line of thinking resembles the consensus argument, with the difference that the teleological argument here serves to legitimise evolutive interpretation *in abstracto* and consensus is required to legitimise the scope of evolutive interpretation *in concreto*. However, if evolutive interpretation can never go beyond an established consensus, the teleological argument is superfluous. It does not add anything to the consensus argument and may be objected to with the same arguments.[174]

A purely subjective-teleological account is defended by those who see the purpose of permanence of treaty relations as the source of legitimacy for evolutive interpretation. This argument is problematic because it equates the object and purpose with the intention of the parties, and thus faces the same problems as all intentionalist arguments.

Regarding the second argumentative strategy referring to specific purposes of the ECHR, the discussion mainly turns on one specific purpose of the ECHR, expressed in the third recital of its Preamble, which states:

> Considering that the aim of the Council of Europe is the achievement of greater unity between its members and that one of the methods by which that aim is to be pursued is the *maintenance and further realisation* of Human Rights and Fundamental Freedoms. (Emphasis added).[175]

This purpose is also highlighted in the Preamble to the Statute of the Council of Europe.[176] In a CoE forum dedicated to evolutive interpretation, ECtHR Judge Françoise Tulkens names the reference of the Preamble to the maintenance and further realisation of fundamental rights as the legitimate basis for evolutive interpretation.[177] Similarly, former president of the ECtHR, Jean-Paul Costa, referred to this passage as legitimising evolutive interpretation.[178] In contrast to this obviously widely supported view, the ECtHR never used this specific purpose in the Preamble for legitimising evolutive interpretation in its case law. In general, it does not even establish a direct connection between evolutive and

[174] For a detailed discussion of the consensus argument see Section IA above.

[175] Convention for the Protection of Human Rights and Fundamental Freedoms (Rome, 4 November 1950) (n 69) recital 3 of the Preamble; for arguments relating to this passage of the Preamble see: Prebensen (n 27) 1125; Bjorge (n 103) 85; *Khamtokhu and Aksenchik v Russia* [GC] EHRR 2017 66, para 37.

[176] Statute of the Council of Europe (London, 5 May 1949) ETS No 1 recital 4 of the Preamble.

[177] Françoise Tulkens, 'Address' in European Court of Human Rights (ed), *Dialogue Between Judges: What Are the Limits to the Evolutive Interpretation of the Convention?* (Strasbourg, Council of Europe Publishing, 2011) 7.

[178] Jean-Paul Costa, 'On the Legitimacy of the European Court of Human Rights' Judgments' (2011) 7(2) *European Constitutional Law Review* 173, 178.

teleological interpretation as such. Only in the concurring opinion by Judges Sicilianos and Raimondi in the case of *Magyar Helsinki Bizottság v Hungary* is evolutive interpretation presented as realising the principle of teleological interpretation as provided by Article 31 VCLT.[179]

Yet, the reference to the purpose of 'maintenance and further realization of human rights' as a source of legitimacy for evolutive interpretation is puzzling. Some commentators refer to the whole phrase, others only to the specific passage of further realisation. It strikes the eye, however, that maintenance and further realisation are two different concepts, which need to be sharply distinguished in the debate about evolutive interpretation. Whereas the term maintenance seems to support a more static than evolutive theory of interpretation, the term further realisation clearly supports evolution. These two diverging purposes show clearly that the ECHR embraces a multitude of purposes, which may also conflict with each other. A mere reference to the passage of 'further realization' is thus only a first step for legitimising evolutive interpretation. A whole theory about its legitimacy must take into account this diversity of purposes, however. It needs to shed light on the interactions between those purposes in order to know whether the dynamic elements dominate in general or in specific circumstances. None of the arguments discussed so far has taken into account this complexity of purposes in the ECHR.

C. Other Rules of International Law Applicable in the Relations between Parties

Scholars regularly point to the relevance of other rules of international law, as mentioned in the general rule of treaty interpretation, for the legitimacy of evolutive interpretation. Article 31(3)(c) VCLT states that treaty interpretation should take into account 'any relevant rules of international law applicable in the relations between the parties'. Prebensen argues that, unlike other international treaties, the ECHR establishes rights of individuals against states, which are hence similar to laws in national legal systems.[180] It follows that the term 'any relevant rules of international law' necessarily embraces any progress in domestic laws.[181] Therefore, legislative developments of national laws and the jurisprudence of national Supreme Courts need to be taken into consideration in interpreting the ECHR according to the rule of Article 31(3)(c) VCLT.[182] According to Prebensen, this interpretive mechanism is evolutive in its very nature. It guarantees that societal changes in the member states of

[179] *Magyar Helsinki Bizottsag v Hungary* [GC] (n 2) 69, para 8.
[180] Prebensen (n 27) 1126.
[181] ibid.
[182] ibid.

the CoE find their way into the jurisprudence of the ECtHR. This is vital for keeping the Convention rights effective and in pace with modern society.[183] Prebensen further substantiates the latter point by the fact that the ECHR as an international treaty is hard to amend in a political process.[184]

Gardiner argues that 'other rules of international law applicable in the relations between the parties' can give rise to an evolutive interpretation.[185] The rule as such is neutral as to whether the interpreter of a treaty should take into account international law which followed the entry into force of the treaty or which was in force at the time of the conclusion of the treaty.[186] For Gardiner, three possible scenarios occur if other rules of international law have changed since the treaty under interpretation has been adopted: '(1) that the treaty envisaged such changes; (2) that the situation remains within the scope of effective interpretation of the treaty; or (3) that the change is so fundamental that the treaty cannot be applied'.[187]

The ILC concludes that 'A treaty may convey'[188] whether Article 31(3)(c) VCLT should be applied in a more dynamic or static manner. It further mentions three indicators for an evolutive approach, which are to be found in the concepts used in a treaty: first, if these concepts imply consideration of further developments in international law; second, if they oblige the parties to further develop the treaty; or third, if they are general to such an extent that they cannot but take into account further developments.[189] It is thus for the specific treaty under interpretation to determine which of these two approaches is legitimate. Yet, Gardiner argues that human rights treaties are a category of treaties in which the drafters have generally envisaged an evolutive theory of interpretation.[190] Therefore, interpreters of human rights treaties need to take into account any relevant rule of international law which is applicable between the parties and which has been adopted after the conclusion of the treaty under interpretation. An evolutive interpretation, which follows from this process, draws its legitimacy from Article 31(3)(c) VCLT in conjunction with the concepts the drafters envisioned.[191] A similar approach is advanced by Fitzmaurice, who sees evolutive interpretation as merging Article 31(3)(c) VCLT with the object and purpose interpretation as laid down in Article 31(1) VCLT.[192]

[183] ibid.
[184] ibid.
[185] Richard K Gardiner, 'The Vienna Convention Rules on Treaty Interpretation' in Duncan B Hollis (ed), *The Oxford Guide to Treaties* (Oxford, Oxford University Press, 2014) 499.
[186] Dörr (n 133) 568, mn 104.
[187] Gardiner, *Treaty Interpretation* (n 99) 254.
[188] A/61/10, Report of the International Law Commission on its 58th session (2006) (United Nations General Assembly) 415 (22).
[189] ibid (23).
[190] Gardiner, *Treaty Interpretation* (n 99) 254.
[191] ibid 256.
[192] Fitzmaurice (n 140) 751.

However, the argument of 'other rules of international law' seems unsuitable to legitimise evolutive interpretation of the ECHR for several reasons. First, the personal scope may be limited. This follows from a report of the ILC in which it explains Article 31(3)(c) VCLT as follows:

> [W]here parties to a treaty … are also parties to the other treaty, where the treaty rule has passed into or expresses customary international law or where they provide evidence of the common understanding of the parties as to the object and purpose of the treaty under interpretation or as to the meaning of a particular term.[193]

This opens a variety of questions. Do all contracting states of the ECHR also need to be parties to the treaty to which the other rule belongs in order for it to be applicable? Is it sufficient if the treaty is signed but not yet ratified? Second, an evolutive interpretation of a Convention right does not necessarily go back to any other international rule or treaty at all. It might as well be established with moral arguments. Contrary to that, the scope of Article 31(3)(c) VCLT is obviously limited to those cases where such a rule of international law may actually be found in a treaty or is part of customary law. This is not enough to encompass all the sources for evolutive interpretations. Furthermore, if the application of that rule depends on the 'common understanding of the parties' the rule of Article 31(3)(c) VCLT ultimately amounts to no more than an intentionalist argument and may be objected to by the arguments presented in Section IIA above.

Prebensen follows a distinct approach to Article 31(3)(c) VCLT, as he argues that 'other rules of international law' may also encompass domestic laws. He develops this argument based on the ECHR's special character as a human rights treaty. He argues that the Convention rights have more similarities with domestic laws than with other international laws as they provide individuals with rights against the state instead of setting up rights between states. Therefore, national developments need to be considered following the rule in Article 31(3)(c) VCLT. According to Prebensen, this constitutes the evolutive element in the interpretation of the ECHR.[194] While it is questionable whether domestic laws can be categorised as rules of international law as referred to by Article 31(3)(c) VCLT, the more troubling feature of the argument for the purposes of this analysis is that it amounts to no more than a consensus argument. He limits the legitimacy of evolutive interpretation to substantive questions, upon which a common ground exists among a great part of the member states. Prebensen's argument shares another characteristic feature with consensus arguments. Democratic legitimacy for him is a basic requirement for the legitimacy of evolutive interpretation, which can only be established if the majority of democracies within the CoE system support a legal development, which can then be promoted by

[193] A/61/10, Report of the International Law Commission on its 58th session (2006) (n 188) 414–15 (21).

[194] Prebensen (n 27) 1126.

the ECtHR on the European level. His argument does not add anything to the typical consensus arguments and is thus subject to the same objections, which I have presented above.

D. Effectiveness

The case law of the ECtHR draws an important connection between evolutive interpretation and the principle of effectiveness in interpretation. In numerous cases of evolutive interpretation the Court stresses the importance of an interpretive approach, which renders the Convention rights 'practical and effective, not theoretical and illusory'.[195] The exact correlation and interplay between the effectiveness principle and evolutive interpretation varies, however, from case to case. In the judgment of *Christine Goodwin v UK* the ECtHR seems to equate to the doctrine of an effective interpretation with the necessity of the Court to 'maintain a dynamic and evolutive approach'.[196] In other cases such as *Hirsi Jamaa and others v Italy* it rather combined the references to the Convention as a living instrument and to the principle of effectiveness in order to support its evolutive approach to the territorial application of the ECHR for cases of extra-territorial expulsions of refugees.[197]

At the CoE's forum 'Dialogue between judges', it was stressed that the combination of the principle of effectiveness on the one hand, and the sequence of maintenance and further realisation in the Preamble on the other, provide the normative basis for evolutive interpretation.[198] In its separate opinion in *Khlaifia and others v Italy*, Judge Serghides adopts the same approach to the relationship between the two interpretive principles.[199] In the justification of its evolutive approach in the recent case of *Magyar Helsinki Bizottsag v Hungary* the Court further emphasised that the effective interpretation of the Convention is rooted in the object and purpose of the Convention.[200]

In the literature, the connection between evolutive interpretation and the principle of effectiveness has also been stressed on various occasions. Some authors argue that evolutive interpretation is based on the 'living instrument' doctrine on the one hand and the principle of effectiveness on the other hand.[201]

[195] *Airey v Ireland* Series A no 32 (1979) para 24; *Christine Goodwin v UK* [GC] (n 1) 74; *Magyar Helsinki Bizottsag v Hungary* [GC] (n 2) para 121.

[196] *Christine Goodwin v UK* [GC] (n 1) 74.

[197] *Hirsi Jamaa and others v Italy* EHRR 2012-II paras 175–77.

[198] Tulkens (n 177) 7.

[199] *Hirsi Jamaa and others v Italy* (n 197) para 175. *Khlaifia and others v Italy* [GC] EHRR 2016 107, para 17.

[200] *Magyar Helsinki Bizottsag v Hungary* [GC] (n 2) para 121.

[201] Bernadette Rainey, Elizabeth Wicks and Clare Ovey, *Jacobs, White and Ovey: The European Convention on Human Rights* (7th edn, Oxford, Oxford University Press, 2017) 76–77. The argument was even more explicit in the fifth edition of the book from 2010, where they defined the two aspects as the 'bedrock of evolutive interpretation' Robin CA White and Clare Ovey, *Jacobs, White,*

Evolutive interpretation in this conception thus encompasses the principle of effectiveness. Other authors have argued the exact opposite, namely that evolutive interpretation only corresponds to one specific aspect of the effectiveness principle.[202]

In order to grasp this argument in its entirety, it is necessary to shed light on how the principle of effectiveness is perceived in general international law literature. The principle consists of two aspects, one being the doctrine of *ut res magis valeat quam pereat* and the second being the guideline for interpreters to follow an interpretation which serves the purpose of a treaty as a whole.[203] The first element demands an interpretation which gives meaning to a right instead of giving no effect to it at all. Thus, an interpreter must not render a treaty impractical regarding its effects in real life.[204] The second aspect of effectiveness aims to give full effect to the aims of a treaty in the interpretation of every single provision of the treaty.[205] The principle of effectiveness as embodied in the first element relates to the more general principle of good faith in international law.[206] Yet, effectiveness as embodied in its second element attaches to a different interpretive principle, the one of object and purpose of a treaty.[207] Hence, although Article 31 VCLT does not explicitly refer to the effectiveness principle, the principles of 'good faith' and 'object and purpose' incorporate it in the general rule of interpretation.[208] In the interpretation of human rights treaties, the effectiveness principle has an even more significant role to play.[209] In its first aspect as *ut res magis valeat quam pereat*, it asks an interpretation of a human rights treaty to have a real effect on the lives of individuals and to protect these rights over time.[210] For Çali, the Court's conception of the effectiveness approach, being that the Convention rights should be rendered 'practical and effective and not theoretical and illusory', corresponds to this first aspect of the effectiveness principle.[211] In its second aspect as purposive effectiveness, it deals with the competing aims of interpreting human rights either in favour of the individual or in favour of the public interest.[212] This account goes further than the first one as it does not investigate the factual effectiveness but the teleological effectiveness.[213] According to Çali, 'The "living instrument" doctrine

and Ovey: The European Convention on human rights (5th ed. Oxford, Oxford University Press 2010) 73.

[202] Başak Çali, 'Specialized Rules of Treaty Interpretation: Human Rights' in Duncan B Hollis (ed), *The Oxford Guide to Treaties* (Oxford, Oxford University Press, 2014) 538.

[203] Gardiner, *Treaty Interpretation* (n 99) 159–60.

[204] ibid 160.

[205] ibid 200.

[206] ibid 160.

[207] ibid.

[208] ibid.

[209] Çali (n 202) 537.

[210] ibid 539.

[211] ibid.

[212] ibid.

[213] ibid.

of the ECtHR … develops this aspect of effectiveness'.[214] Hence, this argument clearly distinguishes between the effectiveness conception in the literature and in the Court's jurisprudence. It concludes that evolutive interpretation does not correspond to the Court's conception of effectiveness, but rather to a different – purposive – aspect of effectiveness.

If one follows the analysis of Çali, the understanding of effectiveness in the ECtHR's case law refers to its first aspect being the *ut res magis valeat quam pereat* doctrine. This first dimension of effectiveness rather constitutes a factual argument which seeks real effects on the lives of individuals. As the ECtHR has stated in so many cases, the rights should be 'practical and effective, rather than theoretical and illusory'.[215] This argument thus looks at the factual consequences of an interpretation in order to classify it as effective or not. As such, it is inappropriate to legitimise evolutive interpretation. It would confer legitimacy only from an *ex post* view. This kind of legitimacy is not enough if we ask the question whether evolutive interpretation is a legitimate approach to interpretation under the ECHR in general and *ex ante*. From this it follows that the first dimension of the effectiveness principle is unable to serve as a source of legitimacy for evolutive interpretation.

In Çali's view, however, evolutive interpretation is based on the second dimension of effectiveness, being purposive effectiveness. However, there is no further explanation why she takes this view. The second conception constitutes a normative argument about which effects should be given to human rights in general.[216] It is about putting either the individual or the interests of the nation states in the focus of human rights interpretation.[217] Contrary to the first dimension of effectiveness, this is an *ex ante* argument, which refers to the effects on the individuals in a more abstract sense. The second dimension of the effectiveness principle thus seems to be a more promising approach for legitimising evolutive interpretation. Yet, this argument would need a further theoretical fundament to be a convincing legitimacy theory.

III. EVOLUTIVE INTERPRETATION AND GENERAL PRINCIPLES OF INTERNATIONAL LAW

The study of the ECtHR's case law reveals three other legitimising patterns for evolutive interpretation, which have not been fleshed out in a detail in the Court's reasoning. Yet, these arguments are worth considering because they have been brought up in some of the most important and contentious cases in the history of the ECtHR. More precisely, this section deals with the arguments

[214] ibid 538.
[215] See, eg, *Airey v Ireland* (n 195) para 24.
[216] Çali (n 202) 539.
[217] ibid 539.

of objectivity of the law, human dignity, and *pro persona*, which are all amply discussed concepts in international law. Notwithstanding their high relevance in general international law, no profound theory has so far established a connection between those principles and evolutive interpretation. In the context of the ECHR, these concepts are less elaborated. Although they have been applied to single cases in the Court's jurisprudence, they lack a thorough conceptual fundament. They only appear occasionally in the Court's reasoning. Interestingly, all arguments of this section have guided the Court's reasoning in cases of equal treatment. Equality rights thus seem to be a special field of application for evolutive interpretation.

A. Objectivity of the Law

In *Marckx v Belgium* the ECtHR had recourse to the notion of 'objectivity of the law' in order to justify its evolutive interpretation.[218] In this case the Court decided that the different treatment of 'legitimate' and 'illegitimate' children could not be established under Article 14 ECHR in conjunction with Article 8 ECHR.[219] Against the legislative reality in the majority of the contracting states, the Court emphasised that there is a noticeable international trend to foster equal treatment of legitimate and illegitimate children.[220] The ECtHR thus referred to an emerging consensus in international law and stressed that the Convention is also relied on 'to accelerate this evolution' in matters of equality.[221] The Court acknowledged that, notably in equality questions, this acceleration through adjudication might bring with it effects that go beyond the specific case at hand.[222] However, it argued that the Court cannot be guided by such consequentialist considerations alone because it must also be mindful of the objectivity of the law in question, which demands equal treatment of all children.[223] The ECtHR has borrowed this line of reasoning from a judgment given by the Court of Justice of the European Union (CJEU) in the case of *Defrenne v Sabena*.[224] However, the Court did not further explain what exactly it meant by its objectivity argument and whether it should guide evolutive interpretation beyond equality cases.

The latter point is interesting insofar as it reduces the foregoing consensus argument to a secondary, supporting argument. This line of reasoning could

[218] *Marckx v Belgium* (n 15) para 58.
[219] ibid para 31.
[220] ibid para 41.
[221] ibid para 58.
[222] ibid.
[223] ibid.
[224] ibid, where the ECtHR refers to the preliminary ruling by the European Court of Justice in Case 43/76 *Gabrielle Defrenne v Société Anonyme Belge de Navigation Aérienne Sabena* (1976) ECR 1976-00455.

be understood as referring to the very nature of the right, as protected by a specific Convention article,[225] dissociated from how the member states interpret it. Although the Court in *Marckx v Belgium* put more emphasis on the emerging consensus in its line of reasoning, the objectivity argument gives an insight into how the Court perceives the Convention rights. It signals that the lack of consensus among the contracting states has only prolonged the process of recognising a right, which had always been inherent in the Convention. It also reflects the Court's willingness to grant the member states time to acknowledge this right expressly, before applying it in its case law. However, it also indicates a certain reluctance by the Court to wait until the very end of the consensus process if this resulted in denying an applicant's protected Convention right. The objectivity argument is quite puzzling, however. First, it remains unclear what exactly is meant by objectively guaranteed rights. This question has already given rise to a huge debate about objectivity in law, especially about objectivity in human rights.[226] Furthermore, it leaves us with the question whether these objective guarantees would imply that there are also objectively valid interpretations. If this were so, this could be an obstacle to rather than support for evolutive interpretation. If one understands objectively valid interpretations as allowing for the discovery of the objective core of a right, it is an inherently static concept. This static connotation could be reduced if one understands the term objective as being equivalent to the concept of reasonable argument. Yet, without any further argumentative fundament on these questions on behalf of the ECtHR, it is difficult to grasp and analyse the objectivity argument of the Court in its entirety. This lack of clarity renders the argument prone to criticism and, in its immature stage, inappropriate as a legitimising argument for evolutive interpretation.

B. Human Dignity

In *I v UK* and the equivalent case of *Christine Goodwin v UK* the Court departed from settled case law on the claim of transgender people to have their post-operative gender registered in official documents. In previous cases the Court had granted the member states a wide margin of appreciation with reference to a common European approach on this matter.[227] The Court attributed the continued lack of consensus within the contracting states to the fact that its own practice of granting a wide margin of appreciation hindered states from

[225] Letsas, 'Strasbourg's Interpretive Ethic' (n 45) 530.

[226] See, eg, Andrei Marmor, *Positive Law and Objective Values* (Oxford, Clarendon Press, 2001); Steven Greer, 'The Interpretation of the European Convention on Human Rights: Universal Principle or Margin of Appreciation' (2010) *UCL Human Rights Review* 1.

[227] *Sheffield and Horsham v UK* [GC] (n 8); *Cossey v UK* (n 7).

developing a common legal approach on the subject.[228] In *I v UK* the Court built its evolutive argument on the general principle of human dignity, which it conceived as constituting 'the very essence of the Convention'.[229] In light of this fundamental principle, the Court argued, equal treatment of transgender people in the twenty-first century could no longer be subject to the margin of appreciation of the contracting states.[230] Again, the Court acknowledged that the effects of its decision would cause repercussions beyond the very case, which is why it engaged in a process of balancing these effects on society with the interest of the applicant. In resolving the balancing exercise, the Court concluded that 'society may reasonably be expected to tolerate a certain inconvenience to enable individuals to live in dignity and worth'.[231]

The human dignity argument in the Court's reasoning in *I v UK* and *Christine Goodwin v UK* bears a considerable resemblance to the objectivity reasoning in *Marckx*. Again, the Court had to deal with an equality right which had previously been the subject of political debate, namely the rights of transsexuals. The ECtHR could not accept the fact that the member states had still not succeeded in respecting equal treatment of transsexuals in the twenty-first century. The Court thus decided to no longer uphold its deferential interpretive practice in this matter and decided the case in an evolutive manner with reference to human dignity. The argument is interesting because, unlike its model convention, the Universal Declaration of Human Rights, the text of the ECHR does not even mention the principle of human dignity.[232] The literature has not yet shed light on the correlation between evolutive interpretation and human dignity. While it has been argued that human dignity supports 'expansive interpretations of human rights',[233] the concept as such does not imply evolutive interpretation. However, it may be argued that human dignity plays a vital role in the further development of equality rights. This is because the concept of human dignity as such promotes that all human beings are of equal worth.[234] The same may be true for human rights protecting the physical integrity of individuals as this is the core field of application for the concept of human dignity in the reasoning of international courts.[235] Whether it may also serve as a legitimising source for evolutive interpretations beyond these core fields of application remains to be clarified. The Court's case law remains silent on this question. I will come back

[228] *Christine Goodwin v UK* [GC] (n 1) para 85; *I v UK* [GC] (n 39) para 65.

[229] *Christine Goodwin v UK* [GC] (n 1) para 90; *I v UK* [GC] (n 39) para 70.

[230] *Christine Goodwin v UK* [GC] (n 1) para 90; *I v UK* [GC] (n 39) para 70.

[231] *Christine Goodwin v UK* [GC] (n 1) para 91; *I v UK* [GC] (n 39) para 71.

[232] Only the Preamble to Protocol No 13 mentions the 'inherent dignity of all human beings': Protocol No 13 to the Convention for the Protection of Human Rights and Fundamental Freedoms concerning the Abolition of the Death Penalty in all circumstances (Strasbourg, 3 May 2003) ETS No 187.

[233] Paolo G Carozza, 'Human Dignity' in Dinah Shelton (ed), *The Oxford Handbook of International Human Rights Law* (Oxford, Oxford University Press, 2013) 345.

[234] ibid 346.

[235] ibid 353.

to the relevance of the human dignity argument for evolutive interpretations later in this book in Chapter 10.

C. *Pro Persona* Interpretation

The third case analysis in this section reveals a pattern similar to that in the two previous ones. Again, the focus of the analysed argument is put on the individual, on human dignity in situations touching upon personal integrity and on the equal treatment of all human beings. The only difference lies in the fact that this line of reasoning was not followed by the Grand Chamber but argued by a single judge. In his dissenting opinion in the case of *Khamtokhu and Aksenchik v Russia*,[236] Judge Pinto de Albuquerque establishes a close connection between evolutive interpretation and the *pro persona* approach to interpretation.[237] He does not expressly deal with the foundational argument of how to legitimise evolutive interpretation, nonetheless his idea is interesting for the purposes of this analysis.

In *Khamtokhu and Aksenchik v Russia*, two Russian prisoners claimed their right to equal treatment concerning the prohibition of whole-life sentences without parole. According to Russian law, this form of imprisonment had been declared inhuman and hence a violation of Article 3 ECHR for vulnerable groups such as women, juveniles and older men, but not for men between the ages of 18 and 65.[238] The applicants sought to contest this differentiation as infringing their rights to equal treatment.[239] The majority of the Court denied the applicants this right by arguing that Russia had fulfilled its obligations under Article 3 ECHR to protect the most vulnerable groups from this inhuman treatment. The Court held that the decision to provide a higher level of protection, which would include other groups, remained within the margin of appreciation of the contracting states.[240] Judge Pinto de Albuquerque attached a detailed dissenting opinion to the judgment, in which he argued in favour of an evolutive and *pro persona* interpretation.[241] He stressed that if a certain type of imprisonment is considered to be inhuman treatment under the absolute right of Article 3 ECHR, protection must be guaranteed for all human beings and not only for groups, which are considered worth protecting by the member states.[242] He maintained that evolutive interpretation is not only about following a majoritarian conception of rights in the member states, but also about putting the

[236] *Khamtokhu and Aksenchik v Russia* [GC] (n 175).
[237] ibid 66, para 37.
[238] ibid para 33.
[239] ibid para 32.
[240] ibid para 81.
[241] ibid 47–72, paras 1–50.
[242] ibid 62, para 31.

human rights of each individual in the focus of interpretation.[243] By this means, the Court gives effect to the main objective of the CoE, being the protection of human rights. According to Judge Pinto de Albuquerque, this protection is best achieved through a *pro persona* interpretation, which thus also contributes to the aim of 'the maintenance and further realisation of human rights and fundamental freedoms'.[244]

The essence of his argument is that a *pro persona* approach would have led to an evolutive interpretation of Article 3 ECHR, so that it would be equally applied to all human beings. Putting the individual at the centre of human rights interpretation may indeed lead to a less deferential approach by the Court concerning human rights-restricting policies of the contracting states. This approach is also very popular in the jurisprudence of the Inter-American Court of Human Rights, which refers to it as *pro homine* interpretation.[245] It may as well be argued that the *pro persona* argument and evolutive interpretation are similar concepts as they both pursue the goal of increased human rights protection.[246] Although, or maybe exactly because, these two approaches share some common features, the *pro persona* argument seems to be inappropriate for legitimising evolutive interpretation. It is itself an underdeveloped principle of the European human rights system. It is neither mentioned in the ECHR nor the subject of any greater discussion in the history of the Convention. It thus seems to face the same legitimacy challenges as evolutive interpretation rather than conferring legitimacy on evolutive interpretation itself.

[243] ibid 65–66, paras 35–38.
[244] ibid 66, para 37.
[245] Çali (n 202) 540.
[246] Fitzmaurice (n 140) 766.

4

The Criticism against Evolutive Interpretation Revisited

A CRITICAL CAMP against evolutive interpretation by the ECtHR has existed since its first use in the case of *Tyrer v UK*. Yet, since the late 2000s, criticism has increased significantly.[1] At the political reform meeting of the ECHR in Brighton some member states argued forcefully that the use of evolutive interpretation in the Court's practice should be stemmed.[2] Such arguments were accompanied and pushed by a parallel critical discussion in academic literature. The public lecture 'The Limits of Law', given by UK Supreme Court Justice Lord Sumption in 2013,[3] had tremendous reinforcing effects on the critical camp against evolutive interpretation.

The academic debate turns on five main legitimacy problems of evolutive interpretation.[4] First, it faces a sovereignty problem as it amounts to legislation without the consent of the member states. Second, it conflicts with the rule of law because evolutive interpretation runs counter to core guarantees such as legal certainty and predictability.[5] Third, evolutive interpretation suffers from democratic illegitimacy as it takes decisions on societal questions, which should be answered in a democratic rather than judicial process. Fourth, in cases of lack of European consensus it gives rise to the factual problem that the interpretation is not sufficiently supported by the legislative realities in the member states. This critique can be rejected from the outset, as I have dismissed the correlation between the factual argument of consensus and the normative legitimacy of evolutive interpretation above in Chapter 3. Fifth, the expansive interpretations

[1] Alice Donald and Philip Leach, *Parliaments and the European Court of Human Rights* (Oxford, Oxford University Press, 2016) 6–10.

[2] For a further discussion of this point see Introduction.

[3] Lord Sumption, 27th Sultan Azlan Shah Lecture: The Limits of Law, 20 November 2013, Kuala Lumpur. The lecture and the academic discussion following the lecture were later published in NW Barber, Richard Ekins and Paul Yowell (eds), *Lord Sumption and the Limits of the Law* (Oxford, Hart Publishing, 2016).

[4] The following paragraph refers mainly to the four legitimacy problems identified by Kanstantsin Dzehtsiarou, 'European Consensus and the Evolutive Interpretation of the European Convention on Human Rights' (2011) 12(10) *German Law Journal* 1730, 1734–35.

[5] See also Lord Sumption, 'The Limits of Law' in NW Barber, Richard Ekins and Paul Yowell (eds), *Lord Sumption and the Limits of the Law* (Oxford, Hart Publishing, 2016) 21.

following from evolutive interpretation widen the scope of the ECHR to an extent that amounts to an inflation of human rights.[6] This will inevitably lead to a flood of complaints, which the Court cannot deal with in a timely fashion.[7] While the increasing number of complaints is obviously challenging for the ECtHR, this practical problem is not linked to the normative question of whether evolutive interpretation is legitimate. I will thus not include this argument in the subsequent analysis.

There are thus three critical arguments which are of special interest for the legitimacy of evolutive interpretation: democratic legitimacy, sovereignty, and the rule of law. By testing the arguments of the critical camp, this chapter will enable us to learn important lessons about the parameters by which any theory for the intertemporal interpretation of the ECHR will be judged.

I. DEMOCRATIC LEGITIMACY OF EVOLUTIVE INTERPRETATION[8]

The democratic illegitimacy critique makes two claims. First, evolutive interpretations are interpretations one can reasonably disagree about and which would be better placed in a political debate. Hence, evolutive interpretation transfers genuine political decisions to the realm of legal interpretation.[9] Second, the use of evolutive interpretations by courts has adverse effects on the democratic system in the long run.[10]

The first claim that evolutive interpretation is a tool of hidden legislation rather than interpretation had been expressed by a judge on the Court's bench as early as the case of *Tyrer v UK*. In his dissenting opinion, Sir Gerald Fitzmaurice had raised the following claim:

> The fact that a certain practice is felt to be distasteful, undesirable, or morally wrong and such as ought not to be allowed to continue is not a sufficient ground in itself for holding it to be contrary to Article 3 … [This] would mean using the Article as a vehicle of indirect penal reform, for which it was not intended.[11]

In the same vein, the more recent critical debate claims that decisions on social policy issues should rather be taken on the national level, as they should be

[6] *Marckx v Belgium* Series A no 31 (1979) 42, dissenting opinion of Sir Gerald Fitzmaurice, para 15.

[7] Marc Bossuyt, 'Should the Strasbourg Court Exercise More Self-restraint' (2007) 28 *Human Rights Law Journal* 321, 330–32.

[8] I have also presented the main ideas of this section in the article Lisa Sonnleitner, 'The Democratic Legitimacy of Evolutive Interpretation by the European Court of Human Rights' (2019) 33(2) *Temple International & Comparative Law Journal* 279.

[9] Lord Sumption (n 5) 21.

[10] Greenawalt considers these two claims as the main democratic arguments against judicial activism: Kent Greenawalt, *Interpreting the Constitution* (New York, Oxford University Press, 2015) 84.

[11] *Tyrer v UK* Series A no 26 (1978) 28, dissenting opinion of Judge Sir Gerald Fitzmaurice, para 14.

preceded by a political process that is sensitive to national interests and traditions.[12] According to Lord Sumption, human rights issues naturally touch upon moral questions, which should be answered in a democratic rather than judicial process. Yet, Lord Sumption distinguishes between 'cases of real oppression'[13] and other cases. In the first category, he acknowledges judicial constraints on the political process. The second category, however, should be an exclusive matter of 'legitimate political debate'[14] within the member states. This is because the latter cases amount to legitimate disagreements in society, which must be answered by democratic majority vote.[15]

Finnis also refers to the argument of reasonable disagreement when he states that evolutive interpretations amount to decisions about 'a morally optional preference for one kind of social life over other reasonable kinds', which is why they are 'reforming the culture by changing the law'.[16] Finnis argues that it should be for the people in the member states to decide upon which rights should be granted in their respective societies. The function of the ECtHR is limited to monitoring whether the member states comply with their obligations.[17] He argues that the Court's role is not to anticipate democratic decisions if new societal questions pose challenges to human rights.[18] Finnis acknowledges the fact that society's decisions may be flawed. Yet, he argues that a court's decision can also be biased and it is thus prone to make mistakes.[19]

The second account of the democratic legitimacy challenge points to the possibility that evolutive interpretation can have adverse effects on democracies in the long run. Lord Sumption argues that evolutive interpretations by the ECtHR repeatedly replace democratic decisions in the member states and thus make democratic deliberation pointless:[20] 'The judicial resolution of major policy issues undermines our ability to live together in harmony by depriving us of a method of mediating compromises among ourselves'.[21] By conveying too much power to external legislators, democracies are imperilled and might subtly develop into different kinds of political system.[22] This claim connects to a debate in constitutional theory in which Waldron had argued that there is a loss of democracy if societal decisions are taken by a non-elected institution rather

[12] Lord Sumption (n 5) 21.
[13] ibid 23.
[14] ibid.
[15] ibid 25.
[16] John Finnis, 'Judicial Law-Making and the "Living" Instrumentalisation of the ECHR' in NW Barber, Richard Ekins and Paul Yowell (eds), *Lord Sumption and the Limits of the Law* (Oxford, Hart Publishing, 2016) 120.
[17] ibid 91.
[18] ibid 90–91.
[19] ibid 91.
[20] Lord Sumption (n 5) 23.
[21] ibid 24.
[22] ibid 26.

than by the people themselves.[23] It reduces the political equality of citizens.[24] In the long run, such a democracy will end up as an 'Aristotelian aristocracy'.[25] He acknowledges the value of perceiving constitutions as 'living organisms' but he warns of the long-term effects on democracy if we exclude citizens from the decisions on how Constitutions should react to new societal challenges.[26]

As will be demonstrated in the following two sections, both arguments of democratic illegitimacy are flawed. As a result, I will demonstrate that it is possible to construct a theory for the legitimacy of evolutive interpretation which is responsive to the democratic illegitimacy critique.

A. The Conceptual Problem of the Critique[27]

The first strand of the critique is problematic in that it remains highly unclear about its two major concepts: evolutive interpretation and legitimate moral disagreement. Yet, by looking deeper into these concepts it becomes obvious that the critique only touches on one aspect of evolutive interpretation.

As I have demonstrated in Chapter 1, the term evolutive interpretation invites us to draw the wrong conclusion that it is a method of interpretation. As I have explained there, evolutive interpretation should rather be qualified as part of a normative theory of interpretation, which is located on a meta-level of the methods of interpretation.[28]

Evolutive interpretation represents one possible outcome of the choice between several interpretive results, of which some are closer to the human rights conceptions at the time of enactment and others are closer to the conceptions at the time of the interpretation. In Chapter 2, following a suggestion by Wróblewski, I have called this dichotomy static and evolutive second-level directives of interpretation. If we discuss the legitimacy of evolutive interpretation we should thus focus on the question of when it is legitimate to choose the evolutive theory of interpretation over the static theory.[29]

[23] Jeremy Waldron, 'Judicial Review and the Conditions of Democracy' (1998) 6(4) *Journal of Political Philosophy* 335, 355.

[24] ibid 342.

[25] Jeremy Waldron, *Law and Disagreement* (Oxford, Clarendon Press, 2004) 264.

[26] Jeremy Waldron, 'A Right-Based Critique of Constitutional Rights' (1993) 13(1) *Oxford Journal of Legal Studies* 18, 43.

[27] An early version of this argument was presented in Sonnleitner (n 8) 285–91 but it has been refined in this book.

[28] Hanneke Senden, *Interpretation of Fundamental Rights in a Multilevel Legal System: An Analysis of the European Court of Human Rights and the Court of Justice of the European Union* (Cambridge, Intersentia, 2011) 72. Djeffal also rejects the conceptualisation of evolutive interpretation as a 'means of interpretation' and describes it as 'a class of results of interpretations': Christian Djeffal, *Static and Evolutive Treaty Interpretation: A Functional Reconstruction* (Cambridge, Cambridge University Press, 2016) 22.

[29] Senden has observed that most of the literature forgets about the crucial question of how to establish an evolutive interpretation: Senden (n 28) 154.

Yet, an evolutive approach to interpretation still takes a choice between interpretive results, which obviously do reveal possible new meanings of a norm. In Chapter 1, I have demonstrated that various authors distinguish between different intensities of evolutive interpretation, reaching from low to high, depending on whether there is an evolution in social facts or in moral values. This conceptual background provides vital insights for the discussion of the arguments of Lord Sumption and Finnis. It now becomes apparent that they both implicitly refer to the higher intensity of evolutive interpretation only. They thus refer to evolutive interpretations, which are responsive to an evolution in moral values. Both authors do not address the question whether they would accept evolutive interpretation in its lower intensity. Their argument against evolutive interpretation must thus be reduced to the following argument: 'if new moral values are in conflict with old moral values, it is in a democracy on the people and not on courts to resolve this conflict, because it constitutes a case of legitimate moral disagreement'.[30] The preliminary conclusion is that their argument is unable to attack evolutive interpretation in its lower intensity.

Still, also the concept of legitimate moral disagreement remains unclear in the critical debate on evolutive interpretation. It is often assumed that a subject matter is one of legitimate moral disagreement, without further justifying this assumption.[31] The crucial question is thus how to distinguish legitimate from illegitimate moral disagreement in human rights matters. Only then will we be able to define the legitimate realm of human rights judicial review, and subsequently of evolutive interpretation. The literature provides us with two arguments. First, illegitimate moral disagreement may occur if a democratic decision-making process is flawed. Kumm lists four possible deficiencies in a democratic process: 'thoughtlessness … illegitimate reasons relating to the good … ideology … capture of the legislative process by rent-seeking special interest groups'.[32] One function of judicial review is to monitor whether these risks have been realised in a democratic process.[33] Føllesdal has raised the point that in addition to democratic decisions, also the national system of judicial review is prone to such risks. National judicial decisions may also be biased due to national interests and traditions.[34] This opens a vital function for international judicial review as a control mechanism for the reasonableness of domestic judicial review.[35] Even though these risks may be realised in political and judicial deliberations, it should be kept in mind that the international court's decision is

[30] Sonnleitner (n 8) 288.

[31] One can particularly observe this in the case of *Hirst v UK (No 2)* [GC] EHRR 2005-IX; see, eg, Lord Sumption (n 5) 23.

[32] Mattias Kumm, 'Democracy is Not Enough: Rights, Proportionality and the Point of Judicial Review' (2009) NYU Public Law Research Paper, 26.

[33] ibid 26.

[34] Andreas Føllesdal, 'Tracking Justice Democratically' (2017) 31(3) *Social Epistemology* 324, 335.

[35] ibid 331–32; Kumm (n 32) 23.

not supposed to replace political deliberation at the national level.[36] As Kumm has stated: 'Courts are not in the business of settling reasonable disagreements. They are in the business of policing the line between disagreements that are reasonable and those that are not'.[37]

The second argument sees a special function of judicial review in the protection of minority rights from majoritarian domination.[38] Lord Sumption has also acknowledged this important role of judicial review. He argued that cases of 'real oppression' of a vulnerable group would justify the overruling of a political decision.[39] His understanding of the term 'real oppression' remains nebulous, however. Instead, Benvenisti's argument on the function of judicial review for the protection of minorities gives vital insights. He argues that domestic conceptions of human rights must always be scrutinised with regard to their ability to effectively protect minorities from arbitrary majoritarian decisions. If such effective protection is granted, a court should respect national conceptions of human rights.[40] The threshold of effective protection is achieved if an interference with minority rights can be reasonably justified. Benvenisti's argument reveals another legitimate function of judicial review. Only 'when these domestic guarantees are non-existent or fail … international institutions must react with resolve'.[41] An international human rights court thus acts as a 'collective supranational voice of reason and morality'[42] if domestic authorities fail to provide an adequate level of minority protection. The two arguments are helpful to narrow down the concept of legitimate moral disagreement by pointing to two situations in which moral disagreement cannot be considered legitimate: if political agreements on moral values do not reach the threshold of reasonableness; and if political agreements amount to an unjustified majoritarian domination of a minority.[43] Consequently, the role of an international court is to scrutinise the rationality of moral disagreements.[44]

This analysis provides two vital insights into the relationship between evolutive interpretation and moral disagreement. First, in cases of legitimate moral disagreement, it is for politics and not for courts to settle the disagreement. In such cases, the Court should not replace domestic human rights conceptions by

[36] Kumm (n 32) 27.

[37] ibid 36.

[38] For the debate on evolutive interpretation see, eg, George Letsas, 'Strasbourg's Interpretive Ethic: Lessons for the International Lawyer' (2010) 21(3) *European Journal of International Law* 509, 527, 540. For the general debate see the seminal work John H Ely, *Democracy and Distrust: A Theory of Judicial Review* (Cambridge, MA, Harvard University Press, 1981) chapter 6, 135ff.

[39] Lord Sumption (n 5) 23.

[40] Eyal Benvenisti, 'Margin of Appreciation, Consensus, and Universal Standards' (1999) 31 *New York University Journal of International Law and Politics* 843, 849.

[41] ibid.

[42] ibid 852.

[43] Sonnleitner (n 8) 290.

[44] Aileen Kavanagh, 'Strasbourg, The House of Lords or Elected Politicians: Who Decides About Rights After Re P?' (2009) 72(5) *Modern Law Review* 815, 843.

evolutive interpretations. Second, in cases of illegitimate moral disagreement, there is a legitimate role for the ECtHR to settle the disagreement. It needs to be stressed again at this point that not all cases of moral disagreement even raise interpretive questions in the time dimension. As we have seen in Chapter 1, the concept of evolutive interpretation also encompasses cases of changes in social facts.[45]

Consequently, the settling of moral disagreement is not an exclusive problem which only occurs in the context of evolutive interpretation. This is a problem of judicial review more generally.[46] It appears that the democratic legitimacy critique against evolutive interpretation should be understood as a more general critique of the ECHR judicial review system. It turns on the question of who is responsible for settling moral disagreement in the European human rights system. Although this question certainly relates to the legitimacy of evolutive interpretation, it cannot be equated with it.[47] As a preliminary conclusion, we can thus say that the argument of legitimate moral disagreement is only able to affect but not to destroy the legitimacy of evolutive interpretation.

The resolution of the conceptual problem reveals that the argument of moral disagreements in a democratic society is unable to render evolutive interpretation illegitimate.[48] It is certainly a vital consideration in the choice between evolutive and static interpretation, but it is only one among several relevant considerations.

B. The Problematic Positioning of Evolutive Interpretation[49]

This section challenges the second argument of democratic illegitimacy, arguing that evolutive interpretation leads to adverse effects on democracies. This critique misconceives the relevance of evolutive interpretation in the interpretive methodology of the ECtHR. Evolutive interpretation neither hinders political deliberation nor dominates the interpretive approach to the ECHR by the Court.

The critique seems to take as a premise that evolutive interpretations constitute the end of political discussions. I argue that evolutive interpretations could also be perceived as valuable contributions to political deliberations.[50]

[45] Sonnleitner (n 8) 290.

[46] See, eg, Waldron's seminal work on this topic: Waldron, *Law and Disagreement* (n 25).

[47] Sonnleitner (n 8) 290.

[48] ibid. Coming to the same conclusion, see Sandra Fredman, 'Living Trees or Deadwood: The Interpretive Challenge of the European Convention on Human Rights' in NW Barber, Richard Ekins and Paul Yowell (eds), *Lord Sumption and the Limits of the Law* (Oxford, Hart Publishing, 2016) 64, conclusion.

[49] This section builds on arguments which I have presented in Sonnleitner (n 8) 291–95.

[50] Richard Bellamy, 'The Limits of Lord Sumption: Limited Legal Constitutionalism and the Political Form of the ECHR' in NW Barber, Richard Ekins and Paul Yowell (eds), *Lord Sumption and the Limits of the Law* (Oxford, Hart Publishing, 2016) 196, 205.

In academia it has been argued that judicial review may have beneficial effects on democratic political deliberation. Hübner Mendes has stressed that 'there is political life after last words'.[51] Similarly, Lafont holds that judicial review realises a vital democratic right of participation, which is the 'right to legal contestation'.[52] This is the right of individuals to have their arguments and cases heard by an institution which commits itself to the use of rational arguments.[53] Whenever an individual goes to court and exercises his or her right to legal contestation, a process of public deliberation is started. The court's function in this process is to enrich the political debate with principled arguments. Lafont describes the court's role as the role of a 'conversation initiator'.[54] This highlights the fact that the political debate is not finished once a matter is brought to court, but rather that the deliberation should continue afterwards. This debate is then accomplished by the rational arguments of the court.[55] The function of judicial review as a forum for enriching political debate has also been identified by Grimm[56] and King.[57] King points to the connection between the court's function as conversation initiator and as an institution for minority protection. He argues that minority issues are often not addressed in political deliberations unless they are brought before a court.[58] King demonstrates this with a case analysis of UK cases before the ECtHR. One-third of the cases in which the ECtHR found a violation of the Convention on the part of the United Kingdom turned on minority rights which had not been the subject of political discussion before.[59] He concludes that 'legislative review … appears to have promoted rather than impeded the value of equality that inspires any convincing conception of democracy'.[60]

Similarly, Føllesdal holds that court decisions will enhance the reasonableness of subsequent political debates as they raise awareness of the minority perspective.[61] It has also been argued that given the fact that the ECtHR does

[51] Conrado Hübner Mendes, *Constitutional Courts and Deliberative Democracy* (Oxford, Oxford University Press, 2013) 186.

[52] Cristina Lafont, 'Philosophical Foundations of Judicial Review' in David Dyzenhaus and M Thorburn (eds), *Philosophical Foundations of Constitutional Law* (Oxford, Oxford University Press, 2016) 271.

[53] ibid 271.

[54] ibid 270.

[55] ibid 276–77.

[56] Dieter Grimm, 'Constitutional Adjudication and Democracy' in Mads T Andenæs (ed), *Judicial Review in International Perspective* (Vol 2, The Hague, Kluwer Law International, 2000) 110.

[57] Jeff King, 'Three Wrong Turns in Lord Sumption's Conception of Law and Democracy' in NW Barber, Richard Ekins and Paul Yowell (eds), *Lord Sumption and the Limits of the Law* (Oxford, Hart Publishing, 2016) 149.

[58] ibid 149. Referring to the United Kingdom, King holds that 'about one-third of these cases involved legislation where the legislature had never even debated the rights-issue at stake in the case'.

[59] ibid.

[60] ibid.

[61] Andreas Føllesdal, 'The Legitimacy of International Human Rights Review: The Case of the European Court of Human Rights' (2009) 40(4) *Journal of Social Philosophy* 595, 603.

not have the power to invalidate domestic statutes, the political debate necessarily has to continue after a decision by the ECtHR.[62] Consequently, rather than ending political debate, evolutive interpretation seems to have the potential to make a vital contribution to public debates in the member states.[63]

A second weakness of the critique is that evolutive interpretation should not be seen in isolation but should be put in its correct place in the ECtHR's methodology. The question of whether the ECtHR should make use of evolutive interpretation should not be answered in an either-or fashion. We should consider the fact that the Convention may also accord a legitimate role to static interpretations. If the Court makes a reasonable choice between these two theories of interpretation, it will not overstep its legitimate role in judicial review. I have already pointed out above that the legitimacy debate should focus on the question of the legitimate choice between evolutive and static interpretation. We should be aware of the difference it makes whether evolutive interpretations must be legitimised on a case-to-case basis or on a once-and-for-all basis.[64] The first scenario requires that the choice between evolutive and static interpretation must be justified in any case, which raises an interpretive question in the time dimension. The second scenario suggests that this choice is taken once, which means that either static or evolutive interpretation is legitimate in all cases of interpretation. This requires no further justification in concrete cases.[65] Having these two options in mind, one can see very clearly that only if one takes a once-and-for-all decision in favour of evolutive interpretation might the critique that it has adverse effects on political deliberation be justified.[66]

Yet, I defend the view that only the first option is legitimate from a normative point of view.[67] Both approaches to interpretation serve core purposes of the ECHR, and of a legal system more generally. While static interpretation protects values such as legal certainty, evolutive interpretation aims at justice.[68] Having these underlying principles in mind, it seems unreasonable to exclude one of them categorically. It would be an unreasonable constraint on doing justice to the individual case.[69] Therefore, we should justify the choice between evolutive and

[62] Bellamy (n 50) 210. But see Aileen Kavanagh, 'What's So Weak About "Weak-form Review"? The Case of the UK Human Rights Act 1998' (2015) 13(4) *International Journal of Constitutional Law* 1008, 1024, who argues that the international law obligation leaves no room for manoeuvre to the member states.

[63] Sonnleitner (n 8) 292–93.

[64] Axel Mennicken, *Das Ziel der Gesetzesauslegung: Eine Untersuchung zur subjektiven und objektiven Auslegungstheorie* (Bad Homburg, Verlag Gehlen, 1970) 85–87.

[65] For detailed discussion see Chapter 2.

[66] Sonnleitner (n 8) 293.

[67] The following paragraph refers to arguments which I have already introduced in ibid 294.

[68] Mennicken (n 64) 86; Mennicken does not address the issue of evolutive interpretation explicitly but rather a similar tension between historical or contemporary interpretations. In the American debate on the living constitution, Friedman comes to the same conclusion: Barry Friedman, 'Dialogue and Judicial Review' (1993) 91(4) *Michigan Law Review* 577, 652.

[69] Mennicken (n 64) 86.

static interpretation in each case with regard to the specific circumstances of the case.[70] Häberle comes to a similar conclusion for constitutional interpretation.[71] This is in line with arguments suggesting that the commitment to a rationally justified casuist reasoning increases the legitimacy of judicial review.[72] The fact that the ECtHR makes use of a bigger set of interpretive principles and methods, which support static as well as evolutive interpretation, shows that the Court also strives for a justification case by case. However, case analysis also shows that its justifications in many cases of evolutive interpretation still lack thoroughness. It is thus crucial to define a theoretical model for justifying the choice between static and evolutive interpretation. This model will be constructed in Part III of this book.

II. SOVEREIGNTY

According to the sovereignty critique, evolutive interpretation amounts to the creation of an obligation which exceeds the concrete commitment of the state parties to the ECHR and hence interferes with states' sovereignty.

Given the fact that sovereignty is one of the fundamental principles of international law,[73] a debate about it necessarily accompanies any debate in international law. Sovereignty is the idea of the supremacy of the state's power within the state.[74] As a legal concept, it confers validity on legal commands.[75] The core legal implication of sovereignty in the realm of international law is that all international obligations depend on the consent of sovereign states.[76] In the common commitment to adhere to the human rights obligations enshrined in the ECHR, the member states of the CoE renounced parts of their sovereignty.[77] This creates no specific problem for sovereignty because sovereign states may subordinate themselves to a binding commitment. Further, the binding nature of the ECtHR's judgments touches upon the sovereignty of the member states because the implementation of the judgments requires no further consent of the state against which the Court has found.[78] Again, this does not

[70] ibid 85, 86, 106.

[71] Peter Häberle, 'Zeit und Verfassung' in Ralf Dreier (ed), *Probleme der Verfassungsinterpretation: Dokumentation einer Kontroverse* (Baden-Baden, Nomos, 1976) 323.

[72] Laurence Helfer and Anne-Marie Slaughter, 'Toward a Theory of Effective Supranational Adjudication' (1997) 107(2) *Yale Law Journal* 273, 323.

[73] Johan D van der Vyver, 'Sovereignty' in Dinah Shelton (ed), *The Oxford Handbook of International Human Rights Law* (Oxford, Oxford University Press, 2013) 395.

[74] Michel Troper, 'Sovereignty' in Michel Rosenfeld (ed), *The Oxford Handbook of Comparative Constitutional Law* (Oxford, Oxford University Press, 2012) 353.

[75] ibid 362.

[76] James Crawford, 'Sovereignty as a Legal Value' in James Crawford, Martti Koskenniemi and Surabi Ranganathan (eds), *The Cambridge Companion to International Law* (Cambridge, Cambridge University Press, 2015) 118.

[77] ibid 122–23.

[78] Troper (n 74) 361.

violate sovereignty as long as the judgment of the European Court of Human Rights amounts to a mere application of the international commitment. It is rather the basic consent requirement that builds the backbone of the criticism against the Court's 'living instrument' doctrine.[79] If consent is the key to an obligation, then the crucial question is what a party consented to, and this is a matter of interpretation of the actual commitment.[80]

Critics argue that evolutive interpretations lack the consent of the contracting parties. The implications of this lacking consent are twofold. First, it implies that evolutive interpretations lead to new obligations for the member states to the Convention. Yet, I will question whether such a sovereignty-friendly understanding of human rights obligations is still convincing in modern international law. The second implication is that these new obligations lack validity because the ECtHR has no sovereign power. I will challenge this second strand of the critique because it bases the concept of validity purely on the requirement of sovereignty.

A. Evolutive Interpretation as the Creation of New Obligations

The sovereignty critique holds that evolutive interpretation exceeds the commitment of the state parties to the ECHR. This argument necessarily builds on the premise that evolutive interpretation leads to the creation of new obligations to which the member states did not agree when drafting the ECHR. This premise will be tested in the following.

This position was first defended in a very famous dissenting opinion of Judge Sir Gerald Fitzmaurice in the case of *Golder v UK*.[81] The rationale behind his argument is that one cannot oblige a state to protect a right of which it had no knowledge at all, and to which it did not consent.[82] Fitzmaurice justifies this argument with the fragile political basement of the Convention system. States were already hesitating before becoming parties to the Convention and before accepting the Court's jurisdiction.[83] In order to merit their continuing acceptance, the Court needs to adopt a more prudent interpretation of the Convention rights, even if they are written in vague terms.[84] The Convention's legitimacy rests on consent of the member states and it is thus on those states to amend the ECHR if its rights are in need of clarification or if it lacks an essential right.[85]

[79] Jan E Helgesen, 'Address' in European Court of Human Rights (ed), *Dialogue Between Judges: What Are the Limits to the Evolutive Interpretation of the Convention?* (Strasbourg, Council of Europe Publishing, 2011) 21.
[80] Crawford (n 76) 123.
[81] *Golder v UK* Series A no 18 (1975).
[82] ibid dissenting opinion, para 28.
[83] ibid dissenting opinion, para 38.
[84] ibid dissenting opinion, para 39.
[85] ibid dissenting opinion, para 37(c).

Consequently, even if a regrettable omission occurred in the drafting process of the Convention, the Court needs to accept them as valid as long as the member states do not amend the Convention.[86]

Although it may be expected that, more than 20 years after the *Golder* case, the discussion has developed substantially, this line of criticism is still defended today. Former UK Supreme Court Justice Baroness Hale argues that the evolutive approach in the jurisprudence of the ECtHR exceeds the obligations to which the member states committed themselves.[87] And also Lord Sumption comes to the conclusion that 'The treatment … as a "living instrument" allows it to make new law in respects which are not foreshadowed by the language of the Convention and which Parliament would not necessarily have anticipated when it passed the Act'.[88]

Whether evolutive interpretation leads to the creation of new obligations is an interpretive question.[89] Possible interferences of evolutive interpretations with the sovereign power of states arise whenever an international commitment is phrased in vague and abstract terms and hence does not give rise to clear-cut obligations for states. This naturally occurs in a human rights treaty such as the ECHR and hence requires interpretation.[90] As I have demonstrated in Chapter 1, the need for the specification of the exact obligations arising from human rights is inherent in the concept of human rights itself. It needs to be recalled that evolutive interpretation is not an interpretive method, which is on its own capable of giving substance to an obligation. It is in fact the result of a choice between various outcomes of the interpretive process, which differ according to their time dimension.[91] Evolutive interpretation thus possibly, but not necessarily, leads to an outcome which extends the human rights obligations of sovereign states. A preliminary reply to the critique is, thus, that the argument is imprecise because it fails to see that evolutive interpretation per se is unable to confer content on a Convention right. Hence, it does not generally interfere with states' sovereignty, but – if at all – only in specific cases.

From this it follows that the critique must be rephrased. Sovereignty must then be perceived as an obstacle to the choice of an evolutive interpretive outcome, which would add substance to the ECHR. Sovereignty in this scenario must lead to the preference for a static outcome in order to avoid outcomes that are not covered by the consent of the member states. The following discussion will examine the persuasiveness of the rephrased critique.

[86] ibid 58; see also: dissenting opinion para 48.

[87] Baroness Hale of Richmond, 'Address' in European Court of Human Rights (ed), *Dialogue Between Judges: What Are the Limits to the Evolutive Interpretation of the Convention?* (Strasbourg, Council of Europe Publishing, 2011) 15.

[88] Lord Sumption (n 5) 24.

[89] Crawford (n 76) 123.

[90] Rudolph Bernhardt, 'Evolutive Treaty Interpretation, Especially of the European Convention on Human Rights' (1999) 42 *German Yearbook of International Law* 11, 12.

[91] For a discussion of my concept of evolutive interpretation see Chapter 2.

Traditional international law provided for an interpretive approach, which made the preference of a sovereignty-sparing interpretation over a sovereignty-restricting interpretation a general rule. This was called the *in dubio mitius* approach to interpretation.[92] Although the *in dubio mitius* rule is not necessarily connected to the time dimension, in which evolutive interpretation is located, it is still an interesting example of the analysis of sovereignty as an argument in the interpretive process. The *in dubio mitius* approach was traditionally assumed by the Permanent International Court of Justice and became an established interpretive principle of international law.[93] In the further development of international law, and especially in the drafting of the VCLT, this approach was not followed, however. Therefore, some authors argue that the *in dubio mitius* principle should no longer be followed today.[94] Bernhardt argues, for example, that

> [t]hese articles [31 and 32] of the Vienna Convention [on the Law of Treaties] are remarkable in several respects. Firstly, one principle of treaty interpretation, which was often invoked in older text books, is not even mentioned. Namely, the principle that treaties should be interpreted restrictively and in favor of State sovereignty, in dubio mitius. This principle is no longer relevant, it is neither mentioned in the Vienna Convention nor has it ever been invoked in the recent jurisprudence of international courts and tribunals. Treaty obligations are in case of doubt and in principle not to be interpreted in favor of State sovereignty.[95]

More recent empirical evidence of its abolishment in international law is the judgment of the ICJ in the *Dispute regarding navigational and related rights (Costa Rica v Nicaragua)*.[96] In this case the ICJ held that sovereignty-limiting treaty provisions should not be interpreted in a restrictive way, but rather like any other treaty provision.[97] The ICJ further held that the use of generic terms in a treaty was a clear sign of the intention of the parties to confer an evolving meaning on those terms.[98]

In the European context, the ECtHR never gave much weight to the *in dubio mitius* principle.[99] ECtHR Judge Pinto de Albuquerque describes it as an outdated 'sovereignist leitmotiv',[100] which contradicts the claim of the ECHR

[92] Luigi Crema, 'Disappearance and New Sightings of Restrictive Interpretation(s)' (2010) 21(3) *European Journal of International Law* 681, 682.

[93] Crawford (n 76) 123; *S.S. Wimbledon* (1923) Series A: Collection of Judgments (1923–1930) 24 (Permanent Court of International Justice).

[94] *Mursic v Croatia* EHRR 2016, dissenting opinion of Judge Pinto de Albuquerque, para 21.

[95] Bernhardt (n 90) 14.

[96] International Court of Justice, *Dispute regarding navigational and related rights (Costa Rica v Nicaragua)* Judgment, ICJ Reports 2009.

[97] ibid para 48.

[98] ibid para 66.

[99] Clovis C Morrisson Jr, 'Restrictive Interpretation of Sovereignty-Limiting Treaties: The Practice of the European Human Rights Convention System' (1970) 19(3) *International and Comparative Law Quarterly* 361, 375.

[100] *Mursic v Croatia* (n 94) 83, para 20.

for the opposing principle of 'in dubio pro persona'.[101] Crema provides two further arguments as to why the international community paved the way for sovereignty-limiting interpretive approaches. First, the international community after 1945 aimed at more substantial international obligations, such as human rights obligations, in order to limit states' power instead of protecting it as the ultimate good.[102] Especially in the European context, states agreed on a mechanism to protect Europe from dictatorships and their atrocious repercussions for human dignity. Sovereignty among European states today must thus be understood as a qualified value, though certainly not an abandoned one.[103] Second, the agents of international relations have shifted from exclusive relations between states to relations between states and individuals.[104] Sovereignty thus became a value which protected only the position of one side of the parties involved, namely states. This is particularly intolerable in the context of human rights treaties, which aim to increase the protection of the individual against state interference.[105] A change of actors in international law took place not only from state parties to individual parties, but also among the state parties to the ECHR. Letsas argues that in the context of the ECHR, attempts to identify the exact commitment of the sovereign drafting states are of little help because the 12 drafting states are not representative of today's 47 member states of the ECHR.[106]

These examples are proof of a certain dissociation of the international community from the sovereignty-friendly interpretation of international obligations. Considering this development, the argument of sovereignty as an absolute obstacle to the evolutive interpretive approach seems to be a weak one. In addition to that, it speaks in favour of sovereignty-limiting approaches to interpretation that they would contribute to achieving a higher level of protection for individual rights. This being said, sovereignty might still be one among other relevant factors in the choice between evolutive and static interpretation. This will be discussed in more detail in Part III of the book.

B. The Contestable Concept of Validity

The sovereignty critique highlights that the ECtHR claims legislative power without having sovereign power. But without possessing sovereign power, these

[101] ibid, dissenting opinion of Judge Pinto de Albuquerque, para 21.
[102] Crema (n 92) 686.
[103] Crawford (n 76) 122.
[104] Crema (n 92) 686.
[105] For a similar argument see George Letsas, 'Intentionalism and the Interpretation of the ECHR' in Malgosia Fitzmaurice and OA Elias (eds), *Treaty Interpretation and the Vienna Convention on the Law of Treaties: 30 Years On* (Leiden, Martinus Nijhoff, 2010) 270–71.
[106] ibid 270.

legislative acts are not valid. Evolutive interpretation thus ultimately leads to invalid obligations for the member states. It needs to be noted from the outset that in light of the foregoing discussion in the previous section, it is questionable whether the critique of the validity of new obligations is relevant at all. This is because I have demonstrated that evolutive interpretation does not create substantively new obligations. If it does not create new obligations, a debate about the validity of these obligations is pointless. Nonetheless, I will briefly comment on the critique and illustrate that the argument employs a highly contestable concept of validity.

The sovereignty critique builds on a very narrow account of validity which focuses exclusively on the transformation of human rights into positive law. Such a narrow concept of the validity of human rights is debatable, however. Indeed, there exist other concepts of validity which argue that positivising human rights is only a means to institutionalise rights which are valid anyway.[107] In such a concept the qualification of human rights as being legally positivised must be differentiated from their qualification as being morally valid. Alexy provides such a concept of validity, which contends that the validity of human rights mainly rests on their moral validity. Their legal validity by being positivised then only adds up to their moral validity.[108] More precisely, it is the justifiability of human rights which confers moral validity on them.[109] According to Alexy's theory, a human right thus validly exists if it can be justified in a rational discourse.[110] Naturally, it is also contestable which human rights obligations are morally valid.[111] This is not the place to embark on a discussion of the various arguments on how to justify human rights, however. Parts of this discussion have been illustrated in the delineation of my concept of human rights in Chapter 1.

The crucial implication of this illustration is to show that there exist alternative concepts of the validity of human rights. They provide convincing arguments as to why the consent of sovereign states to positivise human rights in the ECHR should not be considered to be the only yardstick for determining the validity of human rights obligations in Europe. That being said, it is highly unsatisfactory that the discussed sovereignty critique does not even make an attempt to rebut such competing concepts of validity. It does not provide any reasons why a narrow concept of validity is better than a broad concept of validity. In light of its shaky conceptual fundament, the argument of the lack of validity of evolutive interpretive results is thus not convincing.

[107] Robert Alexy, 'Menschenrechte ohne Metaphysik' (2004) 52(1) *Deutsche Zeitschrift für Philosophie* 15, 16.

[108] Robert Alexy, 'Die Institutionalisierung der Menschenrechte im demokratischen Verfassungsstaat' in Stefan Gosepath and Georg Lohmann (eds), *Philosophie der Menschenrechte* (Frankfurt am Main, Suhrkamp, 2007) 249–50.

[109] Robert Alexy, 'Rights and Liberties as Concepts' in Michel Rosenfeld (ed), *The Oxford Handbook of Comparative Constitutional Law* (Oxford, Oxford University Press, 2012) 290.

[110] Alexy, 'Menschenrechte ohne Metaphysik' (n 107) 16.

[111] Alexy, 'Die Institutionalisierung der Menschenrechte im demokratischen Verfassungsstaat' (n 108) 250.

III. RULE OF LAW

The third line of criticism against evolutive interpretation is based on the rule of law. It is two core aspects of the rule of law which supposedly are in tension with evolutive interpretation. To summarise them with Lord Sumption's words, evolutive interpretation is deemed to be 'subjective' and 'unpredictable'.[112]

The first element refers to the fundamental rule of law guarantee that the law applies to everyone without exception. From this it follows that judges are bound by the given law and should not render subjective judgments following their personal convictions of good law.[113] Some authors consider this principle as the main implication of the rule of law for the judiciary.[114] In the *Marckx v Belgium* case, one of the first cases of evolutive interpretation, this critique was voiced by ECtHR Judge Pinheiro Farinha. He has sought to persuade his colleagues that the judiciary's role is to apply the given Convention rights, but not to redraft the text.[115] By altering the contents of the ECHR, the Court oversteps its jurisdiction and is thus in breach of the rule of law.[116]

With the second element of the critique, namely that evolutive interpretation is 'unpredictable', Lord Sumption refers to the requirement of legal certainty, which is an essential aspect of the rule of law.[117] Legal certainty is vital for avoiding the arbitrary exercise of power over people. Therefore, laws should be publicly proclaimed, accessible to the subjects and applied prospectively.[118] Consistent application of the law is further crucial for achieving equality before the law.[119] The interference of evolutive interpretation with legal certainty is widely defended in the literature. Baroness Hale stressed that whenever evolutive interpretation leads to retrospective changes in obligations, it clearly exceeds the limits of predictability and legal certainty.[120] She argued that the Court did not respect this limit in its case law, especially regarding its expansive interpretation of 'civil rights' in Article 6 ECHR[121] or with the progressive inclusion of social rights into the Convention.[122] It is essential to note, though, that she accepts evolutive interpretations, as long as they are foreseeable for the member states.[123] ECtHR Judge Françoise Tulkens adopts a similar line of argument

[112] Lord Sumption (n 5) 21.
[113] Simon Chesterman, 'Rule of Law' in Rüdiger Wolfrum (ed), *The Max Planck Encyclopedia of Public International Law* (Oxford, Oxford University Press, 2012) 1014, para 2.
[114] Daniel Smilov, 'The Judiciary: The Least Dangerous Branch?' in Michel Rosenfeld (ed), *The Oxford Handbook of Comparative Constitutional Law* (Oxford, Oxford University Press, 2012) 866.
[115] *Marckx v Belgium* (n 6) 58, partly dissenting opinion of Judge Pinheiro Farinha, para 4.
[116] ibid, partly dissenting opinion of Judge Pinheiro Farinha, para 4.
[117] Lord Sumption (n 5) 21.
[118] Chesterman (n 113) 1014, para 2.
[119] ibid para 2.
[120] Baroness Hale of Richmond (n 87) 11.
[121] ibid 14.
[122] ibid 17.
[123] ibid 15.

when she states that evolutive interpretation needs to achieve a balance between legal certainty and flexibility.[124] Concerns about legal certainty were also among the main driving forces behind the political reform process of the ECHR at the Brighton Conference 2012, where member states claimed more consistency in the Court's case law, mostly in 'issues of general principle'.[125]

The rule of law critique faces a major weakness in that it depends on a purely formal concept of the rule of law. Yet, I will demonstrate that we must reject an exclusive formal rule-of-law concept. If we include material aspects into the concept, evolutive interpretation not only conforms with the principle of the rule of law, but also fosters it.

Rule of law is a highly controversial concept. Debate mostly arises between formal and material conceptions, among which one can distinguish between several thinner and thicker conceptions of formal or material rule of law.[126] This is not the place to discuss the various conceptions in detail. Yet, a short recapitulation of the core differences is essential for the sake of the argument. Formal conceptions of the rule of law focus on considerations about the correct enactment of law, its promulgation, clarity, and prospective application. The state has the power to create law following constitutionally defined procedures and is at the same time subject to this duly enacted law.[127] Formal rule of law requires consistency and stability in the application of the law in order to achieve legal certainty.[128] It further requires that law is applied equally to all subjects of the law.[129] Finally, formal rule of law requires the consent of the people through democratic decision making.[130] The elementary principle of formal theories is that the content of law is not relevant for the rule of law.[131] Contrary to that, substantive accounts embrace elements of material justice and thus make the content of law a decisive aspect of the rule of law, understanding it as the rule of good law.[132] Among these substantive theories one may differentiate between thinner versions, which consider the respect for individual rights to be the benchmark of good law and thicker versions, which introduce human dignity or social welfare as the supreme value of a legal order.[133]

Having in mind these basic differentiations, it is striking that the critical arguments against evolutive interpretation presuppose a formal concept of the rule

[124] Françoise Tulkens, 'Address' in European Court of Human Rights (ed), *Dialogue Between Judges: What Are the Limits to the Evolutive Interpretation of the Convention?* (Strasbourg, Council of Europe Publishing 2011) 10.

[125] High Level Conference on the Future of the European Court of Human Rights (Brighton Declaration) Council of Europe 2012 paras 23f.

[126] Brian Z Tamanaha, *On the Rule of Law: History, Politics, Theory* (Cambridge, Cambridge University Press, 2010) 91.

[127] ibid 91–92.

[128] ibid 93.

[129] ibid 94.

[130] ibid 99.

[131] ibid 91–92.

[132] ibid 92.

[133] ibid 91.

of law. The two analysed arguments have criticised the lack of legal certainty and the disregard for correctly enacted law in the case law of the ECtHR. If one adopted a material account of the rule of law, however, evolutive interpretation could even foster the rule of law instead of transgressing it. This is so because arguments on the protection of individual rights or human dignity could provide compelling reasons for the choice of an evolutive interpretation over a static interpretation.

The critical arguments may of course not be rejected due to the mere fact that one could simply adopt a different conception of the rule of law. However, there are convincing arguments why we should include a material account of the rule of law in the concept instead of a purely formal one and why it should guide legal reasoning. The answer to the question why we should integrate a material aspect to the rule of law is inevitably linked with the concept of law in general.

As Klatt has demonstrated, the dual nature of law has important implications for the rule of law. He maintains that if one accepts the dual nature of law, this implies a dual nature of the rule of law and of legal interpretation as well.[134] He thus establishes a substantive version of the rule of law concept, which is based on Alexy's non-positivist concept of the dual nature of law.[135] Rule of law has a dual nature as well, combining a real or formal dimension, which mainly strives for legal certainty, and an ideal or substantive dimension, which aims at correctness.[136]

Klatt further argues that the dual nature of the rule of law informs legal interpretation. This connection is illustrated best in cases of conflict between interpretive arguments.[137] If, for example, a textual interpretation leads to an unjust interpretation, a judge needs to decide whether to follow an unjust but consistent interpretation or to reject it due to considerations of justice.[138] The dual-nature thesis for law and the rule of law provides a solution to this argumentative dilemma by means of reason. The dual nature of the rule of law requires the judge to provide a reasonable justification for this choice instead of giving preference to considerations about legal certainty or justice by default.[139] Consequently, the rule of law serves as a 'rule of reason' in legal argumentation.[140] It requires the interpreter to consider formal as well as substantive elements of the rule of law and, hence, the real and ideal dimension of law.[141] Neither legal

[134] Matthias Klatt, 'The Rule of Dual-Natured Law' in Eveline T Feteris, Harm Kloosterhuis, Jose Plug and Carel Smith (eds), *Legal Argumentation and the Rule of Law* (The Hague, Eleven International Publishing, 2016) 30.

[135] For the concept of the dual nature of law see Chapter 1, Section I.

[136] Klatt (n 134) 30.

[137] ibid.

[138] ibid 33.

[139] ibid 34.

[140] ibid 31.

[141] ibid.

certainty nor justice will enjoy preference in all cases. The preference relation needs to be justified on a case-to-case basis by means of balancing.[142]

Two factors in this balancing model for the rule of law need to be highlighted in particular. First, it is not 'the' rule of law, which is balanced with other values of a legal system, external to the rule of law.[143] Rather, the balancing exercise takes place within the rule of law itself as it encompasses both dimensions of law and hence formal as well as material values. Those internal values of the rule of law are balanced in order to define which dimension of the rule of law should be given more weight in a particular case.[144] Second, the ideal dimension of law is necessarily shown in both possible outcomes. This is because even in the case of preference for the outcome of the real dimension, it is required that this outcome is correct itself.[145] Naturally, this concept of the rule of law places an enhanced argumentative burden on the judge as it requires an assessment of all relevant circumstances in each individual case. Yet, it has the significant advantage of showing equal respect to both facets of the rule of law, the authority of positive law on the one hand, and the protection of fundamental principles of justice on the other.[146]

This theoretical fundament informs the following argument, which provides a reply to the rule-of-law critique expressed against evolutive interpretation. The dual nature of law and hence of the rule of law provides vital insights into how the rule of law connects to evolutive interpretation. If we take a closer look at the nature of evolutive interpretation as one of two poles in the time dimension (see Chapter 2), we see that the dual nature of law also displays in the two poles of the time dimension of interpretation. The static approach to interpretation aims at consistency and legal certainty, whereas the evolutive approach strives for justice in interpretation.[147] Put differently, static interpretation stands for the real dimension in law and evolutive interpretation for the ideal dimension. The dual nature of law provides the basis for the argument as to why none of the two approaches – static or evolutive – can be dominant by default. A purely static approach to interpretation would run counter to the law's claim to correctness, which is raised by the judge who decides the case.[148] A purely evolutive approach, however, would neglect the authoritative force of democratic decisions in cases in which a rational discourse leads to more than one acceptable interpretation of a right. Consequently, both poles of the time dimension of interpretation need to be put in the correct proportion in each case individually. This requires

[142] ibid 37.
[143] ibid.
[144] ibid.
[145] ibid 33.
[146] ibid 38.
[147] Mennicken (n 64) 86.
[148] Robert Alexy, 'The Dual Nature of Law' (2010) 23(2) *Ratio Juris* 167, 168. According to Alexy, the claim to correctness is necessarily raised by people who are officially 'representatives' of the law, and not by the law itself.

a balancing exercise, which defines the preference relation between static and evolutive interpretation. The balancing model will be constructed in Part III of the book.

In accepting the dual-natured account of the rule of law, both poles of the time dimension also correspond to one dimension of the rule of law. Static interpretation corresponds to formal rule of law, whereas evolutive interpretation corresponds to substantive rule of law. Put differently, the outcome of the balancing exercise serves the principle of rule of law either way, either in its formal or in its substantive dimension. If this is so, the critique that evolutive interpretation runs counter to the rule of law is wrong or, at best, imprecise. It is wrong in the sense that a reasonably justified choice between static and evolutive interpretation is always in accordance with the rule of law. Given the fact that the critics all adhere to formal concepts of the rule of law, one might reformulate their criticism and say that the presented balancing model accords too little weight to the static dimension and hence the formal rule of law. A failure to achieve the correct proportion between static and evolutive interpretation would indeed be able to render a particular evolutive interpretation illegitimate. It would not, however, be able to render evolutive interpretation illegitimate in principle, as it is required by the dual nature of law.

It must be noted that the outcome of the balancing exercise itself raises a claim to correctness and must thus be reasonably justifiable. The proposed model guarantees that considerations of justice in the ideal dimension will outweigh considerations of legal certainty in the real dimension only if rational arguments indicate doing so. From this it follows that evolutive interpretation is in conformity with the rule of law if its preference over static interpretation is reasonably justified. For the time being, these preliminary considerations of a theory for the legitimate choice between evolutive and static interpretation should suffice for rebutting the rule of law critique. Whether such a theory can be justified in the context of the ECHR and how it can be constructed in detail is the subject of a closer analysis in Part III of the book.

Part II

The ECHR Constitution

THIS BOOK MAINTAINS that constitutional principles inherent in the Convention determine the legitimacy of evolutive interpretation of the ECHR. Part II sets the cornerstones for this constitutional argument and spotlights the concept of constitutionalism in Chapter 5 as well as the constitutional character of the ECHR in Chapter 6. Chapter 7 constructs a constitutional framework for the Convention, which enables us to determine a normative theory of interpretation for the ECHR later in this book.

When investigating constitutionalism beyond the nation state, two different questions may be of interest. The first looks at constitutionalism from within an international organisation and hence at the constitutional effects on the international body itself.[1] The second sheds light on the dimension of what has been called 'multi-level constitutionalism',[2] with a focus on the mutual impact and constraints of constitutional norms between various legal orders.[3] I will focus on the second perspective as I will not examine structural or organisational constitutional elements within the CoE. A vast branch of literature has done so already.[4] This line of literature points to the Statute of the Council of Europe as the main constitutional source as it establishes the political as well as judicial organs of the community, determines the relationship among these bodies, and manifests the adherence of the political community to democratic principles.[5] The core interest of this study is different, however. It lies in the substantial, constitutional guarantees of the Convention system and its effects on the interpretation of the Convention. This amounts to an investigation into the ECtHR's role in interpreting the Convention in the light of these constitutional guarantees, and

[1] Martin Loughlin, 'What Is Constitutionalisation?' in Petra Dobner and Martin Loughlin (eds), *The Twilight of Constitutionalism?* (Oxford, Oxford University Press, 2010) 63.

[2] ibid 66.

[3] ibid 67.

[4] See, eg, Andreas Føllesdal, Birgit Peters and Geir Ulfstein (eds), *Constituting Europe: The European Court of Human Rights in a National, European, and Global Context* (Cambridge, Cambridge University Press, 2013); Evert A Alkema, 'The European Convention as a Constitution and Its Court as a Constitutional Court' in Paul Mahoney, Franz Matscher, Herbert Petzold and Luzius Wildhaber (eds), *Protecting Human Rights: The European Perspective: Studies in Memory of Rolv Ryssdal* (Cologne, Heymanns, 2000).

[5] Florence Benoît-Rohmer and Heinrich Klebes, *Council of Europe Law: Towards a Pan-European Legal Area* (Strasbourg, Council of Europe Publishing, 2005) 17.

consequently, an investigation into the legitimate limits, which evolutive interpretation puts on the authorities of the member states. The argument takes as a premise that the ECHR constitutes a constitutional system, which constrains the member states to the Convention and the reasons underlying this premise will be provided in what follows.

5

The Argument of Constitutionalism

THIS CHAPTER PRESENTS the underlying constitutionalist concepts which inform the approach of this research. First, I will have a brief look at the classic concept of constitutionalism and its transfer to the international realm (Section I). I will demonstrate how the constitutionalist method may contribute to the argument on the legitimacy of evolutive and static interpretation. Then I will go on to present in more detail those theories in the constitutionalist discourse which specifically inform this investigation. The second section will take up the theory of cosmopolitan constitutionalism, whereas the third section will present the idea of deliberative or discursive constitutionalism.

I. CONSTITUTIONALISM IN THE INTERNATIONAL REALM

There is no such thing as a general definition of constitutionalism.[1] It is a political theory, which focuses on the limits on government, and which goes hand in hand with the process of the coming into being of a constitution.[2] This process of 'constitution-hardening'[3] is usually referred to as constitutionalisation.[4] Constitutionalism is thus the political theory behind constitutionalisation. In a broad sense, any entity with an organised governance structure could be said to have a constitution.[5] However, a normative concept of the constitution goes beyond mere descriptive, structural elements and requires the constitution to fulfil certain further requirements.[6] According to a suggestion by Rosenfeld, constitutionalism stands for three core claims: constraint on the power of government, commitment to the rule of law, and the protection of fundamental

[1] Michel Rosenfeld, 'Introduction' in Michel Rosenfeld (ed), *Constitutionalism, Identity, Difference, and Legitimacy: Theoretical Perspectives* (Durham, NC, Duke University Press, 1994) 3.

[2] Martin Loughlin, 'What Is Constitutionalisation?' in Petra Dobner and Martin Loughlin (eds), *The Twilight of Constitutionalism?* (Oxford, Oxford University Press, 2010) 55.

[3] Nicholas Tsagourias, 'Introduction – Constitutionalism: A Theoretical Roadmap' in Nicholas Tsagourias (ed), *Transnational Constitutionalism* (Cambridge, Cambridge University Press, 2007) 1.

[4] Anne Peters, 'Rechtsordnungen und Konstitutionalisierung: Zur Neubestimmung der Verhältnisse' (2010) 65(1) *Zeitschrift für öffentliches Recht* 3, 10.

[5] Thomas Cottier and Maya Hertig, 'The Prospects of 21st Century Constitutionalism' in Armin von Bogdandy and Rüdiger Wolfrum (eds), *Max Planck Yearbook of United Nations Law* (Vol 7, Leiden, Brill, 2003) 279.

[6] ibid 279–80.

rights.[7] Cottier and Hertig suggest a slightly richer normative concept, which embraces the constraining function on government through fundamental rights, the commitment to the rule of law, the organisation of governance, the separation of powers, and democratic legitimacy.[8] With a focus on the role of the judiciary, Loughlin suggests that constitutionalism builds on an independent judiciary, separation of powers, fundamental rights and the function of the judiciary to safeguard the constitution.[9] This latter perspective, which accords the role of safeguarding constitutional guarantees to the judiciary, amounts to a liberal or legal constitutionalist perspective.[10] The counterpart of this view would be republican or political constitutionalism, which accords this role to a political and, hence, democratic process.[11] In what follows, the focus will be on the first alternative, being legal or liberal constitutionalism. This is because the aim of this investigation is to clarify whether the ECHR – as intertemporally interpreted by the ECtHR – legitimately constrains the authority of states' power. More precisely it is an investigation into whether evolutive and static interpretations raise a legitimate claim to authority, which must be obeyed by the member states of the CoE. Either this can be achieved by a model of legal constitutionalism or it is doomed to fail.

Traditionally, constitutionalism focused on legitimacy questions within a nation state. As a consequence, legal orders beyond the nation state are often measured by the normative functions which have been established for the national domain.[12] It is clear from the outset, however, that international legal orders do not yet or may never achieve exactly the same level of constitutionalism as nation states.[13] For example, the international judiciary has much less power than national (constitutional) courts regarding its inability to review the constitutionality of international law due to the lack of a constitutional document and, consequently, its inability to ultimately strike down legal acts.[14] This has led to the criticism that the language of constitutionalism should be limited to the domain of states and should not be transferred to the international sphere.[15] Contrary to that, it has been argued that we should free constitutional analysis beyond the nation state from the narrow framework of constitutional analysis within the nation state.[16] A constitutionalist argument beyond the nation state

[7] Rosenfeld (n 1) 3.

[8] Cottier and Hertig (n 5) 281.

[9] Loughlin (n 2) 55.

[10] ibid 58.

[11] ibid 57.

[12] Neil Walker, 'The EU and the WTO: Constitutionalism in a New Key' in Gráinne de Búrca and Joanne Scott (eds), *The EU and the WTO: Legal and Constitutional Issues* (Oxford, Hart Publishing, 2003) 33; Tsagourias (n 3) 4.

[13] Cottier and Hertig (n 5) 281.

[14] Christopher A Ford, 'Judicial Discretion in International Jurisprudence: Article 38(1)(C) and "General Principles of Law"' (1994) 5 *Duke Journal of Comparative and International Law* 35, 38.

[15] Dieter Grimm, *Constitutionalism: Past, Present, and Future* (Oxford, Oxford University Press, 2016) 376.

[16] Walker (n 12) 32.

needs to be sensitive to the different structures and relations in the international sphere.[17]

> [S]paces beyond the state … may lack a common or coherent organisational or normative charter or lack common governmental structures. However, even in such spaces, questions arise about conditions of membership, about relations, or about the organisation and regulation of power.[18]

These are typical constitutional questions. A modern, pluralist conception of constitutionalism thus needs to break with a fixed, state-focused view on constitutionalism.[19] Constitutionalism should not be conceived in an either-or fashion, which is measured by some template of a nation state, but rather in a gradual fashion.[20] It is a process, the progress of which can be measured by reference to factors of constitutionalisation.[21] Walker suggests a set of seven factors which help to determine the progress in the process of constitutionalisation: 'discursive maturity, authority, jurisdiction, interpretive autonomy, institutional capacity, citizenship and representation'.[22]

By means of these factors, the degree of constitutionalisation of a polity – at the national or post-national level – can be measured.[23] Therefore, a legal order may in the course of history be at different stages of constitutionalisation.[24] Such a conception of constitutionalism does not herald the end of national constitutions, 'which remain[] at the heart of Constitutionalism'.[25] It seeks to properly acknowledge the increasing influence of the international sphere on domestic constitutions within a concept of contemporary constitutionalism. This influence is to be understood as a mutual process, in which values and general principles of the international order affect local orders and vice versa.[26] It can be described as a 'communicative constitutional process'.[27]

The presented normative concepts agree that the main idea behind constitutionalism is the constraining function on the government.[28] The concept of constraint is thus crucial for understanding constitutionalism. The nature of these constraints has been defined as limits on the 'scope of authority', limits on the 'mechanisms used in exercising the power' and limits based on

[17] Tsagourias (n 3) 5.
[18] ibid 4.
[19] Walker (n 12) 32.
[20] ibid 33.
[21] ibid.
[22] ibid 35.
[23] ibid.
[24] Cottier and Hertig (n 5) 297.
[25] ibid 302.
[26] ibid 316–17.
[27] ibid 317.
[28] Samantha Besson, 'Whose Constitution(s)? International Law, Constitutionalism and Democracy' in Jeffrey L Dunoff and Joel P Trachtman (eds), *Ruling the World? Constitutionalism, International Law, and Global Governance* (Cambridge, Cambridge University Press, 2009) 387.

fundamental rights.[29] In Loughlin's words, state authority is limited by 'the structures, processes, principles, and values of a "constitution"'.[30] According to Besson, the power is constrained by rule of law, democracy, and fundamental rights.[31] Furthermore, the idea of equality as a constraint has gained increasing importance in the context of constitutionalism beyond the state. Equality in this context requires that fundamental rights are granted to every human being equally.[32]

Formally speaking, these constraints are equipped with legal superiority in the constitutional order in order for them to be effective.[33] Two factors are thus relevant for speaking of a constitutionalised legal order beyond the nation state. First, there needs to be a legal order that guarantees material rights and principles, which are able to constrain public authority. Second, these material constraints need to be formally legitimate, in the sense of a 'self-constitutive process by a democratic constituent power'.[34] Besson calls this the 'paradox of constitutionalism':[35]

> A constitution constrains the legal order, thus making it (materially) legitimate in a constitutional democracy. But it can do so democratically only if those constitutional constraints also constitute that democratic order … And this in turn requires a self-constitutive process by a democratic constituent power.[36]

This requires that an international community binds itself by norms.[37] This self-binding constraining effect is of particular interest in international law where new rules were classically induced from states' declarations of will only.[38] Interestingly, the international debate on constitutional constraints puts the focus almost exclusively on the purpose to protect the rights of the individual from state interference.[39] Therefore, it has been argued that the international community only has a material constitution, without the formal legitimacy of a self-binding community.[40] The latter requires an enhanced role of the individuals in this community to define and shape these material constraints.[41] This will vary from one international order to the other, which is why this requirement needs to be checked in each order individually. Whether this holds true for the ECHR as well will be tested in Chapter 6.

[29] Wil Waluchow, 'Constitutionalism' (The Stanford Encyclopedia of Philosophy (2018), Edward N Zalta (ed)) https://plato.stanford.edu/archives/spr2018/entries/constitutionalism/.
[30] Loughlin (n 2) 47.
[31] Besson (n 28) 387.
[32] Rosenfeld (n 1) 8–9.
[33] Besson (n 28) 386.
[34] ibid 389.
[35] ibid.
[36] ibid.
[37] ibid 397.
[38] Robert Uerpmann, 'Internationales Verfassungsrecht' (2001) 56(11) *JuristenZeitung* 565, 572.
[39] Tsagourias (n 3) 5.
[40] Besson (n 28) 392–93.
[41] ibid.

So far, we have seen that constitutionalism is employed to justify a legal system as well as to provide constraints to the authorities in this system.[42] However, constitutionalism also proves to be useful for the assessment of the legitimacy of an interpretative approach. Kumm notes that 'Questions of interpretative methodology … call for answers that ultimately make reference to the moral grounds for legitimate constitutional authority'.[43]

Generally speaking, constitutional law gives valuable information on how to resolve interpretive problems.[44] Constitutionalism provides a cognitive framework for identifying the substantive values and the methods of interpretation in a constitutional system.[45] It investigates the normative foundations of why we should consider a constitution or any other constitution-like document as supreme.[46] This normative frame provides vital substantive principles, which the interpretive approach to this constitution strives to achieve.[47] More specifically, discursive constitutionalism provides a framework of analysis which measures the legitimacy of an interpretive approach by its argumentative quality. Also, cosmopolitan constitutionalist models are committed to the 'meta-principle of impartial reasoning',[48] which tests whether the justification of political outcomes and norms pass a threshold of reasonableness.[49]

Consequently, constitutionalist arguments equip the set of legal reasoning with arguments that are responsive to diversity in legal systems. This is particularly attractive for transnational legal orders such as the CoE, in which the norms of an international legal system may possibly collide with domestic norms. Cosmopolitan constitutionalism does not seek to resolve such conflicts with strict hierarchical structures. Rather, it seeks to allow for multiple options of compliance with obligations, which are thus responsive to local particularities while respecting a common set of values.[50] This way of resolving conflicts between norms necessitates an enhanced judicial role in interpretation[51] and balancing.[52]

Cosmopolitan and discursive constitutionalist arguments thus provide a convincing framework of analysis for the legitimacy of an interpretive approach such as evolutive interpretation of the ECHR, which seeks to maintain a high

[42] HP Glenn, *The Cosmopolitan State* (Oxford, Oxford University Press, 2013) 126.

[43] Mattias Kumm, 'The Cosmopolitan Turn in Constitutionalism: On the Relationship Between Constitutionalism in and Beyond the State' in Jeffrey L Dunoff and Joel P Trachtman (eds), *Ruling the World? Constitutionalism, International Law, and Global Governance* (Cambridge, Cambridge University Press, 2009) 267.

[44] Aharon Barak, *The Judge in a Democracy* (Princeton, NJ, Princeton University Press, 2006) 126.

[45] Kumm (n 43) 266.

[46] ibid 267.

[47] ibid 267, 269.

[48] David Held, 'Principles of Cosmopolitan Order' in Gillian Brock and Harry Brighouse (eds), *The Political Philosophy of Cosmopolitanism* (Cambridge, Cambridge University Press, 2005) 19.

[49] ibid 22.

[50] Glenn (n 42) 276, 282.

[51] ibid 275.

[52] ibid 283.

level of protection of individual rights. These constitutionalist arguments will thus be spotlighted in the following two sections.

II. COSMOPOLITAN CONSTITUTIONALISM

In a cosmopolitan conception of constitutionalism the focus is on the position of the individual within a legal system, not as a citizen but as a human being.[53] This approach to the individual as a human being may be called the principle of 'equal worth and dignity'.[54] It can thus be said that the constitutional quality of a legal system is measured by the position it accords to individuals and their rights. In particular, cosmopolitan constitutionalism provides a framework for analysing human rights practice of adjudicative bodies.[55] In the international realm, the constitutionalist framework helps in approaching the interpretation of the relevant legal documents because there is usually no explicit constitution which could provide guidance.[56]

The primary concern of cosmopolitan constitutionalism lies in the responsiveness of constitutional structures to individual rights in heterogenic communities. The main claim of cosmopolitan constitutionalism is that state authority is restrained by substantial guarantees of diversity and equality, protection of minorities, religious liberty and individual rights.[57] Consequently, cosmopolitan theories are also strongly committed to the idea of separation of state authority, not only with regard to federal constitutional structures, but also regarding an enhanced role of judicial review.[58] Although cosmopolitan features can be found in almost all constitutions worldwide,[59] the substantive guarantees were usually limited to citizens only.[60] In contemporary constitutionalism the focus has shifted from citizens' rights to human rights, which individuals have due to their nature as human beings, not as citizens: 'A cosmopolitan legal order [CLO] is a transnational legal system in which all public officials bear the obligation to fulfil the fundamental rights of every person within their jurisdiction, without respect to nationality or citizenship'.[61] Of course, also cosmopolitan constitutional theory comes in various ways. Strong versions of it argue that there is a 'single, world community'[62] to which every individual belongs by being

[53] Held (n 48) 12.
[54] ibid.
[55] Kumm (n 43) 262.
[56] ibid 266.
[57] Glenn (n 42) 135.
[58] ibid 139–40.
[59] ibid 135.
[60] ibid 144–46.
[61] Alec Stone Sweet, 'A Cosmopolitan Legal Order: Constitutional Pluralism and Rights Adjudication in Europe' (2012) 1(1) *Global Constitutionalism* 53, 53.
[62] Glenn (n 42) 173; according to Glenn, authors arguing in favour of weakening the concept of nation states, abandoning borders, etc defend strong versions of cosmopolitanism.

human. Following a strong version of cosmopolitan constitutionalism results in breaking with the tradition of the nation state as the source of individual rights.[63] However, 'There are more conciliatory versions of it, more cognizant of the value of the local as well as universal values'.[64] The argument presented in this book will draw on Kumm's mitigated conception of cosmopolitan constitutionalism, which connects constitutionalism on the national and the international level.[65]

Kumm's 'cosmopolitan paradigm'[66] draws the authority of a constitution from its justifiability to the people.[67] The authoritative character of a constitution ultimately depends on public reason and not on the will of the people.[68] Kumm's model stands in contrast to statist constitutionalist models, which put democratic legitimacy as the core criterion for constitutional authority.[69] With regard to the legitimacy of an interpretive approach, such models would measure interpretations by their compliance with democratic decisions. Kumm's cosmopolitan constitutionalist framework, however, introduces a criterion of reasonableness for the legitimacy of an interpretive approach.[70]

Kumm's model of cosmopolitan constitutionalism can be further refined when connecting it to another model of constitutionalism, namely deliberative or discursive constitutionalism. As the next section will show, deliberative or discursive constitutionalism establishes a more thorough connection between constitutionalism and legal argumentation.

III. DELIBERATIVE OR DISCURSIVE CONSTITUTIONALISM

The model of deliberative or discursive constitutionalism is particularly relevant to the argument in this book because it provides a constitutionalist argument for judicial review and legal argumentation. Following the academic discourse, I will use the two terms of deliberative and discursive constitutionalism interchangeably.

Discursive constitutionalism seeks to harmonise constitutional review with democracy.[71] The two concepts are usually perceived as being in conflict with each other, as the judiciary exercising constitutional review is neither democratically elected nor accountable. Discursive or deliberative constitutionalism

[63] ibid 173.
[64] ibid 176.
[65] Kumm (n 43) 264.
[66] ibid 268.
[67] ibid.
[68] ibid.
[69] ibid 269.
[70] ibid.
[71] Robert Alexy, 'Balancing, Constitutional Review, and Representation' (2005) 3(4) *International Journal of Constitutional Law* 572, 578.

regards constitutional review as a form of democratic representation of the people through its inherent feature of reason-giving in the argumentative judicial process.[72] Alexy labels this 'argumentative representation'.[73] In the rationale of discursive constitutionalism, argumentative representation is thus added to the parliamentary representation of the people through elections.[74] Legal reasoning by a judge thus has to be based on rational arguments, and the binding force of precedents or political decisions has to be checked in each and every case for their constitutionality.[75] This idea of reason-giving goes back to Habermas, who has argued that good argumentation renders authorities legitimate.[76] The legitimacy of an authority thus depends on its embeddedness in a 'discursive process'.[77] More precisely, the legitimate authority of constitutional or human rights review depends on its embeddedness in a democratic, discursive process.[78]

Discursive constitutionalism is the political philosophy behind the dual nature of law.[79] It is the attempt of 'institutionalizing reason' in a legal system.[80] Constitutional review has to consider not only the real dimension of representation as expressed in democratic elections, but also the ideal, discursive dimension of representation as expressed in the ideal values of a society.[81] There are constraints on this model of argumentative representation in discursive constitutionalism, however. First, the court's argumentation must only employ good or rational arguments.[82] Second, the court's argumentation must fulfil the requirement that 'a sufficient number of people must, at least in the long run, accept these arguments for reasons of correctness'.[83]

Only then can one speak of true institutionalisation of reason as well as of human rights in a democratic society.[84] These constraints have been expressed in a slightly different way by Forst in the context of deliberative democracy.

[72] ibid 578–79.

[73] ibid 578.

[74] ibid 579.

[75] Pavlos Eleftheriadis, 'Constitutional Change through Deliberation' in Ron Levy (ed), *The Cambridge Handbook of Deliberative Constitutionalism* (Cambridge, Cambridge University Press, 2018) 200.

[76] Jürgen Habermas, *Communication and the Evolution of Society* (Boston, MA, Beacon Press, 1979) 178 and 204f.

[77] Cormac Mac Amhlaigh, 'Harmonising Global Constitutionalism' (2016) 5(2) *Global Constitutionalism* 173, 192.

[78] Robert Alexy, 'Die Institutionalisierung der Menschenrechte im demokratischen Verfassungsstaat' in Stefan Gosepath and Georg Lohmann (eds), *Philosophie der Menschenrechte* (Frankfurt am Main, Suhrkamp, 2007) 264.

[79] Robert Alexy, 'The Dual Nature of Law' (2010) 23(2) *Ratio Juris* 167, 167.

[80] Alexy, 'Balancing, Constitutional Review, and Representation' (n 71) 581.

[81] ibid 579.

[82] ibid 580. Eleftheriadis has further argued that deliberation is constrained by the requirements of the rule of law as well as the procedural requirements in a particular legal system: Eleftheriadis (n 75) 200.

[83] Alexy, 'Balancing, Constitutional Review, and Representation' (n 71) 580.

[84] Alexy, 'Die Institutionalisierung der Menschenrechte im demokratischen Verfassungsstaat' (n 78) 264.

Legitimate reasons are those which are 'reciprocally and generally justifiable'.[85] According to him, these requirements are expressions of the right to justification, which is a basic moral right of every human being.[86] The main purpose of judicial review is then to ensure this basic right by scrutinising the reciprocity and generality not only in a political decision-making process, but also in the judicial decisions, which the judges take themselves.[87]

Mac Amhlaigh has transferred the concept of discursive constitutionalism to the international realm.[88] He argues that its core feature of legitimacy through reason-giving is able to answer legitimacy questions of actors beyond the nation state. This is because discursive constitutionalism focuses on the more general problem of the legitimacy of an authority, which is abstracted from the specificities of a particular state authority.[89] Furthermore, the requirement of providing reasons for achieving legitimacy ensures that the model of discursive constitutionalism is flexible enough to be responsive to the particularities and challenges of global authorities.[90] It is not tailored to the practices and features of a specific legal system.[91]

Consequently, both cosmopolitan constitutionalism and discursive constitutionalism inform the argumentation in this book. This is to say that constitutionalism in the context of human rights adjudication needs to be responsive to both the focus on the individual as the main addressee of human rights and the requirement of rational justification in the argumentation in human rights cases.

[85] Rainer Forst, *The Right to Justification: Elements of a Constructivist Theory of Justice* (Jeffrey Flynn trans, New York, Columbia University Press, 2012) 173.

[86] ibid 177.

[87] ibid 182.

[88] Mac Amhlaigh (n 77).

[89] ibid 203.

[90] ibid 205.

[91] ibid 203, 205.

6

The Constitutional Nature of the ECHR

THE ARGUMENT OF constitutionalism in the context of the ECHR implies that the authority of domestic state actors is constrained by constitutionalised principles of the CoE legal system. Though the ECHR as such is clearly not a constitution but a multilateral treaty, it shares some core features with national constitutions such as the empowerment of individuals with rights against the state or the institutionalisation of judicial review.[1] Therefore, one could describe the ECHR as an international contract with constitutional elements.[2] This idea is highly contestable. Grimm has dismissed the argument that the ECHR, the ECtHR and the CoE as such can be characterised as a constitutional system.[3] While Grimm acknowledges that the Court's judgments may even demand constitutional amendments, he points to the fact that the power of the Court is not comparable to that of a constitutional court and nor does the power of the other CoE organs come close to the public power exercised by state organs in a constitutional system.[4] Similarly, Alkema rejects the constitutional nature of the ECHR.[5] He points to the fact that the protection level for individuals among the CoE member states is still too diverse to be comparable to a constitutional system.[6] Furthermore, states remain the central actors as they hold the legislative as well as executive power, thus hindering the Court in exercising its monitoring function properly.[7] Yet, following the idea of gradual

[1] George Letsas, 'The ECHR as a Living Instrument: Its Meaning and Legitimacy' in Andreas Føllesdal, Birgit Peters and Geir Ulfstein (eds), *Constituting Europe: The European Court of Human Rights in a National, European, and Global Context* (Cambridge, Cambridge University Press, 2013) 108.

[2] Christian Walter, 'Die Europäische Menschenrechtskonvention als Konstitutionalisierungsprozeß' (1999) 59 *Zeitschrift für ausländisches öffentliches Recht und Völkerrecht* 961, 971.

[3] Dieter Grimm, *Constitutionalism: Past, Present, and Future* (Oxford, Oxford University Press, 2016) 369.

[4] ibid 369.

[5] Evert A Alkema, 'The European Convention as a Constitution and Its Court as a Constitutional Court' in Paul Mahoney, Franz Matscher, Herbert Petzold and Luzius Wildhaber (eds), *Protecting Human Rights: The European Perspective: Studies in Memory of Rolv Ryssdal* (Cologne, Heymanns, 2000) 62.

[6] ibid 43.

[7] ibid 45.

constitutionalism, this chapter proves this general conclusion wrong. Instead, it unfolds the current stage of constitutionalism in the ECHR legal system.

I. THE CONSTITUTIONAL STATUS OF THE ECHR'S JUDICIAL REVIEW MECHANISM

The idea of the Convention as a constitution or 'bill of rights' does not originate in constitutionalist literature or in the case law of the ECtHR, but goes back to the early days of the Convention.[8] Sir Humphrey Waldock, the first President of the European Commission of Human Rights (EComHR, the Commission), addressed the matter directly in a speech delivered on the fifth anniversary of the Convention.[9] He emphasised that if the Convention was to be a constitutional document, the creation of an individual petition procedure was indispensable. If the ECHR was rather to be a treaty of collective action to avoid the rise of another dictatorship, then the right to individual petition had a less important role to play. The crucial point for conceiving the ECHR as a constitutional instrument was thus the right to individual petition. And it was for the member states to decide which kind of instrument the Convention should be.[10] Although the drafting states decided to make the right to individual petition an optional clause in the Convention, they all gradually accepted the right to individual petition within the first 25 years of the Convention's existence.[11] By 1990 all member states had adopted the optional clauses.[12] The ECtHR in its case law also made very clear that this right to individual petition had to be accepted by the member states without any reservations.[13] The final step for fully institutionalising the right to individual petition had been taken with Additional Protocol No 11 to the ECHR, which made the right to individual petition mandatory for all member states to the Convention.[14]

In the course of time, the strengthened role of the individual also became visible in the Court's proceedings. Whereas in the beginning the individual's position had been represented exclusively by the Commission, the individual

[8] Ed Bates, *The Evolution of the European Convention on Human Rights: From Its Inception to the Creation of a Permanent Court of Human Rights* (Oxford, Oxford University Press, 2010) 365.

[9] Address by Sir CHM Waldock at the Council of Europe, in celebration of Council of Europe Day at the Brussels Exhibition, 3 September 1958, also published as Humphrey Waldock, 'The European Convention for the Protection of Human Rights and Fundamental Freedoms' in Humphrey Waldock (ed), *The British Yearbook of International Law* (vol 34, London, Oxford University Press, 1958).

[10] ibid 359.

[11] Bates (n 8) 376.

[12] ibid 401.

[13] *Loizidou v Turkey (Preliminary Objections)* Series A no 310 (1995) para 89.

[14] Protocol No 11 to the European Convention for the Protection of Human Rights and Fundamental Freedoms, restructuring the control machinery established thereby (Strasbourg, 11 May 1994) ETS No 155, which introduced the right to individual petition in Art 34.

applicant has been at the heart of the proceedings ever since the early 1980s.[15] Furthermore, the Court, in its case law, has significantly shaped today's enhanced role of the payment of just satisfactions for human rights violations. This development is attributed to the high importance that the Court accords to the interests of the individual applicant.[16]

The Strasbourg system of judicial review has undergone significant changes from its creation up to today's functioning. The initial system with two institutions, being the EComHR and the ECtHR, was not fully depoliticised. The Committee of Ministers (CM, the Committee) as a political organ was involved in the review mechanism. The Committee not only received reports of the Commission if no solution had been achieved in a case, it also had to decide in the referred case if it was not referred to the Court instead.[17] Although a practice had been established that the CM would simply follow the Commission's decision,[18] it was only from Protocol No 11 onwards that the review mechanism had officially become 'fully judicialized'.[19] The newly established Court united the roles of the Commission and the previous Court in one single instance and hence decided not only upon the merits, but also upon the admissibility of an application.[20] No longer was there any role accorded to a political organ as had been done before with respect to the CM.[21] Moreover, the member states initially only agreed upon an optional jurisdiction of the ECtHR, which forced the Court to prove its quality to the member states.[22] Although all member states had actually accepted the Court's jurisdiction by 1990, this became mandatory for the member states only by Protocol No 11 in 1998.[23]

Yet, the question remains whether all these changes have contributed to the fact that the review mechanism of the ECHR may today be labelled constitutional. The power of judicial review of a constitutional court can be categorised along several lines, among which the most important distinction is drawn between strong or weak review.[24] The distinction between strong and weak review relates to whether a court may decide not to apply a legislative act or even declare it void

[15] Bates (n 8) 402–04.

[16] ibid 407.

[17] See Arts 31 and 32 of the European Convention for the Protection of Human Rights and Fundamental Freedoms in the original version of 1950.

[18] Bates (n 8) 466.

[19] ibid 462.

[20] ibid.

[21] ibid.

[22] Mikael R Madsen, 'The Protracted Institutionalization of the Strasbourg Court: From Legal Diplomacy to Integrationalist Jurisprudence' in Jonas Christoffersen and Mikael R Madsen (eds), *The European Court of Human Rights Between Law and Politics* (Oxford, Oxford University Press, 2011) 45.

[23] Protocol No 11 to the European Convention for the Protection of Human Rights and Fundamental Freedoms (n 14).

[24] Jeremy Waldron, 'The Core of the Case against Judicial Review' (2006) 115(6) *Yale Law Journal* 1346, 1354.

if it is incompatible with individual rights and hence force the legislator to revise the law (strong review) or whether the court's judgment on the incompatibility of a legislative act with individual rights is of mere declaratory value, leaving the implementation measures to the legislator (weak review).[25] There is another dichotomy between abstract and concrete judicial review, which is particularly widespread in European constitutional review debate.[26] This concerns whether a court has jurisdiction only for deciding in individual cases brought before it (concrete review) or whether it extends also to the review of the compatibility of legislative measures with the constitution beyond a concrete case at hand (abstract review).[27]

Article 32 ECHR defines the jurisdiction of the ECtHR as 'extend[ing] to all matters concerning the interpretation and application of the Convention and the Protocols thereto'.[28] Its jurisdiction, according to the text of the Convention, extends to concrete review only, thus barring it from the abstract review of legislative acts. This limitation is often used as an argument against the constitutional nature of the ECHR.[29] Whether the Convention's review mechanism amounts to strong or weak review is contestable, however. Judicial review by the ECtHR has even been described as 'a "soft" version of strong review'.[30] It is strong in the sense that it is the last instance in human rights disputes in Europe and that its judgments are binding on the contracting states. It is weak in the sense that it cannot invalidate domestic laws.[31] The limitation of the Court's power to weak review is one of the main arguments against its classification as a constitutional court.[32] However, the CoE member states were willing to accept that the effects of the Court's case law go way beyond the individual case at hand and hence have a sustained influence on the domestic legal systems.[33] Early on after the

[25] ibid 1354–55.

[26] Wojciech Sadurski, *Rights Before Courts: A Study of Constitutional Courts in Postcommunist States of Central and Eastern Europe* (Dordrecht, Springer, 2008) 65–66; Mark Tushnet, *Advanced Introduction to Comparative Constitutional Law* (Cheltenham, Edward Elgar Publishing, 2014) 50–51, referring to it as 'a priori' review, which belongs to the 'Kelsenian model' of judicial review and which has influenced the civil law tradition of judicial review more than the common law tradition. But see Alec Stone Sweet and Martin M Shapiro, 'Abstract and Concrete Review in the United States' in Martin M Shapiro and Alec Stone Sweet (eds), *On Law, Politics, and Judicialization* (Oxford, Oxford University Press, 2002).

[27] Waldron (n 24) 1358–59; Waldron refers to concrete review as 'ex post' review because it takes place after the entry into force of a legislative act. He refers to abstract review as 'ex ante' review because it can – but must not necessarily – take place prior to the entry into force of a legislative act.

[28] Convention for the Protection of Human Rights and Fundamental Freedoms (Rome, 4 November 1950) (Council of Europe).

[29] Alkema (n 5) 59f.

[30] Richard Bellamy, 'The Limits of Lord Sumption: Limited Legal Constitutionalism and the Political Form of the ECHR' in NW Barber, Richard Ekins and Paul Yowell (eds), *Lord Sumption and the Limits of The law* (Oxford, Hart Publishing, 2016) 210.

[31] ibid.

[32] Helen Keller and Alec Stone Sweet (eds), *A Europe of Rights: The Impact of the ECHR on National Legal Systems* (Oxford, Oxford University Press, 2008) 13.

[33] Bates (n 8) 418–19.

establishment of the EComHR and the ECtHR, it became obvious that it was not only a forum for disputing cases of the most serious human rights violations, but rather an institution for settling 'ordinary' human rights issues arising in the daily lives of individuals.[34] Many cases concerned the length of proceedings or other procedural guarantees or the protection of family life and personal integrity.[35] It has even been criticised that the Court keeps itself from delivering constitutional justice by defining the Convention rights in too much detail.[36] Yet, the upshot of this development was that the judgments soon began to shape the domestic laws of the member states, which initially gave rise to the applications of the affected individuals and which were in most cases adapted in the aftermath of the decision.[37] While the ECtHR maintained the declaratory character of its decisions, many member states would not confine their implementation measures to the payment of just satisfaction but would voluntarily take general measures such as amending their domestic laws in order to keep pace with the European standard of human rights protection.[38] A study of the relationship between the legal systems of the member states and the ECHR has demonstrated that the Convention rights have been steadily integrated into domestic laws and have thus shaped the national legal systems sustainably.[39] A further yardstick for measuring constitutional review is whether a court also defines abstract principles, which address not only the parties of the case, but the legal system as a whole.[40] While the Court usually stresses its strict confinement to the facts of the case, there are cases in which it shows a tendency to formulate more general principles.[41] Case analysis reveals that nowadays the Court also assumes a law-making function in addition to delivering individual justice.[42] The principles established in some cases, eg cases of non-discrimination, which hardly allow for interference, are addressed to all member states of the Convention rather than exclusively to the parties of the case.[43] It can thus be said that the Court sometimes defines abstract principles in its case law. Consequently, one can classify the Court's review mechanism as quite strong in practice.

A constitutionalist perspective on the Convention was also visible in the case law of the Commission and the Court from the beginning. As early as in the

[34] ibid 396f; see also 374.

[35] ibid 397–99.

[36] Alkema (n 5) 58, 62.

[37] Bates (n 8) 419; see also 399.

[38] ibid 418.

[39] Keller and Stone Sweet (eds), *A Europe of Rights* (n 32) 682.

[40] Helen Keller and Alec Stone Sweet, 'Assessing the Impact of the ECHR on National Legal Systems' in Helen Keller and Alec Stone Sweet (eds), *A Europe of Rights: The Impact of the ECHR on National Legal Systems* (Oxford, Oxford University Press, 2008) 703–04.

[41] Luzius Wildhaber, 'Rethinking the European Court of Human Rights' in Jonas Christoffersen and Mikael R Madsen (eds), *The European Court of Human Rights Between Law and Politics* (Oxford, Oxford University Press, 2011) 217–19, referring to cases such as *Hirst v UK (No 2)* [GC] EHRR 2005-IX and *Marckx v Belgium* Series A no 31 (1979).

[42] Keller and Stone Sweet (eds), *A Europe of Rights* (n 32) 703.

[43] Wildhaber (n 41) 219.

1961 inter-state case of *Austria v Italy*, the Court held that the conclusion of the ECHR was built on the idea of establishing a 'common public order' and not an order based on the principle of reciprocity.[44] More explicitly, in the case of *Loizidou v Turkey*, the ECtHR called the Convention 'a constitutional instrument of European public order'.[45] Furthermore, in the case of *Soering v the United Kingdom* the Court called the Convention 'an instrument for the protection of individual human beings', which is again a sign for the significant role accorded to the interests of the individual.[46]

II. LOCATING THE ECHR IN THE INTERNATIONAL CONSTITUTIONALISM DEBATE

In academia the constitutionalisation of international law is the subject of lively discussion. While the previous section has demonstrated that the Convention's judicial review mechanism displays many characteristic features of constitutional review, this section seeks to define the Convention's constitutional status regarding its wider context in modern international law. It is an attempt to transfer the parameters of constitutionalisation from the international debate to the regional human rights system of the CoE.

In the wider international law context, Besson has argued that the international community is indeed a political community as it shares common interests and goals and sticks to a feeling of solidarity.[47] This analysis is all the more true for the regional community within the CoE, which shares the common interest of the protection of human rights, democracy and the rule of law.[48] As far as the requirement of a 'self-constituting' political community is concerned, Besson has argued that the international community is still too state centred to speak of a democratic, self-constituting community, which would be able to legitimise self-binding norms.[49] Regardless of whether this analysis actually fits the international community, one can definitely argue that this does not quite hold true for the regional community protecting the ECHR. Although the CoE is a union among nation states, the role of the individual is much stronger compared to the wider international level. Not least since the adoption of Additional Protocol 11 to the ECHR and its introduction of the individual application procedure, the

[44] *Austria v Italy* (1961) no 788/60; this principle was recalled, eg, in the case of *Mamatkulov and Askarov v Turkey* [GC] EHRR 2005-I, [2005] para 100.

[45] *Loizidou v Turkey (Preliminary Objections)* (n 13) para 75.

[46] *Soering v UK* Series A no 161 (1989) para 87.

[47] Samantha Besson, 'Whose Constitution(s)? International Law, Constitutionalism and Democracy' in Jeffrey L Dunoff and Joel P Trachtman (eds), *Ruling the World? Constitutionalism, International Law, and Global Governance* (Cambridge, Cambridge University Press, 2009) 397–98.

[48] Statute of the Council of Europe (London, 5 May 1949) ETS No 1 at Preamble para 3.

[49] Besson (n 47) 398.

role of individuals in shaping the legal system of the ECHR has become a significant one.

> The personal interest of the individual who takes the trouble to prepare such a case and bring it before the Convention organs should be seen as one of the most important instruments to make the Convention really a living and meaningful instrument.[50] … In this way the individual who wants to protect his own rights becomes the promoter of European integration through fundamental rights.[51]

The constitutional status of the ECHR may be derived from several further factors. A first, and arguably modest, factor is that the Convention is directly applicable in all member states of the CoE.[52] Although only few states accord a supreme status to the ECHR, it takes up a sort of supreme function in practice.[53] This is because the ECtHR serves as a quasi-constitutional court with compulsory jurisdiction on government acts which touch upon individual rights. Domestic authorities must abide by the binding judgments of the Court and hence keep national laws in conformity with the Convention rights.[54] This stands in stark contrast to other international courts, which have less strong enforcement mechanisms.[55] What is even more relevant in this aspect is the degree to which the case law of the ECtHR is internalised even by those states and national courts that are not directly bound by a specific judgment.[56] The ECHR system has achieved a high level of compliance in most of the member states, which leads to a constant adaptation process of national laws to the Court's jurisprudence across the 47 member states.[57] Although the Court cannot declare national laws void if they run counter to the Convention, this factual influence of the Court's case law manifests a 'governance function' built on its case law.[58] This governance function is what makes the Court shift from delivering 'individual justice' to 'constitutional justice', with effects that reach beyond the individual case.[59] Second, the compulsory jurisdiction of the ECtHR manifests a vital step from a

[50] Jochen A Frowein, 'The European Convention on Human Rights as the Public Order of Europe' in Andrew Clapham (ed), *Collected Courses of the Academy of European Law: The Protection of Human Rights in Europe* (vol 2, Dordrecht, Martinus Nijhoff Publishers, 1991) 287.

[51] ibid 288.

[52] Stephen Gardbaum, 'Human Rights and International Constitutionalism' in Jeffrey L Dunoff and Joel P Trachtman (eds), *Ruling the World? Constitutionalism, International Law, and Global Governance* (Cambridge, Cambridge University Press, 2009) 247.

[53] ibid.

[54] ibid.

[55] Christopher A Ford, 'Judicial Discretion in International Jurisprudence: Article 38(1)(C) and "General Principles of Law"' (1994) 5 *Duke Journal of Comparative and International Law* 35, 55.

[56] Keller and Stone Sweet, 'Assessing the Impact of the ECHR on National Legal Systems' (n 40) 683.

[57] ibid 703–04.

[58] Alec Stone Sweet and Helen Keller, 'The Reception of the ECHR in National Legal Orders' in Helen Keller and Alec Stone Sweet (eds), *A Europe of Rights: The Impact of the ECHR on National Legal Systems* (Oxford, Oxford University Press, 2008) 14.

[59] Keller and Stone Sweet, 'Assessing the Impact of the ECHR on National Legal Systems' (n 40) 703–04.

mere international treaty to a non-consensual obligation of states.[60] Third, the ECHR goes further than many national bills of rights in Europe – if they exist at all – in that it creates stronger positive obligations.[61] From this it follows that the ECHR system has become a pivotal pillar of global constitutionalism, which sets up international limits to domestic acts of governments and which accomplishes the role of domestic constitutional courts where they exist.[62]

This analysis of the ECHR legal system substantiates the premise underlying this research that the ECHR entails a constitutionalised order of norms. The normative upshot of this categorisation as a constitutional system is that it binds its state parties to 'substantive constitutional principles' of this legal system, which go beyond mere procedural rules.[63] A crucial task of this study is thus to define the nature of the constraints which are brought about by the legal order of the ECHR. An obvious restraint can of course be found in the human rights catalogue itself, which the Convention imposes. Human rights and constitutional rights share the core characteristic function of limiting governance in a legal order.[64] Arguably, the exact shape of these obligations may give rise to controversy. Following the ideal of a discursive constitutional system, the constitutional authority of the Court's decisions – and hence the constitutional authority of the concrete human rights obligations arising from evolutive interpretation – needs to be measured by a high standard of rationality in the Court's reasoning. In Part III, I will elaborate on a model for the legitimacy of intertemporal interpretation, which is responsive to this requirement.

[60] Gardbaum (n 52) 249.

[61] ibid 253.

[62] ibid 255.

[63] Brun-Otto Bryde, 'International Democratic Constitutionalism' in Ronald J St Macdonald and Douglas M Johnston (eds), *Towards World Constitutionalism: Issues in the Legal Ordering of the World Community* (Leiden, Martinus Nijhoff, 2005) 106.

[64] Gardbaum (n 52) 251–52.

7

Three Basic Constitutional Principles of the ECHR

THE MAJOR IMPLICATION of the Convention's constitutional character is that the member states of the Convention are bound by the unifying fundamental values. These unifying values should be understood as a normative fundament consisting of more abstract constitutional principles, which have shaped the interpretation of the Convention rights. This relates to Barak's observation in the context of constitutional interpretation, who argues that 'The values and principles underlying the constitution … form a normative umbrella that extends over the constitution itself'.[1] Yet, the question remains as to which constitutional principles we speak of in the context of the ECHR. If we want to identify the normative constitutional framework, which informs the interpretation of the Convention rights, we have to dig deeper than the Convention text itself.[2] These values are evident if we shed more light on the most fundamental concepts to which a community is committed. This commitment may be visible in foundational documents of a legal community and in the significance which is accorded to these principles within the community.[3] I argue that these fundamental principles are shown in the CoE's enduring commitment to the principles of human rights, democracy, and the rule of law.

In Section I, I will support this claim with further arguments and thoroughly analyse the three concepts of human rights, democracy, and the rule of law. The analysis of the three foundational principles will give a more thorough insight into the cornerstones of the Convention's constitutional system. While this analysis will be descriptive in the first step, analysing the concepts as defined by the political bodies of the CoE and the ECtHR, it will be followed by a normative argument demonstrating how the three concepts all reflect aspects of the real as well as the ideal dimension of law. In Chapter 1, I introduced Alexy's concept of the dual nature of law, which embraces a real or authoritative dimension and an ideal dimension, which raises a claim to correctness. This is the first investigation so far to transfer the discussion of the dual nature of law to the

[1] Aharon Barak, *The Judge in a Democracy* (Princeton, NJ, Princeton University Press, 2006) 134.
[2] Compare the argument of Barak in the context of a national constitution: ibid.
[3] ibid 135.

discourse about evolutive interpretation. The following analysis supports the thesis that static and evolutive interpretation are intimately connected with the dual-natured concept of law as expressed in the constitutional fundaments of the ECHR.

The subsequent Section II will show that the institutionalisation of both dimensions of law in the Convention system can be traced on various levels. It is expressed in the intentions of the drafters of the ECHR and in their commitment to the foundational values of the whole CoE system, being human rights, democracy, and the rule of law. It is further evident in how the political bodies of the CoE have shaped these fundamental values throughout the years. Lastly, it is the ECtHR which has upheld and strengthened the realisation of both dimensions of law in its case law. The second section will reveal that the dual nature of law is unwittingly shown in all institutions of the CoE. The Convention's three constitutional principles thus fully endorse the dual-natured concept of law. This has vital repercussions for the subsequent argument in Part III on how the constitutional fundaments influence the interpretive approach of the ECtHR.

Lastly, Section III will connect the findings of the first two sections to the Court's reasoning in cases of static and evolutive interpretation. This section will reveal that the ECtHR intuitively connects the principles of the ideal dimension of law to cases of evolutive interpretation, and the principles of the real dimension of law to cases of static interpretation. The justification for evolutive and static interpretations in a concrete case is thus ultimately rooted in the two dimensions of law.

I. THE THREE PILLARS OF THE COUNCIL OF EUROPE AS CONSTITUTIONAL PRINCIPLES

The legal system of the CoE is based on the three pillars of human rights, democracy, and the rule of law.[4] They were introduced in the Statute of the CoE,[5] reaffirmed in the Preamble to the ECHR,[6] and their fulfilment is the prerequisite for acceptance of new members of the CoE.[7] A serious violation of one of these principles may lead to the suspension of a state's representation rights or its withdrawal from the CoE.[8] They further assume the function of a legitimacy standard for international law within the CoE legal system.[9] In its 2005 Warsaw

[4] Florence Benoît-Rohmer and Heinrich Klebes, *Council of Europe Law: Towards a Pan-European Legal Area* (Strasbourg, Council of Europe Publishing, 2005) 141.

[5] Statute of the Council of Europe (London, 5 May 1949) ETS No 1 recital 3 of the Preamble.

[6] Convention for the Protection of Human Rights and Fundamental Freedoms (Rome, 4 November 1950) (Council of Europe) recitals 4 and 5 of the Preamble.

[7] Art 3, Statute of the Council of Europe (n 5).

[8] ibid Art 8.

[9] Benoît-Rohmer and Klebes (n 4) 20.

Declaration, the heads of state reinforced the strict commitment of the CoE to the preservation and promotion of human rights, democracy, and the rule of law. They declared that 'All its activities must contribute to this fundamental objective'.[10] These three principles are thus the most fundamental principles to which the CoE community adheres. If we accept that the Statute of the CoE serves as the constitutional law of its community,[11] the strict subordination of all law to the principles of human rights, democracy, and the rule of law allows for the suggestion that these principles are the most important constitutional principles of this community.

They are perceived as mutually intertwined principles, which cannot be fulfilled separately. The full achievement of one of these principles depends on the implementation of the other two principles respectively. The CoE's Committee of Ministers has expressed it in the following way:

> There can be no democracy without the rule of law and respect for human rights; there can be no rule of law without democracy and respect for human rights, and no respect for human rights without democracy and the rule of law.[12]

This approach of the CoE to its fundamental principles constitutes a vital indicator for the full institutionalisation of the ideal dimension in its legal system. I will demonstrate this first by taking a closer look at the CoE's approach to each of the fundamental principles, and second by connecting the concepts to the dual nature of law.

A. Rule of Law

According to the CM, the rule-of-law concept of the CoE consists of the three components of 'state based on the rule of law',[13] legality, and due process, each of which unites another set of sub-principles under its heading.[14] Key aspects of a 'state based on the rule of law' are the separation of powers, the enhanced role of the judiciary and the fact that authoritative acts are based on law.[15] Legality groups the principles of lawfulness, legal certainty, and equality before the law.[16] Finally, due process requires that state action is subject to effective control and that everyone has the right to a fair trial.[17] In a more recent study of 2013, the

[10] Third Summit of Heads of State and Government of the Council of Europe (Warsaw Declaration) 2005 recital 1.

[11] Benoît-Rohmer and Klebes (n 4) 17 and 28.

[12] CM(2008)170, The Council of Europe and the Rule of Law – An overview, 21 November 2008 (Committee of Ministers of the Council of Europe) 5, para 27.

[13] This relates to the French term *état de droit* or the German term *Rechtsstaat*.

[14] CM(2008)170 (n 12) 7–10.

[15] ibid paras 37–42.

[16] ibid paras 43–53.

[17] ibid paras 54–58.

CoE Commission for Democracy through Law (Venice Commission) concludes that six aspects form the rule-of-law concept: legality, legal certainty, prohibition of arbitrariness, access to justice, respect for human rights, and the principles of non-discrimination and equality before the law.[18]

The political organs of the CoE expressly defend a substantive[19] or thick concept of the rule of law, which is necessarily connected to the commitment to human rights.[20] The PACE even explicitly rejects a purely formalistic understanding of the rule of law, which would confine itself to legality or the rule by law.[21] Rather, also these formal aspects of the rule of law are perceived as being informed by the substantive concept of the rule of law.[22] Legality, thus understood, requires that state authorities not only act on the basis of law, but that they act on the basis of laws which fulfil certain quality requirements as set forth by the ECtHR.[23] Certainly, the quality standard mostly relates to procedural Convention rights, such as, for example, Articles 5, 6, 7 and 13.[24] It has been argued in the literature that a substantive concept of the rule of law only makes sense in a society in which a shared set of values informs this substantive concept,[25] and in which an institution has the mandate to determine the concrete obligations which flow from the protection of these values.[26] Arguably, the member states of the CoE both share common values, which are best expressed in the ECHR, and accept the jurisdiction of the ECtHR to interpret these rights. Hence, the requirements for a meaningful substantive concept of the rule of law are fulfilled in the context of the ECHR.

Arguments based on the rule of law play a central role in the case law of the ECtHR. A closer examination of the Court's jurisprudence reveals further insights into the concept of the rule of law, which applies to the Convention. In the early case of *Golder v UK*, the Court emphasised that the principles set forth in the Preamble to the Convention are more than mere rhetoric.[27] Taking into account the role which the interpretive rules in the VCLT accord to the preamble of a treaty, the ECtHR considered the principle of the rule of law a guiding principle for the interpretation of Article 6 ECHR.[28] It was only a short time after that that the Court consolidated its stance on the relevance of

[18] CDL-AD(2016)007, Study No 711/2013, Rule of Law Checklist, 18 March 2016 (European Commission for Democracy through Law) 7, para 18.

[19] Resolution 1594 (2007), The principle of the Rule of Law 2007 (Council of Europe Parliamentary Assembly) para 6.1.

[20] CM(2008)170 (n 12) 6, para 32.

[21] Resolution 1594 (2007) (n 19) para 4.

[22] CM(2008)170 (n 12) para 44.

[23] ibid para 46.

[24] Geranne Lautenbach, *The Concept of the Rule of Law and the European Court of Human Rights* (Oxford, Oxford University Press, 2013) 191.

[25] ibid 23.

[26] ibid 61.

[27] *Golder v UK* Series A no 18 (1975) para 34.

[28] ibid.

the rule of law and declared that the principle pervades the whole Convention text.[29] It is today established case law that the principle of the rule of law is 'inherent in all the Articles of the Convention'.[30] One of the most fundamental elements of the ECtHR's conception of the rule of law is the aspect of legal certainty.[31] Just like the principle of the rule of law itself, the Court perceives it to be inherent in all Convention articles.[32] Another important element of the rule of law is the principle of 'lawfulness', which the Court scrutinises whenever the Convention demands that state action be 'prescribed by law'[33] or 'in accordance with the law'.[34] The principle of lawfulness requires that the domestic law lives up to a certain quality standard,[35] such as foreseeability and accessibility.[36] Although the ECtHR continually highlights the importance of more formal aspects of the rule of law, its concept does not restrict itself to formal elements either.[37] The quality requirements of lawfulness explicitly embrace a substantive element as well.[38] It requires that the domestic laws, which serve as a basis for state action, themselves have to be in accordance with the substantive guarantees of the ECHR.[39] It needs to be noted, though, that the ECtHR is less straightforward in fostering a substantive understanding of the rule of law than the Parliamentary Assembly, which explicitly supports the substantive concept of the rule of law.[40] Still, particularly in cases relating to torture and inhuman or degrading treatment under Article 3 ECHR, the Court has established a direct connection between the rule of law and substantive human rights guarantees. Accordingly, the argument of the rule of law served as the argumentative basis to prohibit the extradition of fugitives to countries in which they run the risk of torture and inhuman or degrading treatment,[41] and to prohibit the use of evidence achieved contrary to the guarantees of Article 3 at trial.[42] The Court

[29] *Engel and others v the Netherlands* Series A no 22 (1976) para 69.

[30] *Amuur v France* (1996) EHRR 1996-III para 50; *Iatridis v Greece* (1999) EHRR 1999-II para 58; *Baka v Hungary* [GC] (2016) EHRR 2016 para 117; *Béláné Nagy v Hungary* [GC] EHRR 2016 para 112; *Broniowski v Poland* [GC] EHRR 2005-IX para 147.

[31] *Beian v Romania* EHRR 2007-V para 39; *Lupeni Greek Catholic Parish and Others v Romania* [GC] EHRR 2016 para 116; *Béláné Nagy v Hungary* (n 30) para 89.

[32] *Beian v Romania* (n 31) para 39; *Lupeni Greek Catholic Parish and Others v Romania* (n 31) para 116.

[33] eg Art 5(1) ECHR: 'No one shall be deprived of this liberty save in the following cases and in accordance with a procedure prescribed by law'; Art 10(2) ECHR: 'The exercise of these freedoms … may be subject to such formalities, conditions, restrictions or penalties as are prescribed by law'.

[34] eg Art 8(2) ECHR: 'There shall be no interference by a public authority with the exercise of this right except such as is in accordance with the law'.

[35] *Amann v Switzerland* [GC] (2000) EHRR 2000-II para 57.

[36] ibid para 55; *Broniowski v Poland* (n 30) para 147.

[37] Lautenbach (n 24) 212.

[38] This was mentioned for the first time in *Winterwerp v The Netherlands* Series A no 33 (1979) para 39.

[39] *Ilaşcu and others v Moldova and Russia* [GC] EHRR 2004-VII para 461.

[40] Resolution 1594 (2007) (n 19) para 6.1.

[41] *Soering v UK* Series A no 161 (1989) para 88.

[42] *Othman (Abu Qatada) v UK* EHRR 2012-I para 264; *Gäfgen v Germany* [GC] EHRR 2010-IV para 175.

has further connected the rule of law guarantee to positive obligations under the right to private and family life in Article 8 ECHR.[43] Consequently, the rule of law requires that the member states provide adequate protection against arbitrary interference with Convention rights[44] and that they take 'all the measures that could reasonably be expected to enforce'[45] the protection of Convention rights. Furthermore, member states need to guarantee an effective mechanism for the individual application procedure to the ECtHR. Any hindrance of the right to individual application as provided by Article 34 ECHR has been regarded as a breach of the core guarantee of the rule of law.[46] Finally, the ECtHR also explicitly accords a constitutional character to the principle of the rule of law, when it states that the rule of law is 'One of the fundamental components of European public order'.[47]

This analysis of the CoE's concept of the rule of law allows for an interesting interim conclusion. It reveals that the political as well as the judicial organs of the organisation fully endorse formal and substantive elements of the rule of law. Both are thus inherent elements of the ECHR, which need to be taken into consideration when interpreting the Convention.

B. Democracy

The Preamble to the Statute of the CoE states that 'individual freedom, political liberty and the rule of law, … form the basis of all genuine democracy'.[48] Likewise, the Preamble to the ECHR maintains that the 'fundamental freedoms … are best maintained … by an effective democracy'.[49] Although democracy is one of the main pillars of the CoE's political action, the Parliamentary Assembly today still sees a need for further conceptualisation.[50] In 1983 the Parliamentary Assembly adopted a Resolution on the 'principles of democracy'.[51] The Resolution roots the concept in human dignity and equal respect for every individual,[52] and subdivides it into four dimensions, namely 'social and professional life', 'political and institutional life', 'international relations' and 'legal standards'.[53] The first dimension embraces freedom of expression, the right

[43] *Sylvester v Austria* (2003) nos 36812/97 and 40104/98 para 63; *P.P. v Poland* (2008) no 8677/03 para 88.

[44] *Tysiac v Poland* EHRR 2007-I para 112.

[45] *Sylvester v Austria* (n 43) para 72; *P.P. v Poland* (n 43) para 95.

[46] *Ilaşcu and others v Moldova and Russia* (n 39) paras 317, 481.

[47] *Al-Dulimi and Montana Management Inc. v Switzerland* [GC] EHRR 2016 para 145.

[48] Statute of the Council of Europe (n 5) recital 3 of the Preamble.

[49] Convention for the Protection of Human Rights and Fundamental Freedoms (n 6) recital 4 of the Preamble.

[50] Resolution 1746 (2010) Democracy in Europe: Crisis and Perspectives (Council of Europe Parliamentary Assembly).

[51] Resolution 800 (1983) Principles of Democracy (Council of Europe Parliamentary Assembly).

[52] ibid para 4.

[53] ibid; see sections A, B, C and D.

to information, and the importance of human rights education.[54] The political dimension focuses on democratic elections and the enhanced integration of individuals in the political decision-making process.[55] The international dimension highlights the element of global justice in the concept of democracy.[56] The final legal dimension connects the concept of democracy to the guarantees of rule of law and separation of powers, and stresses the role of judges in scrutinising the compliance of other state powers with their legal obligations.[57] It further highlights the importance of achieving a fair balance between protecting individual rights and national interests.[58] Lastly, the legal dimension of democracy also stresses the need to be 'open-minded … to new provisions affording fuller protection of human rights'.[59] A 2010 Resolution of the Parliamentary Assembly gives further insights into some of these elements. It stresses the deliberative character of democracy[60] and demands an even more enhanced role for individuals in the democratic decision-making process.[61] Furthermore, it maintains that democracy not only amounts to procedural guarantees of decision making, but also depends heavily upon a society which seeks to achieve social justice and equal respect.[62]

A more accentuated concept appears if one analyses the jurisprudence of the ECtHR. The Court reiterated in several cases the fundamental character of this principle when holding that 'the Convention was designed to maintain and promote the ideals and values of a democratic society'.[63] The Convention establishes vital prerequisites for the democratic decision-making process in the member states. One indispensable aspect of a democratic state is protected under Article 3 of the first additional Protocol,[64] which provides for the right to free elections. It is thus one of the core connections between the ECHR and the principle of democracy.[65] In one of its earliest cases, the Court held with regard to Article 6 ECHR that

> [i]n a democratic society within the meaning of the Convention, the right to a fair administration of justice holds such a prominent place that a restrictive interpretation

[54] ibid section A.
[55] ibid section B.
[56] ibid section C.
[57] ibid section D, i.
[58] ibid section D, ii.
[59] ibid section D, ii.
[60] Resolution 1746 (2010) (n 50) para 6.1.1.
[61] ibid paras 2.1. and 2.2.
[62] ibid para 2.3.
[63] *Kjeldsen, Busk Madsen and Pedersen v Denmark* Series A no 23 (1976) para 53; *United Communist Party of Turkey and Others v Turkey* [GC] (1998) EHRR 1998-I para 45; *Zdanoka v Latvia* [GC] EHRR 2006-IV para 98.
[64] Protocol to the Convention for the Protection of Human Rights and Fundamental Freedoms (Strasbourg, 20 March 1953) ETS No 009.
[65] *Mathieu-Mohin and Clerfayt v Belgium* Series A no 113 (1987) para 47; *Zdanoka v Latvia* (n 63) para 103; *Yumak and Sadak v Turkey* [GC] EHRR 2008-III para 107; *Karácsony and Others v Hungary* [GC] EHRR 2016 para 141.

> of Article 6 para. 1 (art. 6-1) would not correspond to the aim and the purpose of that provision.[66]

Although the democratic principle in the ECHR is certainly focused on the procedural legitimacy of authoritative decisions, it also bears an essential substantive demand for their legitimacy.[67] The fundamental guarantees as set forth in the Convention are thus vital yardsticks for the democratic quality of domestic laws.[68] Some of the substantive Convention rights are thus intimately connected to the concept of democracy in the CoE.[69] This intimate connection between democracy and the substantive Convention guarantees has already been highlighted by the French representative, Mr Teitgen, in the drafting process of the Convention:

> [S]ecurity of person; exemption from slavery and servitude; freedom from arbitrary arrest, detention, exile and other measures; freedom from arbitrary interference in private and family life, to home and correspondence; freedom of thought, conscience and religion; freedom of opinion and expression of opinion; freedom of assembly; to marry and found a family; the right of parents to have a prior right regarding the kind of education to be given to their children, and finally, the right to own property … Is there any State which can, by violating these rights and fundamental freedoms, claim that its country enjoys a democratic regime?[70]

In the Court's case law it is first and foremost the right to free speech as protected in Article 10 ECHR,[71] and the freedom of the press as a prerequisite for free political deliberation,[72] which are seen as vital elements of democracy. The same holds true for the right to freedom of assembly as set forth in Article 11 ECHR.[73] Also the aspects of 'pluralism, tolerance and broadmindedness'[74] are key elements of the concept of democracy in the ECtHR's case law. Hence, respect for minorities and their inclusion in the decision-making process are

[66] *Delcourt v Belgium* Series A no 11 (1970) para 25.

[67] See also Evert A Alkema, 'The European Convention as a Constitution and Its Court as a Constitutional Court' in Paul Mahoney, Franz Matscher, Herbert Petzold and Luzius Wildhaber (eds), *Protecting Human Rights: The European Perspective: Studies in Memory of Rolv Ryssdal* (Cologne, Heymanns, 2000) 51; Gerhard van der Schyff, 'The Concept of Democracy as an Element of the European Convention' (2005) 38(3) *Comparative and International Law Journal of Southern Africa* 355, 356.

[68] van der Schyff (n 67) 356.

[69] Conor A Gearty, 'The European Court of Human Rights and the Protection of Civil Liberties: An Overview' (1993) 52(1) *Cambridge Law Journal* 89, 116–17, who sees this connection especially in Arts 8 and 10 ECHR.

[70] *Collected Edition of the 'Travaux Préparatoires'* Volume I (The Hague, Martinus Nijhoff, 1975) 269–70.

[71] *Handyside v UK* Series a no 24 (1976) para 49; *Lingens v Austria* Series A no 103 (1986) para 41; *Gorzelik and Others v Poland* [GC] EHRR 2004-I; *Yumak and Sadak v Turkey* (n 65) para 107.

[72] *Lingens v Austria* (n 71) para 42; *Castells v Spain* Series A no 236 (1992) para 43.

[73] *Stankov and The United Macedonian Organisation Ilinden v Bulgaria* EHRR 2001-IX para 97.

[74] *Handyside v UK* (n 71) para 49; *Lingens v Austria* (n 71) para 41; *Gorzelik and Others v Poland* (n 71) para 90.

vital for the pluralist democracy.[75] The Court stresses that in a democracy, the views of the majority must not automatically dominate the decision-making process.[76] Likewise, the protection of religious communities under Article 9 ECHR is intimately connected to a pluralist democratic society.[77] Furthermore, the prohibition of slavery and forced labour as protected in Article 4 ECHR,[78] the right to life in Article 2 ECHR and the prohibition of torture in Article 3 ECHR[79] are taken to be core values of the concept of democracy.

The substantive elements of the ECHR's democratic principle can be connected to the notion of 'democratic society', which permeates the Convention.[80]

> The democratic society represents a commitment to engendering respect and acceptance of values such as individual autonomy and collective and institutional autonomy as illustrated by its guarantee of fundamental freedoms and rights.[81]
>
> True democracy entails the justification of action or inaction, whether by the democratic state or other societal actors, against the background of the freedoms created and parameters set by the democratic society envisaged by the convention.[82]

As with the principle of the rule of law, the ECtHR also accords constitutional status to the democratic principle of the ECHR, which is part of the European public order.[83]

The analysis of the democratic principle in the ECHR demonstrates that there is less clarity on the concrete concept of democracy among the CoE bodies than regarding the principle of the rule of law. It has become clear, though, that the concept of democracy in the CoE embraces not only formal, but also substantive elements. The study of the case law of the ECtHR has revealed a multifaceted principle, which puts the focus on procedural guarantees of the democratic state and procedural rights of the democratic society. However, it has further revealed that the concept of the democratic society is also deeply interwoven with several substantive Convention guarantees. Moreover, the analysis of the Parliamentary Assembly's approach to democracy has revealed a dynamic element in the concept, which demands open-mindedness towards new

[75] *Gorzelik and Others v Poland* (n 71) para 93.

[76] *Leyla Sahin v Turkey* [GC] EHRR 2005-XI para 108.

[77] *Kokkinakis v Greece* Series A no 260-A (1993) para 31; *Metropolitan Church of Bessarabia and Others v Moldova* EHRR 2001-XII para 118; *Refah Partisi (The Welfare Party) and Others v Turkey* [GC] EHRR 2003-II para 90; *Leyla Sahin v Turkey* (n 76) para 104.

[78] *Siliadin v France* EHRR 2005-VII para 112.

[79] *Akpinar and Altun v Turkey* (2007) no 56760/00 para 47; regarding Art 3 see also *Kudla v Poland* [GC] (2000) EHRR 2000-XI para 90.

[80] van der Schyff (n 67) 357; This connection is also well established in the Court's case law: *Handyside v UK* (n 71) para 49; *Lingens v Austria* (n 71) para 42.

[81] van der Schyff (n 67) 371.

[82] ibid 372.

[83] *United Communist Party of Turkey and Others v Turkey* (n 63) para 45; *Refah Partisi (The Welfare Party) and Others v Turkey* (n 77) para 86; *Karácsony and Others v Hungary* (n 65) para 141; *Gorzelik and Others v Poland* (n 71) para 89.

human rights obligations. Although this concept seems to be a very vague one, the insights gained will allow me to draw some vital conclusions in Section III below.

C. Human Rights

The third of the three core guarantees also goes back to the Statute of the CoE, which not only lists the importance of 'individual freedom' and 'political liberty' for democracy,[84] but also makes the acceptance of 'human rights and fundamental freedoms' a precondition for membership in the CoE.[85] The drafting of the ECHR constituted an attempt by the member states to further define the concrete human rights obligations in this regard.[86]

Unlike the principles of the rule of law and democracy, it is thus difficult to define the concept of human rights in the CoE in a more abstract way as it is intimately connected to the concepts of the various Convention rights. However, the abstract concept receives further elucidation on the one hand by its interconnectedness with the other two fundamental values, and on the other by the subordination of concrete human rights obligations to the human rights principle.

As has been noted in the introduction to this section, according to the CM, the three core values of the CoE are intertwined.[87] Likewise, the ECtHR upholds the intimate connection between the Convention guarantees of democracy, rule of law, and human rights.[88] Consequently, rule of law as well as democracy constitute inherent elements of the concept of human rights. From this it follows that the commitment to human rights goes beyond the concrete Convention rights to a more abstract sphere. As has been expressed by the CM, the concrete Convention rights are subordinate to the three fundamental principles:

> Democracy, rule of law and human rights can be seen as three partly overlapping circles. Some principles, such as equality and non-discrimination, belong to all three notions … Others are more directly associated with two of the three notions, such as the fair trial principle (rule of law and human rights) or the principles of freedom of expression, assembly and association (democracy and human rights). Still other principles operate principally in relation to one of the three notions (e.g. the human rights principles of freedom of movement).[89]

[84] Statute of the Council of Europe (n 5) recital 3 of the Preamble.

[85] ibid Art 3.

[86] Arthur H Robertson, *The Council of Europe: Its Structure, Functions and Achievements* (London, Stevens & Sons, 1961) 12.

[87] CM(2008)170 (n 12) para 23.

[88] *Klass and Others v Germany* Series A no 28 (1978) para 55.

[89] CM(2008)170 (n 12) para 26.

This clearly indicates that there is a more fundamental commitment to human rights than the rights enshrined in the text of the Convention. The same holds true for the other values of democracy and the rule of law. It thus seems legitimate to say that these three values form the constitutional core of the ECHR, which undergirds all articles of the Convention and its protocols. It will now be made explicit how this constitutional core acknowledges the dual nature of law and, thus, how the dual nature of law is deeply rooted in the legal system of the ECHR.

II. THE IDEAL AND REAL DIMENSION IN THE ECHR

The study of the concepts of human rights, democracy, and the rule of law in the ECHR shows clearly that both the political bodies of the CoE and the ECtHR foster an understanding of these fundamental values which fully corresponds to the real and ideal dimensions of law in the dual-nature concept of law.[90]

This conclusion can be exemplified most clearly by means of the rule-of-law concept. On the one hand, the Court stresses the importance of formal elements of the rule of law such as legal certainty, which correspond to the real, authoritative dimension of law. On the other, the ECtHR also maintains that domestic laws can be qualified as 'lawful' only if they respect the substantive rights set forth in the Convention. The PACE goes even further by stating explicitly that the rule of law amounts to more than the 'supremacy of statute law'[91] and that the rule of law is not a formalistic, but a substantive concept.[92] These latter aspects thus establish substantive constraints for domestic legislation, which amount to a threshold of correctness as required by the ideal dimension of law.

Likewise, the concept of democracy in the ECHR is much richer than a mere procedural guarantee of a political system, which grants an equal right to participation to everyone. First, the substantive connotation of the democratic principle in the ECHR stems from its intimate connection to the principles of human dignity, equality, and justice, which were acknowledged by the PACE in 1983 and reaffirmed in 2010.[93] Second, the concept as acknowledged by the PACE also stresses the dynamic character of human rights obligations in a democratic society,[94] which constitutes a clear separation of the concept of democracy from the formal element of legal certainty, as expressed in the real dimension of law. Third, the ECtHR has established a rich case law on the conceptual interrelations between the substantive Convention guarantees and democracy, which clearly go beyond political rights such as the right to free elections or the right to the free expression of opinions.

[90] See Chapter 1, Section I.
[91] Resolution 1594 (2007) (n 19) para 4.
[92] ibid paras 4–6.
[93] Resolution 800 (1983) (n 51).
[94] ibid section D. ii.

These substantive elements of democracy thus constrain the democratic decision-making process in the sense that they cannot be overruled by majority vote.[95] As such, the concept of democracy also establishes a threshold of correctness, as required by the ideal dimension of law. As van der Schyff has put it, 'the democratic society is both the reality and the ideal against which the actions of the state must be measured'.[96]

Consequently, values of the real and ideal dimension pervade the constitutional core of the Convention. This dual nature has been widely acknowledged by the ECtHR in its case law as well as by the political bodies of the CoE since the beginning. This is to say that although the Convention system grants a certain leeway to national democratic decision making and upholds values such as consistency and legal certainty, it also seeks to realise an ideal of human rights, which is best expressed in the organisation's commitments to justice, human dignity, and the values of a democratic society.

The fact that the dual nature of law permeates the Convention's legal system allows us to go one step further in the analysis. The next section will study the implications of the Convention's adherence to the competing ideals of the real and ideal dimension for interpretation of the Convention rights.

III. TIME DIMENSION OF INTERPRETATION AND THE DUAL NATURE OF THE ECHR

I have demonstrated above how the dual nature of law is shown in the time dimension of interpretation.[97] I have argued that static interpretation, which aims for consistency and legal certainty, represents the real dimension of law. Evolutive interpretation, which strives for justice in law, stands for the ideal dimension of law. While I have raised this claim in Chapter 4 in a more abstract way to demonstrate that evolutive interpretation is not necessarily in conflict with the rule of law, I will now link this claim to the concrete context of evolutive interpretation of the ECHR.

The attribution of static and evolutive interpretation to the real and ideal dimension is generally supported by the way the ECtHR uses evolutive interpretation in its case law. It needs to be noted, though, that in most cases the Court backs its evolutive interpretations by a consensus argument.[98] As I have demonstrated above, an exclusive consensus justification of evolutive interpretation must be rejected as it builds on purely factual arguments.[99] A normative project for the legitimacy of evolutive interpretation, as suggested in this book, seeks

[95] Lautenbach (n 24) 197.
[96] van der Schyff (n 67) 364.
[97] See Chapter 4, Section III.
[98] See, eg, *Tyrer v UK* Series A no 26 (1978).
[99] See Chapter 3, Section IA.

to build upon a more thorough justification. It is thus even more interesting to study the reasoning of the Court in those cases in which it was not possible to establish a consensus among the contracting states because then the judges had to resort to a more thorough justification for their evolutive interpretation. Case analysis of these cases shows that by means of evolutive interpretation the Court primarily strives for effective human rights protection.[100] The standard line of argument reads: 'It is of crucial importance that the Convention is interpreted and applied in a manner which renders its rights practical and effective, not theoretical and illusory'.[101]

A further argumentative basis for evolutive interpretations can be found in the value of human dignity.[102] In the cases of *I v UK* and *Christine Goodwin v UK* on the right of transsexuals to official recognition of their chosen gender, the ECtHR argued that human dignity and human freedom constitute 'the very essence of the Convention'.[103] At the time of these cases, there was still no European consensus on the rights of transsexual people.[104] Yet, the Court rejected the requirement of consensus and held that

> [i]n the twenty first century the right of transsexuals to personal development and to physical and moral security in the full sense enjoyed by others in society cannot be regarded as a matter of controversy requiring the lapse of time to cast clearer light on the issues involved.[105]

The evolutive interpretation of Article 8 ECHR was thus justified by its effect 'to enable individuals to live in dignity and worth in accordance with the sexual identity chosen by them'.[106]

The argument from human dignity further served to justify an evolutive interpretation of Article 4 ECHR, prohibiting slavery and forced labour, in order for it to also encompass situations of trafficking of human beings.[107] The effective protection of human rights as well as the principle of human dignity are moral ideals or ideals of justice, which correspond to the ideal dimension of law. Consequently, evolutive interpretation corresponds to values of the ideal dimension of law.[108]

Static interpretation, on the other hand, focuses on the procedural or formal dimension of rights as it is primarily concerned with respect for the historical

[100] See, eg, *Demir and Baykara v Turkey* [GC] EHRR 2008-V para 146; *Sergey Zolotukhin v Russia* [GC] EHRR 2009-I para 80.

[101] See, eg, *Christine Goodwin v UK* [GC] EHRR 2002-VI para 74; *Bayatyan v Armenia* [GC] EHRR 2011-IV para 98.

[102] See Chapter 3, Section IIIB; see also *L v Lithuania* EHRR 2007-IV para 56.

[103] *I v UK* [GC] (2002) no 25680/94 para 70; *Christine Goodwin v UK* (n 101) para 90.

[104] *I v UK* (n 103) paras 64–65; *Christine Goodwin v UK* (n 101) paras 84–85.

[105] *I v UK* (n 103) para 70; *Christine Goodwin v UK* (n 101) para 90; *Y.Y. v Turkey* EHRR 2015-I para 109.

[106] *I v UK* (n 103) para 71; *Christine Goodwin v UK* (n 101) para 91.

[107] *Rantsev v Cyprus and Russia* [GC] EHRR 2010-I para 282.

[108] See also Chapter 4, Section III.

legislator or for precedents. The case law of the ECtHR clearly supports the categorisation of static interpretation as representing the real dimension of law. Static interpretation is put in a direct relation with the values of legal certainty, predictability and equality before the law.[109] In cases in which the Court considers applying evolutive interpretation, it always highlights the importance of fidelity to precedents when it holds that 'it is in the interests of legal certainty, foreseeability and equality before the law that it should not depart, without good reason, from precedents laid down in previous cases'.[110] From this it follows that static interpretation corresponds to the values of the real dimension.

Consequently, there is an intimate tie between the Convention's constitutional core, the evolutive and static approach to interpretation, and the dual nature of law. The connection of evolutive interpretation with the concept of law provides the analytical nexus for its general legitimacy in a legal system. In a nutshell, this analytical link is established by the fact that the ideal dimension of law necessarily leads to moral correctness in law, and evolutive interpretation seeks to establish moral correctness in law. However, as has been demonstrated, the dual nature of law also provides legitimacy to the counterpart of evolutive interpretation, being static interpretation. Whereas both approaches to interpretation are thus legitimate in general, we need to establish a model for legitimising the application of evolutive interpretation in a concrete case. For this purpose, I need to link the analytical model to a theory of legal argumentation, which provides justification for the specific application of evolutive interpretation. This will be done in Part III of this book. I will argue that the case-by-case legitimacy of evolutive and static interpretation rests in normative arguments, which are to be found in the constitutional framework of the ECHR.

[109] *Bayatyan v Armenia* (n 101) para 98.

[110] See, eg, *Christine Goodwin v UK* (n 101) para 74; *Bayatyan v Armenia* (n 101) para 98.

Part III

Balanced Legitimacy Model

HOW CAN WE determine the right degree of evolution in the interpretation of the ECHR? And how can we do justice to the competing constitutional principles in the Convention system, which call for restraint and dynamism in interpretation at the same time? I defend the thesis that in order to legitimise its temporal theory of interpretation, the ECtHR needs to balance the competing constitutional values behind static and evolutive interpretations on a case-by-case basis.

The analysis in this book so far supports the conclusion that arguments of intertemporal interpretation, which confer exclusive legitimacy on either static or evolutive interpretation, fail to comply with the fundamental constitutional principles of the ECHR. The Convention's constitutional system has a dual nature, serving values of the ideal and real dimension of law. As we have seen in the foregoing chapters, human rights, democracy, and the rule of law all have a formal and substantive side. It is neither recommended to have a system which completely denies any of these values, nor is it possible that a system always serves all of them in the same manner. Therefore, any legal system naturally needs to establish a balance between these values, which must be open to change in the course of time.[1] This is in line with Friedman's observation that dynamism and finality are both vital elements of a constitution. Instead of fostering only one of these values, a constitutional system needs to strive for a balance between them.[2] In the same vein, Robert Post argues for a case-sensitive choice of an intertemporal theory of interpretation.[3]

In light of these considerations, the legitimacy of evolutive or static interpretation is not a matter of absoluteness, but a matter of degree. This degree may vary from case to case. Certain circumstances of a case and certain human rights violations demand a more static approach to interpretation, while others demand a more evolutive account. The final justification of the interpretive approach is to be found in the constitutional principles of the ECHR. The

1 Daniel Smilov, 'The Judiciary: The Least Dangerous Branch?' in Michel Rosenfeld (ed), *The Oxford Handbook of Comparative Constitutional Law* (Oxford, Oxford University Press, 2012) 862.

2 Barry Friedman, 'Dialogue and Judicial Review' (1993) 91(4) *Michigan Law Review* 577, 652.

3 Robert Post, 'Theories of Constitutional Interpretation' (1990) 30 *Representations* 13, 35; in his terms this is to say a theory that considers both historical and responsive interpretation. This terminology mainly corresponds to static and evolutive interpretation.

following chapters construct a rational balancing procedure for choosing the correct approach to intertemporal interpretation, which is in accordance with the Convention's constitutional fundaments.

Chapter 8 establishes the fundaments of this balancing model. It sheds light on the norm-theoretical background of the values in the real and ideal dimension of law. They should be constructed as principles rather than rules. This analysis provides the theoretical fundament for establishing a conditional preference relation between two competing normative arguments in the Court's reasoning of whether to choose a static or evolutive approach to interpretation. Chapter 8 will also locate the balancing model in the process of the application of law, and will differentiate it from balancing models, which have been established for proportionality analysis and for competing competences. I will further differentiate it from models for the balancing of interpretive canons and demonstrate why a balancing of the values behind evolutive and static interpretation is preferable.

Chapter 9 develops the balancing-based model for determining the legitimacy of evolutive and static interpretation of the ECHR in a specific case. It also reacts to the critical discussion on balancing in human rights assessment. I will outline the internal structure of such a model as well as its weight formula for balancing the competing principles. This section will take Alexy's balancing model for proportionality analysis as its starting point and will adapt it to the requirements of balancing in the time dimension of interpretation.

Chapter 10 elaborates on the external justification of the balancing model. It will identify the relevant factors which influence the weight of the competing principles. This section contains a thorough analysis of the case law of the ECtHR as well as the fundamental principles of the Convention in order to identify as many of the relevant arguments for static and evolutive interpretation as possible. I will give them the shape of weighting rules. This chapter finally sheds light on the factor of the epistemic reliability of the underlying premises, which has a tremendous impact on the concrete weight of a principle.

8

Setting the Scene for Balancing at the Interpretation Stage

Balancing is a method of legal argumentation which seeks to achieve the correct proportion between two competing principles.[1] This is a conditional proportion instead of a strictly hierarchical relation.

The dual-nature theory of law so far has demonstrated that static and evolutive interpretations serve higher normative requirements, as expressed in the constitutional values belonging to the real and ideal dimensions of law. I have demonstrated in Chapter 7 that these values of the real and ideal dimension are mirrored in the Convention's three constitutional values of human rights, democracy, and the rule of law. The nature of these normative requirements, which influence the choice between static and evolutive interpretation, can either be one of rules or principles. The first two sections of this chapter defend their categorisation as principles and build the norm-theoretical fundament for the balancing model. The final two sections locate the balancing model for evolutive and static interpretation within the different stages of law application and differentiate it from other balancing models.

I. THE DISTINCTION BETWEEN RULES AND PRINCIPLES

If the values of the real and ideal dimension are constructed as rules, they are to be perceived as definitive imperatives,[2] commanding that a norm be interpreted evolutively or not. Given the fact that both the real and ideal normative requirements of the ECHR cannot be fulfilled at the same time, the rule-like conception would lead to a conflict between the two. The resolution of a conflict between rules demands that either one of the competing rules is invalidated or that an exception clause is added to one of the two rules.[3] A rule conception of the normative requirements in the real and ideal dimension would thus require that one of the two is hierarchically superior. This is to say that either the real

[1] Robert Alexy, *A Theory of Constitutional Rights* (Julian Rivers trans, Oxford, Oxford University Press, 2010 (repr)) 50f.

[2] ibid 57.

[3] ibid 49.

dimension is given priority in the ECHR, which would lead to an obligation for the ECtHR to interpret statically, or that the ideal dimension should be superior, which would create an imperative to interpret evolutively. However, as has been demonstrated above, both dimensions are fully endorsed by the constitutional core of the Convention and are vital elements of human rights protection in general. It would be difficult to maintain that the three foundational concepts of human rights, democracy, and the rule of law should be reduced to either their formal or substantive aspects. Consequently, the normative constitutional requirements of the real and ideal dimension compete at an equal level. This conflict is not an accidental one, which can easily be resolved by omitting one of the two dimensions in the ECHR. Rather, the conflict between the values underpinning static and evolutive interpretation is a deliberate one as both dimensions serve vital goals of the European human rights protection system. The drafters of the Convention have committed themselves to the constitutional values of both dimensions and the political organs today uphold this commitment.[4]

If the normative requirements are constructed as principles, however, the command to interpret a norm evolutively depends on the factual and legal circumstances of the case.[5] Then the conflict between the normative requirements no longer poses a problem as they can both be realised to varying degrees.[6] The principle-theoretical background opens the possibility of a conditional preference relation between two competing constitutional principles, which is sensitive to the specific circumstances of the case. It is important to note that such a case-dependent preference relation between static and evolutive interpretation does not lead to pure contingency in the interpretive approach of the ECtHR. In the long term, the determination of preference relations in concrete cases will lead to a rich dogmatic of preference relations, which allows for a certain degree of predictability for future cases.[7] Consequently, it is more reasonable to construct the constitutional values of the real and ideal dimension in the ECHR as principles which determine the choice between evolutive and static interpretation.

The literature on principles theory so far provides us with the distinction between formal and material principles,[8] or, in Dworkin's wording, 'conservative principles' and 'substantive principles'.[9]

[4] For a detailed discussion, see Chapter 7.

[5] This is due to the nature of principles as optimisation requirements, which demand 'that something be realized to the greatest extent possible given the legal and factual possibilities': Alexy, *A Theory of Constitutional Rights* (n 1) 47.

[6] ibid 48.

[7] ibid 108; this effect results from Alexy's 'Law of Competing Principles', which states that the concrete preference relation in a specific case takes the character of a rule and thus constitutes a definitive imperative: ibid 54.

[8] Initially, Alexy considered the category of material principles or substantive principles, see ibid 65; in the Postscript added later, he also considered formal principles, see ibid 414.

[9] Ronald Dworkin, *Taking Rights Seriously* (Cambridge, MA, Harvard University Press, 1978) 38.

Material principles are substantive individual rights, such as constitutional rights or human rights.[10] They are material because they represent substantive values, which ultimately refer to moral correctness, fairness or justice.[11] Alexy argues that collective goods constitute material principles as well,[12] whereas Dworkin distinguishes between substantive principles, as requirements of morality, and policies, as economic, political or social community goals.[13] For the purposes of this study, it suffices to bear in mind that a principle is material if it stands for moral correctness.

Formal principles share the main characteristic feature of material principles, which is the feature of being an optimisation requirement.[14] It is the object of this optimisation, in which formal principles differ from material principles. Formal principles focus on the procedural requirements of a democratic decision-making process only, leaving the qualification of its content aside.[15] Put differently, formal principles confine themselves to the real dimension of law instead of the ideal dimension.[16] A principle is thus formal if it stands for formal or procedural values. Examples of formal principles are democracy in the sense of an authoritative decision by a democratic legislator.[17] Borowski further specifies that it is the 'respect' for a previous authoritative decision by the competent body which constitutes what he calls an 'accessory formal principle'.[18] Dworkin further adds the doctrine of precedent as a formal principle.[19] According to Dworkin, formal principles seek to maintain the 'status quo'[20] or, in other words, legal certainty.

How can we transfer the categories of formal and material principles to the discussion about evolutive and static interpretation? The following section demonstrates that there is an intimate connection between static interpretation and formal principles as well as between evolutive interpretation and material principles.

II. CONNECTING STATIC AND EVOLUTIVE INTERPRETATION TO FORMAL AND MATERIAL PRINCIPLES

Naturally, legal interpretation raises questions of formal and material principles. Should a court follow formal considerations such as legal certainty

[10] Alexy, *A Theory of Constitutional Rights* (n 1) 65; Dworkin (n 9) 82, 90.

[11] Dworkin (n 9) 22.

[12] Alexy, *A Theory of Constitutional Rights* (n 1) 65.

[13] Dworkin (n 9) 22.

[14] Robert Alexy, 'Formal Principles: Some Replies to Critics' (2014) 12(3) *International Journal of Constitutional Law* 511, 515.

[15] ibid 516.

[16] ibid.

[17] Martin Borowski, 'Formelle Prinzipien und Gewichtsformel' in Matthias Klatt (ed), *Prinzipientheorie und Theorie der Abwägung* (Tübingen, Mohr Siebeck, 2013) 184.

[18] ibid 192.

[19] Dworkin (n 9) 38, 'formal' being 'conservative' in his wording.

[20] ibid 38.

and democratic legitimacy and thus strive for consistency in its case law and respect for legislative intent? Or should it rather safeguard material principles such as justice and thus aim at achieving morally correct outcomes?

I have demonstrated above how the justification of the ECtHR in cases of evolutive interpretation relates to the ideal dimension of law.[21] The Court employs arguments such as human dignity, personal freedom or the effective protection of human rights in order to justify evolutive interpretation. These arguments clearly correspond to material principles, which are concerned with the substantive content of a right instead of its procedural legitimacy. In static interpretations, however, the Court resorts to arguments such as legal certainty, predictability and lack of consensus. It thus puts the focus on procedural requirements, which are not related to the substance of a right, but which amount to formal principles. Consequently, material principles provide the normative reasons for evolutive interpretation, whereas formal principles provide the normative reasons for static interpretation.

The categorisation of the arguments in support of evolutive and static interpretation as principles has major implications for the resolution of the conflict between the two approaches to interpretation. Principles, in contrast to rules, can be contradictory and conflict with each other, without the consequence that one of them necessarily needs to give way to the other principle. Rather, the preference relation between them is conditional as it depends on the factual and legal possibilities of the case of conflict.[22] This is achieved by means of balancing of the two competing principles. Consequently, to resolve the conflict between evolutive and static interpretation in a concrete case, one needs to balance the competing normative arguments behind the two approaches to interpretation. It is thus the constitutional principles which have to be balanced.[23]

Consequently, the choice between evolutive and static interpretation opens a new field of application for the theory of balancing as well as for the theory of formal and material principles.[24]

III. BALANCING IN THE DIFFERENT STAGES OF LAW APPLICATION

Three scenarios of balancing in the application of law need to be distinguished from each other: balancing at the competence level, balancing at the interpretation stage, and balancing at the proportionality stage. The model of balancing

[21] See Chapter 7, Section III.

[22] Alexy, *A Theory of Constitutional Rights* (n 1) 47.

[23] Compare: Aharon Barak, *The judge in a democracy* (Princeton, Princeton University Press 2006) 126.

[24] See Alexy, *A Theory of Constitutional Rights* (n 1); Klatt has further demonstrated the applicability of formal principles to the balancing of competences: see Matthias Klatt, *Die praktische Konkordanz von Kompetenzen: Entwickelt anhand der Jurisdiktionskonflikte im europäischen Grundrechtsschutz* (Tübingen, Mohr Siebeck, 2014).

will probably not be the same for each stage of the application of law. Therefore, it is highly unlikely that one can construct an abstract one-size-fits-all model of balancing for all stages of the application of the law. Although the discourse on balancing in the other stages of law application may provide relevant insights, one needs to scrutinise carefully the transferability of these discourses to the stage of interpretation.

The standard case of balancing refers to the field of colliding fundamental rights, and hence to the proportionality analysis of an interference with a right. Proportionality analysis amounts to a three-pronged test, which consists of the steps of suitability, necessity and balancing in the strict sense, preceded by the examination of the legitimate aim.[25] In the case of limitations on Convention rights, also the ECtHR resorts to proportionality analysis, which more or less strictly follows the steps of legitimate aim,[26] necessity[27] and balancing in the strict sense.[28] The step of balancing in the strict sense amounts to the determination of the weight of the fundamental right on the one hand, and the intensity of the interference on the other. Once the weights have been accorded to each side, it can be determined which of the colliding interests is more important according to the circumstances of the specific case.[29]

Balancing has also been suggested as a solution for colliding competences of judicial organs in the multi-layered human rights protection in Europe.[30] Klatt has suggested a model for the balancing of competences which leads to a conditional preference relation, depending on the weight of the competences in a concrete case of overlapping competences between different institutions.[31] This is particularly relevant in the international and European realm, where jurisdictions beyond the nation state complement domestic jurisdictions.

The status of balancing in the interpretation stage is less explored in the academic discourse today.[32] It needs to be recalled here that static and evolutive interpretations are not interpretive canons themselves. As has been demonstrated in Chapter 3, they are located on a meta-level of the interpretive canons. This meta-level refers to the time dimension of interpretation, which is seen in every canon of interpretation. Notwithstanding this structural difference, the discussion on the balancing of interpretive canons may provide useful insights

[25] Robert Alexy, 'Balancing, Constitutional Review, and Representation' (2005) 3(4) *International Journal of Constitutional Law* 572, 572.

[26] Janneke H Gerards, *General Principles of the European Convention on Human Rights* (Cambridge, Cambridge University Press, 2019) 220f.

[27] See generally Janneke Gerards, 'How to Improve the Necessity Test of the European Court of Human Rights' (2013) 11(2) *International Journal of Constitutional Law* 466, 466–490.

[28] Gerards (n 26) 242f.

[29] Robert Alexy, 'On Balancing and Subsumption. A Structural Comparison' (2003) 16(4) *Ratio Juris* 433, 437f.

[30] Klatt, *Die praktische Konkordanz von Kompetenzen* (n 24) 16–19.

[31] ibid 194 and in chapter 9.

[32] But see Matthias Klatt, 'The Rule of Dual-Natured Law' in Eveline T Feteris, Harm Kloosterhuis, Jose Plug and Carel Smith (eds), *Legal Argumentation and the Rule of Law* (The Hague, Eleven International Publishing, 2016).

for a model of balancing interpretive theories such as evolutive and static interpretation. The literature provides us with some models of conditional preference relations relating to the canons of interpretation, which will be presented in more detail in the following.

IV. BALANCING OF INTERPRETIVE CANONS

The model of balancing interpretive arguments or canons is an alternative approach to the classic discussion of a hierarchical order of interpretive canons. At the time of writing, no generally accepted model for a ranking of the interpretive canons can be found in the literature.[33] From a discourse-theoretical perspective on legal argumentation, a conditional preference relation among interpretive canons is preferable to a strict hierarchical order of interpretive canons.[34] This section sheds light on three arguments of this kind.

A. Alexy's Model of a Preference Relation for Canons

Alexy has described the cornerstones of a model of balancing canons, although he did not call it a balancing model.[35] The fundamental principle of such a model is the principle of universalisability, which requires that the choice of argument must be based on rationally justifiable rules.[36] The principle of universalisability is expressed in the following rule of Alexy's model: '(J.8) Determinations of the relative weight of arguments different in form must conform to weighting rules'.[37]

The weight accorded to a specific type of argument must thus be justified according to weighting rules. This exercise is called 'external justification' and links any balancing exercise to legal argumentation.[38]

Alexy has defined two further rules, which apply to the choice among interpretive canons. The first one defines a prima facie preference relation in favour of textual and intentionalist arguments, unless they are outweighed by other rational arguments:

> (J.7) Arguments which give expression to a link with the actual words of the law, or the will of the historical legislator, take precedence over other arguments, unless rational grounds can be cited for granting precedence to the other arguments.[39]

[33] See generally Robert Alexy, *A Theory of Legal Argumentation: The Theory of Rational Discourse as Theory of Legal Justification* (Ruth Adler and Neil MacCormick trans, Oxford, Oxford University Press, 2011) 247.

[34] ibid 248.

[35] ibid 248f.

[36] ibid 249.

[37] ibid.

[38] ibid 230f; see also Matthias Klatt and Johannes Schmidt, 'Epistemic Discretion in Constitutional Law' (2012) 10(1) *International Journal of Constitutional Law* 69, 74.

[39] Alexy, *A Theory of Legal Argumentation* (n 33) 248.

This rule was later called the 'Radbruch formula of legal argumentation'.[40] Finally, a third rule ensures that every possible interpretive argument must be taken into consideration: '(J.9) Every possibly proposable argument of such a form that it can be counted as one of the canons of interpretation must be given due consideration'.[41]

According to Alexy's model, we thus have to justify the choice of interpretive arguments by means of three rules. First, we must define weighting rules. Second, textual and intentionalist arguments have a higher prima facie weight. Third, all canons of interpretation have to be considered. Rule (J.7) is of particular interest because it establishes a prima facie preference relation of textual and historical arguments due to more fundamental considerations of legal certainty. It thus appears to build on the premise that legal certainty is the decisive guiding principle of interpretation, without providing further justification for this premise. At the same time, the rule states that rational grounds can outweigh the prima facie preference of textual and historical arguments. Put differently, considerations of justice or moral correctness can outweigh considerations of legal certainty. If we look at the rule like this, it ultimately seems to boil down to a conflict of meta-level theories of interpretation, which is simply mirrored in the canons of interpretation. It thus seems more reasonable to resolve the conflict at the bottom, which is the conflict between legal certainty and material justice. However, the model proposed by Alexy rather helps to reveal this conflict, instead of resolving it.

B. Klatt's 'Balancing-dependent Subsumption'

Klatt suggests a balancing model for interpretive canons. His model bridges the dual nature of law as a concept of law with legal argumentation and illustrates how the former is seen in the latter. In a first step, Klatt clarifies that the process of subsumption of social facts under a legal rule sometimes necessarily involves balancing. He calls this 'balancing-dependent subsumption'.[42] In a second step, he demonstrates that every canon of interpretation displays either the real or ideal dimension of law, or even both dimensions.[43] Conflicts in legal interpretation often boil down to conflicts between arguments that represent the real dimension of law, and arguments that represent the ideal dimension of law. He argues that 'When the wording of a statute suggests a certain alternative of interpretation, which is however unjust, the judge must choose between giving preference to either legal certainty or to justice'.[44] Therefore, the choice of argument ultimately depends on the determination of the correct relation between

[40] Klatt, 'The Rule of Dual-Natured Law' (n 32) 38.
[41] Alexy, *A Theory of Legal Argumentation* (n 33) 250.
[42] Klatt, 'The Rule of Dual-Natured Law' (n 32) 32.
[43] ibid.
[44] ibid 33.

the principles of legal certainty and justice.[45] Instead of a strict hierarchy of interpretive canons, Klatt's model thus focuses on the 'correct integration of the real and the ideal dimension of the law in legal argumentation'.[46]

Contrary to Alexy's model, Klatt's model rightly identifies the source of interpretive problems as a conflict between the more fundamental values of legal certainty and justice, and he provides the valuable idea of solving this problem by means of balancing of these values instead of the canons. However, such a balancing model raises many questions in detail. First, and most fundamentally, can legal certainty as a formal principle be balanced against justice as a material principle at all? There is a controversial discussion in the literature, which remains unaddressed by the author. Second, Klatt's model puts the focus on canons of interpretation, which he attributes to values of legal certainty and justice. However, I have demonstrated that all canons bear both dimensions and cannot be attributed to one or the other. Third, and more formally, what would be the exact structure and relevant variables of such a balancing model? The literature so far does not provide us with a well-elaborated model of a balancing of interpretive arguments, which he could simply transfer to his model. In order for Klatt's balancing model to be convincing, a more profound outline of such a model is vital.

C. Wróblewski's 'Second-level Directive of Interpretation'

Another conditional preference relation of interpretive canons according to the specific circumstances of the case has been suggested by Wróblewski. He acknowledges that any text can be interpreted in various ways according to first-level interpretive directives or canons, but also that each of these interpretations can be reasonably justified.[47] This conflict necessitates a second level of interpretive directives belonging to a specific normative theory of interpretation, which determine the choice among the interpretive results at the first level.[48] In his early work, Wróblewski has formulated the following possible second-level directive of interpretation:[49] 'If there are various possible meanings of an interpreted rule one ought to choose the meaning in which the rule is most consistent with the approved extra-legal social rules and evaluations'.[50]

According to Wróblewski, the set of 'extra-legal social rules and evaluations' is the subject of ongoing controversy.[51] Wróblewski does not further define

[45] ibid.
[46] ibid.
[47] Jerzy Wróblewski, *Judicial Application of Law* (Dordrecht, Springer, 1992) 91.
[48] Jerzy Wróblewski and Neil MacCormick, 'On Justification and Interpretation' (1994) 53 *ARSP Beiheft* 255, 261. See also Chapter 2, Section I.
[49] Wróblewski, *Judicial Application of Law* (n 47) 91.
[50] ibid 107.
[51] ibid.

whether a specific set of rules and evaluations would be normatively desirable. He rather formulates in a neutral way that whatever rules and evaluations are approved, they should be applied consistently.[52] In his later writings with MacCormick, he maintains even more generally that second-level directives 'authorise a process of weighing of relative values [which] should incorporate some reference to general principles of law, and perhaps also to certainly widely held moral principles'.[53]

Building on Wróblewski's findings, MacCormick and Summers have further specified that any interpretive argument, well justified as it may be, can be 'outweighed' by 'a counter-argument leading to a different interpretation which counts as a weightier argument in the prevailing circumstances'.[54]

The authors acknowledge that this is still a rather general model of preference relation when they say that 'The whole topic of conflict-settling, especially in the weighing mode, requires much further work. We can only stress here that what really carries the weight may not be so much the arguments themselves as the values which underlie them'.[55] It needs to be stressed that the model suggested by Wróblewski, and refined by MacCormick and Summers, is primarily aimed at defining a general theory of interpretation, which is detached from any specific legal system.[56] Their model thus intentionally demonstrates in a fairly general way that in any legal system the justification of the choice of an interpretive meaning should be guided by the weighing of normative arguments. They maintain that any further specification of the second-level directives is highly dependent on the individual legal system in which the interpretation takes place.[57] They further stress that such a specification for a concrete legal system is a 'deeply complex and problematic'[58] task. However, the authors do acknowledge that one of the most fundamental aspects of any model for second-level directives is the resolution of the 'evident dichotomy between a cluster what might be called "static values" … and "dynamic values"'.[59] Wróblewski even maintains that the conflict between static and dynamic values lies at the bottom of the conflict of interpretive results.[60]

The model by Wróblewski, taken in combination with the arguments provided by MacCormick and Summers, faces a similar problem as Klatt's model. They have identified the problem properly, as a conflict which needs

[52] ibid.

[53] Wróblewski and MacCormick (n 48) 261.

[54] Neil MacCormick and Robert S Summers, 'Interpretation and Justification' in Neil MacCormick (ed), *Interpreting Statutes: A Comparative Study* (London, Taylor and Francis, 1991) 528.

[55] ibid.

[56] Wróblewski and MacCormick (n 48) 262; also 264.

[57] ibid 262.

[58] ibid.

[59] ibid 265.

[60] Jerzy Wróblewski, 'Statutory Interpretation in Poland' in Neil MacCormick (ed), *Interpreting Statutes: A Comparative Study* (London, Taylor and Francis, 1991) 282.

to be resolved at a second level of interpretation, and more fundamentally at the level of a normative theory of interpretation. However, given their claim to provide a general theory of justification in interpretation, they do not provide further insights on this second level of interpretation. Therefore, the details on how to determine the preference relation in a specific case, and on which factors influence the weight of the competing second-level directives, remain far from clear. Moreover, Wróblewski's reference to 'extra-legal social rules and evaluations' is puzzling as it seems to be preferable to justify the choice of interpretive arguments by legal standards, which are binding on the interpreter, instead of extra-legal standards.

D. Interim Conclusions

All the discussed models stress the importance of according weight to interpretive arguments in order to determine a conditional preference relation between them in each individual case. The analysis of the three arguments provides a vital fundament for the balancing model, which will be presented subsequently. Klatt, Wróblewski and MacCormick support the thesis that the conflict of interpretive arguments needs to be resolved on a level of interpretation which is superior to the canons of interpretation. Furthermore, Wróblewski and MacCormick support the thesis that this conflict resolution requires the investigation of a specific legal system. Lastly, they also support the thesis that the conflict between static and evolutive interpretations lies at the heart of this interpretive conflict and thus needs to be addressed with priority.

Consequently, it is maintained here that the balancing of more fundamental principles of interpretation is preferable to a balancing of interpretive canons. This thesis builds on the following considerations. Conflicts between static and evolutive or dynamic interpretations build the core of interpretive problems.[61] As any canon of interpretation displays a static and evolutive dimension, a balancing of interpretive canons does not respond properly to this problem of how to define a preference relation between static and evolutive interpretation. A balancing of the more fundamental constitutional principles, which support evolutive or static interpretation, thus constitutes the most straightforward and promising model for resolving not only the tension in the time dimension of interpretation, but also the more fundamental conflict underlying interpretation in general.

[61] ibid.

9

The Balancing Model for Evolutive and Static Interpretation

THE KEY FOR determining the correct proportion between evolutive and static interpretation in an individual case is to balance the underlying evolutive and static constitutional principles of the ECHR. This argument is guided by the idea that the choice between interpretive arguments must follow rational grounds.[1] I put the principle of universalisability at the core of this argument as it is a key requirement of justification in interpretation.[2] Consequently, the reasons provided for the justification of an interpretation must not be based exclusively on the specific circumstances of the case, but also on more pervasive principles of the legal system.[3] This is achieved by reference to the evolutive and static constitutional principles. The principle of universalisability further requires that the determination of the weight of arguments must follow rationally justifiable weighting rules.[4]

As has been demonstrated in the previous chapter, the suggested balancing model must not be confused with the standard case of balancing of colliding fundamental rights. This being said, the theoretical fundaments of balancing, which have been developed for proportionality analysis, serve as a point of departure for the design of the balancing model for evolutive and static interpretation.

I. BASIC IDEAS ON THE BALANCING MODEL

How exactly can a balancing model satisfy the rationality requirement, which is needed for the justification of evolutive and static interpretation? Legal interpretation as one part of judicial reasoning is primarily based on interpretive

[1] For an embryonic version of this idea, see Lisa Sonnleitner, 'The Democratic Legitimacy of Evolutive Interpretation by the European Court of Human Rights' (2019) 33(2) *Temple International & Comparative Law Journal* 279, 294f.

[2] Robert Alexy, *A Theory of Legal Argumentation: The Theory of Rational Discourse as Theory of Legal Justification* (Ruth Adler and Neil MacCormick trans, Oxford, Oxford University Press, 2011) 249; Jerzy Wróblewski and Neil MacCormick, 'On Justification and Interpretation' (1994) 53 *ARSP Beiheft* 255, 257.

[3] Wróblewski and MacCormick (n 2) 257.

[4] Alexy, *A Theory of Legal Argumentation* (n 2) 249.

methods, which can lead to different, competing interpretations of a norm. Conflicts very often occur between interpretations relating to time, namely if one interpretation strives for a meaning that is consistent with precedents or the will of the legislator, and another interpretation strives for a more contemporary reading of the norm. In the literature, Wróblewski and MacCormick have described this conflict in the following way:

> There is an evident dichotomy between a cluster of what might be called 'static values', such as those of certainty and stability in law, security of legal expectations, and respect for the constitutional division of power as between law-maker and law-applier, and 'dynamic values' concerning the importance of adjusting legal norms to common social expectations, or to the supposed needs of a changing society, or to some substantive conception(s) of justice.[5]

These competing interpretations can thus be described as static interpretations on the one hand and evolutive interpretations on the other. This conflict relating to time is inherent in any method of interpretation. Put differently, the time dimension of interpretation is an integral part of all interpretive arguments.[6] The conflict is rooted in a more fundamental feature of the concept of law, which Alexy has described as the dual nature of law. It demonstrates that there is a dichotomy in law between consistency and justice. As I have demonstrated in Chapter 8, static interpretation can ultimately be subordinated to the values of the real dimension of law, whereas evolutive interpretation can be subordinated to the values of the ideal dimension in law. The dual nature is thus seen in static and evolutive interpretation. Consequently, if the time dimension is seen in all methods of interpretation, the dual nature is apparent in all of them as well. Therefore, the resolution of this conflict in the time dimension needs to take place on a level beyond the methods of interpretation. It needs to vest the justification for static or evolutive interpretation in the most fundamental principles of the Convention's constitutional framework. The constitutional principles of the ECHR reflect the values of the real and ideal dimension, or more concretely the values of legal certainty and justice. A balancing exercise does not accord absolute dominance to any of these constitutional principles but forces us to justify the preference relation between the constitutional principles in each case. It thus ensures that the justification of intertemporal interpretations is guided by a normative theory of interpretation which respects the plurality of the Convention's constitutional demands.

The structure of such a balancing model is either that the formal principle of legal certainty is balanced against the material principle of justice, or that the plurality of formal principles supporting static interpretation is balanced against the plurality of material principles supporting evolutive interpretation.

[5] Wróblewski and MacCormick (n 2) 265.
[6] See Chapter 3.

The resolution of the conflict will lead to a conditional preference relation between static and evolutive interpretation, instead of an unconditional preference relation.

II. CRITICAL ASPECTS OF BALANCING IN HUMAN RIGHTS INTERPRETATION

Is the use of balancing arguments by the ECtHR detrimental to the effective protection of human rights? Whereas the theory of balancing provides a model for the solution of colliding material principles, the role of formal principles in this exercise is the subject of ongoing controversy.[7] The main argument against a direct balancing between a formal and a material principle in proportionality analysis is that this could lead to a situation in which interference with a fundamental right would be justified for the sole reason that the authority of the democratic legislator is then more effective. This would render effective human rights protection *ad absurdum*.[8] Put differently, critics argue that in the balancing exercise human rights might be subjected to community interests.[9] Putting public morality in proportion to individual rights might have a detrimental effect on the latter.[10] This critique may be split up into various aspects.

In his critique of Alexy's balancing model, Allan argues:

> These reflections must cast some doubt on Alexy's view that, in constitutional adjudication, a substantive rights principle might be weighed against a purely *formal* principle of democracy … There is no virtue in allowing the clear convictions of the majority, or its representatives, to procure an *unjustified* infringement of constitutional rights.[11]

The critique thus claims that in such a model, a purely procedural, majoritarian decision could lead to the justification of a substantively unjust violation of a fundamental right.

Several compelling arguments can be put forward against Allan's critique. First, in the stage of interpretation, the effect of the direct involvement of a formal principle in balancing is different from in the stage of proportionality analysis. Determining the preference relation between static and evolutive interpretation does not yet lead to a justification of an interference with the

[7] Robert Alexy, 'Formal Principles: Some Replies to Critics' (2014) 12(3) *International Journal of Constitutional Law* 511, 511, 512, 516.

[8] Robert Alexy, *A Theory of Constitutional Rights* (Julian Rivers trans, Oxford, Oxford University Press, 2010 (repr)) 423.

[9] Başak Çali, 'Balancing Human Rights? Methodological Problems with Weights, Scales and Proportions' (2007) 29(1) *Human Rights Quarterly* 251, 260.

[10] ibid.

[11] TRS Allan, 'Constitutional Rights and the Rule of Law' in Matthias Klatt (ed), *Institutionalized Reason: The Jurisprudence of Robert Alexy* (Oxford, Oxford University Press, 2012) 135–36.

fundamental right in the concrete case. Even if the formal principles of static interpretation prevail in the balancing at the interpretation stage, this does not determine the outcome of a subsequent balancing at the proportionality stage. A court could still find a violation of a right due to a disproportionate interference, even though it has previously opted for a restrained interpretation of this right.

Second, the consequence of Allan's argument in interpretation would be that we have to exclude all static arguments of interpretation in order to ensure effective protection of material principles. This would lead to the absurd effect that arguments from legal certainty or legislative intent would play no role whatsoever in interpretation. This cannot be upheld for treaty interpretation. On the one hand, positive international law accords an explicit role to historical arguments in treaty interpretation, even though this role is only a secondary one according to Article 32 VCLT. On the other, the analysis of the ECHR's constitutional values has revealed that static values form a considerable part of the Convention's constitution. These principles cannot simply be kicked out in the interpretation of the Convention, again also considering the fact that the aims and purposes of a treaty constitute the primary source of interpretation according to Article 31 VCLT. Consequently, formal and material principles need to be balanced directly against each other in the stage of interpretation. The critique can thus be rejected for this stage of the application of law.

Critics also express scepticism regarding the scales used in balancing models. Most prominently, Habermas has pointed to the arbitrariness of balancing arguments because they equate constitutional rights with collective values. He argues that values may never be put on the same scales as rights because the latter 'possess a greater justificatory force than values'.[12] Habermas' critique specifically targets balancing in the context of proportionality analysis and may not be transferred to balancing at the interpretation stage because in this model only constitutional principles are balanced with each other. However, if rephrased, the critique attacks the kinds of arguments used in balancing in a more general manner. For example, Çali argues:

> If the scale chosen is not empirically quantifiable, its invocation and consideration will most likely be arbitrary and subject to the personal viewpoints of the decision maker and the judge. Larger scales reflect political, cultural or economic preferences of their times rather than empirical assessments of a particular situation. Empirical considerations aim to de-personalize the grounds for the restrictions of rights as much as possible, however, the choice of which considerations count is in itself an interpretive exercise.[13]

Çali further argues that balancing models are prone to consequentialist arguments, which accord more weight to communal interests as 'they have

[12] Jürgen Habermas, *Between Facts and Norms: Contributions to a Discourse Theory of Law and Democracy* (Cambridge, MA, MIT Press, 1996) 259.

[13] Çali (n 9) 265.

significance for greater numbers in the society'.[14] This kind of reasoning would not only neglect the subjective standpoint of individuals and minorities, but also disregard the aspect of diversity as a key feature of human rights.[15]

This critique is vulnerable to several arguments. Balancing can certainly not be equated with the consequential argument of the greater good for the greater number. While Çali dismisses normative arguments as arbitrary, they are actually key for legitimate decision making if they pass the threshold of reasonableness. The balancing model for the intertemporal interpretation of the ECHR conforms to the idea of discursive constitutionalism.[16] The interpreter needs to give rationally justifiable reasons for the choice of an evolutive or static approach to interpretation. If we recall Forst's argument, legitimate reasons are those which are 'reciprocally and generally justifiable'.[17] Hence, a qualitative criterion applies to arguments employed in balancing. This being said, we have to accept that there is still a risk of making mistakes in judicial reasoning as there is in any human act.[18] Yet, balancing gives us a means to structure judicial reasoning and to control its reasonableness. Çali's suggestion to rely on more objective empirical considerations, however, renders balancing in human rights assessment vulnerable to exactly the kind of risk she is trying to avoid. While empirical facts certainly are objectively measurable, they cannot confer legitimacy on human rights reasoning. It is an 'is-ought fallacy' to argue that empirical facts determine what ought to be.[19] Put differently, while we can measure the correctness of normative arguments by a qualitative criterion such as the threshold of reasonableness, we cannot apply such a threshold to empirical facts. The use of empirical arguments is thus even more prone to reflect discriminating majoritarian views than the use of rationally justified normative arguments.

III. INTERNAL STRUCTURE OF THE BALANCING MODEL

What does the balancing model for evolutive and static interpretation look like? How does it contribute to a rational justification of intertemporal interpretations? The 'Law of Balancing', as developed by Alexy for proportionality analysis,[20] leads to a specific internal structure of the balancing exercise. Alexy

[14] ibid 263.

[15] ibid.

[16] See Chapter 5, Section III.

[17] Rainer Forst, *The Right to Justification: Elements of a Constructivist Theory of Justice* (Jeffrey Flynn trans, New York, Columbia University Press, 2012) 173.

[18] Steven Greer, '"Balancing" and the European Court of Human Rights: A Contribution to the Habermas-Alexy Debate' (2004) 63(2) *Cambridge Law Journal* 412, 414.

[19] Hans Kelsen, *Pure Theory of Law* (Max Knight trans, Berkeley, CA, University of California Press, 2005 (repr)) 6.

[20] Alexy, *A Theory of Constitutional Rights* (n 8) 102. The Law of Balancing: 'The greater the degree of non-satisfaction of, or detriment to, one principle, the greater must be the importance of satisfying the other'.

describes three stages of balancing: first, determining the degree of non-satisfaction of the first principle; second, determining the importance of satisfaction of the competing principle; third, determining whether the importance of satisfying the competing principle justifies interference with the other principle.[21] While the intensity of interference regarding the first principle is always a 'concrete quantity',[22] the importance of the principle which has been interfered with is one of abstract weight.[23] However, the importance of the competing principle is not necessarily one of concrete weight only, but can be a combination of both abstract and concrete weights.[24] According to Alexy, the scale for determining the weights of the intensity of interference, as well as the importance of a principle, has three points, being 'light', 'moderate' and 'serious'.[25] Consequently, the final outcome of the balancing exercise can be rationally justified by categorising each of the competing principles on the scale and deducing the relevant conclusions from the proportion between the two categorisations.[26] This step is called 'internal justification',[27] which allows for a logical deduction of the balancing result from the weights accorded to the competing principles.[28]

If we want to transfer the internal structure of the model of balancing in proportionality analysis to the case of balancing in the time dimension of interpretation, minor adaptations are necessary. The structure for determining the prevalence of an evolutive or static interpretation in a specific case also follows three steps. In a first step, the intensity of the interference of an evolutive interpretation with the static principles, or the real dimension, of the ECHR needs to be determined. In a second step, the importance of the competing evolutive principles, or the ideal dimension, of the ECHR has to be established. The third and final step determines whether the importance of the evolutive principles in the ideal dimension can justify the interference with the static principles in the real dimension.

If I follow Alexy's classification of light (l), moderate (m) and serious (s), the following outcomes of the balancing exercise are possible.[29] There are three scenarios in which the evolutive constitutional principles of the ideal dimension are more important than the static principles of the real dimension:

(1) if the importance of the ideal dimension is serious (s) and the intensity of interference with the real dimension only light (l);

[21] ibid 401.
[22] ibid 405.
[23] ibid.
[24] ibid 406.
[25] ibid 405.
[26] ibid 404.
[27] Alexy, *A Theory of Legal Argumentation* (n 2) 221.
[28] Matthias Klatt and Johannes Schmidt, 'Epistemic Discretion in Constitutional Law' (2012) 10(1) *International Journal of Constitutional Law* 69, 88, 100.
[29] See Alexy, *A Theory of Constitutional Rights* (n 8) 407–08.

(2) if the importance of the ideal dimension is serious (s) and the intensity of interference with the real dimension moderate (m);
(3) or if the importance of the ideal dimension is moderate (m) and the intensity of interference with the real dimension is only light (l).

As a consequence, the choice of the evolutive interpretation is the best justifiable outcome in these cases as it is required by the constitutional principles of the ECHR.

If these three scenarios are changed to the exact opposite, they amount to cases in which the static constitutional principles of the real dimension are more important than the evolutive principles of the ideal dimension. These can also be demonstrated as three scenarios:

(1) if the importance of the ideal dimension is light (l) and the intensity of interference with the real dimension is serious (s);
(2) if the importance of the ideal dimension is moderate (m) and the intensity of interference with the real dimension is serious (s);
(3) or if the importance of the ideal dimension is only light (l) and the intensity of interference with the real dimension is moderate (m).

As a consequence, the choice of the static interpretation is the best justifiable outcome in these cases as it is required by the constitutional principles of the ECHR.

Finally, there are three further cases, which lead to a stalemate between the colliding constitutional principles. This is so if the importance of the evolutive principles in the ideal dimension can be classified with the same grade as the intensity of the interference with the static principles of the real dimension. This is the case if both sides are categorised as either light (l), moderate (m) or serious (s):

(1) if the importance of the ideal dimension is serious (s) and the intensity of interference with the real dimension is also serious (s);
(2) if the importance of the ideal dimension is moderate (m) and the intensity of interference with the real dimension is also moderate (m);
(3) or if the importance of the ideal dimension is light (l) and the intensity of interference with the real dimension is also light (l).

In such a case, it is not for the ECtHR but for the member states to decide whether they want to opt for a static or evolutive interpretation regarding the specific legal question. Therefore, this third scenario demonstrates a new field of application for the margin of appreciation in the ECHR. It is a margin of appreciation which refers to the interpretation of the Convention, and could thus be named 'interpretive margin of appreciation'. This stands in contrast to Greer's finding that 'there is no genuine domestic margin of appreciation concerning how the rights themselves should be understood'.[30] Yet, accepting

[30] Greer (n 18) 434.

an interpretive margin of appreciation of member states in the case that the constitutional principles are indifferent towards evolutive or static interpretation seems to be reasonable with an eye to putting the individual at the centre of human rights assessment. This is because the interpretive margin of appreciation allows member states to interpret the Convention rights more extensively than the ECtHR but never more narrowly than the Court. It must be noted that the identification of a certain leeway of parties in the interpretation of an international treaty is not new to international law literature. The work of the ILC Study Group on treaties over time, led by Professor Georg Nolte, has resulted in the finding that the taking into consideration of subsequent agreements and practices 'may result in narrowing, widening, or otherwise determining the range of possible interpretations, including any scope for the exercise of discretion which the treaty accords to the parties'.[31] This identification of interpretive discretion by state parties in the interpretation of an international treaty is comparable to the interpretive margin of appreciation identified above. Yet, the process of identifying this leeway for interpretation using subsequent agreements and practice is not further determined in the ILC report. It is clear, however, that it is not embedded in a structured balancing model and that it does not result from a stalemate position of competing constitutional principles of an international treaty. The general tone of the ILC report gives the impression that it relates to the intentions of the parties as determined by means of subsequent agreements and practice.

IV. WEIGHT FORMULA

Alexy has developed a 'Weight Formula', which stands for the weight of a principle in a specific case.[32] The formula displays the following variables: the intensity of the interference with the first principle according to the circumstances of the case; the importance of satisfying the competing principle in the circumstances of the case; and the abstract weights of the competing principles.[33] This results in the concrete weight of the first principle in the specific circumstances of the case.[34] The formula can be extended with regard to the epistemic reliability of the underlying premises. While Alexy originally included only one reliability variable for empirical premises in his weight formula,[35] Klatt and Schmidt

[31] Conclusion 7 para 1 of the ILC draft conclusions on subsequent agreements and subsequent practice in relation to the interpretation of treaties, International Law Commission, 'Report of the International Law Commission (A/73/10)' (Seventieth Session (30 April–1 June and 2 July 2018)) para 51.

[32] Alexy, *A Theory of Constitutional Rights* (n 8) 408.

[33] ibid; the last variable of abstract weights is only necessary if the abstract weights of the competing principles are not identical.

[34] ibid 409.

[35] ibid 419, especially fn 97.

suggest that a variable for the reliability of normative premises should be added to Alexy's weight formula.[36] This is because empirical or normative uncertainties may appear with regard to the categorisation of the weights accorded to the competing principles.[37] Consequently, the adapted weight formula for balancing has four variables, which appear on both sides of the competing principles: the abstract weights; the intensity of the interference on the one side and the importance of the principle on the other side; the reliability of the empirical premises; and the reliability of the normative premises.[38] It must be noted that the abstract weights of the competing principles could be identical.[39] The same holds true for the empirical and normative premises, which may also be equal on both sides. This leads to a situation where these three variables – if identical on both sides – compensate each other.[40] Therefore, in many cases, the weight formula may be reduced to a simplified formula, which only includes the determination of the concrete intensity and importance of the colliding principles in a specific case.[41]

This weight formula, as developed for the standard case of balancing as part of proportionality analysis, can be transferred to the model of balancing in the time dimension of interpretation without any further modifications. All the variables are vital components for determining the weight of arguments in interpretation as well. It needs to be examined, though, whether the abstract weights can be determined for both sides in all cases of interpretation. If this is the case and if they are equal, the variables could be omitted in the balancing exercise.

I have demonstrated above that the constitutional principles which conflict in the time dimension of interpretation can be accorded to the real and ideal dimension of law.[42] I have further demonstrated that both dimensions are equally rooted in the constitutional fundaments of the ECHR, and that they are thus of equal importance for achieving the main objectives of the Convention.[43] It thus seems reasonable to conclude that the abstract weights of the colliding principles in the time dimension of interpretation are identical and hence equalise themselves. This is different from balancing as part of proportionality analysis, where it is accepted that colliding principles can have either equal or varying abstract weights.[44] This difference makes sense as the weight in the balancing exercise for evolutive and static interpretation does not refer to the weight of

[36] Matthias Klatt and Johannes Schmidt, *Spielräume im öffentlichen Recht: Zur Abwägungslehre der Prinzipientheorie* (Tübingen, Mohr Siebeck, 2010) 51, 56.

[37] ibid 19, 46.

[38] ibid 52.

[39] See Alexy, *A Theory of Constitutional Rights* (n 8) 406.

[40] Matthias Klatt, *Die praktische Konkordanz von Kompetenzen: Entwickelt anhand der Jurisdiktionskonflikte im europäischen Grundrechtsschutz* (Tübingen, Mohr Siebeck, 2014) 214.

[41] ibid.

[42] See Chapter 7, Section III.

[43] See Chapter 7, Section II.

[44] Alexy, *A Theory of Constitutional Rights* (n 8) 406.

a principle as fundamental right, but rather to the weight of a principle as an argument in interpretation. Consequently, any prima facie preference for the static or evolutive dimension is rejected. In the context of the balancing of interpretive canons, Klatt has suggested his 'Radbruch Formula of legal argumentation',[45] which accords a prima facie preference to the authoritative dimension of law in order to establish a higher argumentative burden for interpretations which depart from the wording of the law or the will of the historical legislator.[46] However, such a prima facie preference for static values in the interpretation of the ECHR would not reflect the constitutional structure of the ECHR appropriately. For example, it would be difficult to argue that in a treaty for the protection of human rights the abstract weight of legal certainty should be higher than the weight of human dignity. For the same reason, a prima facie preference for evolutive values needs to be rejected. It would lead to an almost insurmountable argumentative burden for the side of static values, and hence eclipse the authoritative dimension of law in the application of the ECHR. Therefore, the equal abstract weight on both sides leads to the situation that the variable of abstract weights can be omitted once and for all in the weight formula of balancing in the time dimension of interpretation. Consequently, only the remaining factors of the concrete weight and the reliability of the empirical and normative premises remain as components of the weight formula.

The following chapter sheds further light on the question of how to accord weight to the competing principles at stake.

[45] Matthias Klatt, 'The Rule of Dual-Natured Law' in Eveline T Feteris, Harm Kloosterhuis, Jose Plug and Carel Smith (eds), *Legal Argumentation and the Rule of Law* (The Hague, Eleven International Publishing, 2016) 38. The formula is based on an argument by Alexy that interpretations which are closer to the wording of the law or the will of the historical legislator take precedence over other arguments: Alexy, *A Theory of Legal Argumentation* (n 2) 248.

[46] Klatt, 'The Rule of Dual-Natured Law' (n 45) 38.

10

External Justification

EVERY BALANCING EXERCISE requires the determination of the concrete weights of the colliding principles by categorising the intensity of the interference as well as the importance of the colliding principles. This has been demonstrated by means of the internal structure of balancing as described above.[1] Principles theory calls the reasons we provide for determining the weights 'external justification'.[2] External justification thus backs the premises underlying the accordance of concrete weight to a principle.[3] While Alexy has introduced the idea of the external justification of premises to legal argumentation more generally, Klatt and Schmidt have transferred this idea to the domain of balancing. Wróblewski and MacCormick argue in a similar vein when they say that the justification of legal interpretation requires a mix of premises, which refer to the law and the facts of the case on the one hand, and to axiological and other values on the other.[4] Alexy classifies six groups of rules of external justification: 'rules and forms of (1) interpretation, (2) dogmatic argumentation, (3) use of precedents, (4) general practical reasoning, (5) empirical reasoning, and (6) the so-called special legal argument forms'.[5]

The weight of a principle can thus be backed by valid rules of positive law, by proven empirical facts or by legal reasoning in the classic sense.[6] It is the latter which is of special interest. The relevant arguments for the external justification are not part of a balancing exercise themselves. Rather, these are arguments stemming from legal argumentation in general. Herein lies the connection of balancing with a general theory of legal argumentation.[7]

[1] See Chapter 9, Section III.

[2] Robert Alexy, *A Theory of Legal Argumentation: The Theory of Rational Discourse as Theory of Legal Justification* (Ruth Adler and Neil MacCormick trans, Oxford, Oxford University Press, 2011) 230; see also Matthias Klatt and Johannes Schmidt, *Spielräume im öffentlichen Recht: Zur Abwägungslehre der Prinzipientheorie* (Tübingen, Mohr Siebeck, 2010) 74, 88.

[3] Alexy, *A Theory of Legal Argumentation* (n 2) 230; Matthias Klatt and Johannes Schmidt, 'Epistemic Discretion in Constitutional Law' (2012) 10(1) *International Journal of Constitutional Law* 69, 74, 88.

[4] Jerzy Wróblewski and Neil MaCcormick, 'On Justification and Interpretation' (1994) 53 *ARSP Beiheft* 255, 264.

[5] Alexy, *A Theory of Legal Argumentation* (n 2) 231–32.

[6] ibid 230.

[7] Robert Alexy, *A Theory of Constitutional Rights* (Julian Rivers trans, Oxford, Oxford University Press, 2010 (repr)) 107. See also Matthias Klatt, 'Robert Alexy's Philosophy of Law as System' in Matthias Klatt (ed), *Institutionalized Reason: The Jurisprudence of Robert Alexy* (Oxford, Oxford University Press. 2012) 20–21.

If we connect this idea to the constitutionalism debate, we can argue that discursive constitutionalism plays a vital role for external justification. Constitutionalised principles provide the referential, normative framework for the judicial application of law. According to Kleinlein, constitutionalised principles are embedded in a discursive process of development, which serves flexibility regarding new developments on the one hand and strives for coherence by constantly referring to the same fundamental principles on the other.[8] Similarly, Kumm's cosmopolitan constitutionalism assumes that constitutionalised principles are employed in order to determine the preference relation in a concrete case.[9] As Kumm has put it, 'Questions of interpretative methodology … call for answers that ultimately make reference to the moral grounds for legitimate constitutional authority'.[10]

The weight of a principle can only be determined in accordance with the circumstances of the specific case. Notwithstanding this necessary connection to the concrete case, it is possible to shed light on the factors which must be taken into account.[11] Discourse theory requires that the determination of the concrete weight follows rationally justified rules. It is possible to define such rules, which guide the determination of these weights. They are called 'weighting rules'.[12] The following sections will determine the necessary weighting rules with regard to balancing in the time dimension of interpretation in the ECHR. The requirement of rationally justified rules for the determination of the concrete weight of arguments is also in line with the principle of reasonableness, which is deeply embedded in the ECHR.[13] For this purpose, I will first analyse the use of weighting rules by the ECtHR in the standard case of balancing in proportionality analysis, before going on to formulate concrete rules for balancing at the interpretation stage.

I. HOW TO ACCORD WEIGHTS IN THE ECHR?

By examining the factors which guide the ECtHR in the standard case of balancing of colliding fundamental rights and interests, it turns out that the

[8] Thomas Kleinlein, *Konstitutionalisierung im Völkerrecht: Konstruktion und Elemente einer idealistischen Völkerrechtslehre* (Heidelberg, Springer, 2012) 683.

[9] Mattias Kumm, 'Rethinking Constitutional Authority: On the Structure and Limits of Constitutional Pluralism' in Matej Avbelj and Jan Komárek (eds), *Constitutional Pluralism in the European Union and Beyond* (Oxford, Hart Publishing, 2012) 39.

[10] Mattias Kumm, 'The Cosmopolitan Turn in Constitutionalism: On the Relationship between Constitutionalism in and Beyond the State' in Jeffrey L Dunoff and Joel P Trachtman (eds), *Ruling the World? Constitutionalism, International Law, and Global Governance* (Cambridge, Cambridge University Press, 2009) 267.

[11] Matthias Klatt, 'Balancing Competences: How Institutional Cosmopolitanism Can Manage Jurisdictional Conflicts' (2015) 4(2) *Global Constitutionalism* 195, 214.

[12] Alexy, *A Theory of Legal Argumentation* (n 2) 249: '(J.8) Determinations of the relative weight of arguments different in form must conform to weighting rules'.

[13] Evert A Alkema, 'The European Convention as a Constitution and Its Court as a Constitutional Court' in Paul Mahoney, Franz Matscher, Herbert Petzold and Luzius Wildhaber (eds), *Protecting*

Court follows some standard rules in the balancing process. These rules might be able to inform the determination of factors relevant for the balancing at the interpretation stage. These factors then influence the weight of the colliding interests on the one hand and the breadth of the margin of appreciation of the member states on the other.[14] There are two categories of factors, as some of them are of a more general nature, being applicable to all Convention rights, and some of them are rights specific.

The first of the general factors is that the more closely an interest is connected to the core rights and principles of the ECHR, the more weight is accorded to this interest.[15] Second, the weight of an interest at stake is heightened if it is backed by a strong European consensus.[16] The third factor looks at whether a 'particularly important facet of an individual's existence or identity is at stake'.[17]

Apart from these general factors, some weighting factors have been established with regard to specific Convention rights. For example, a rule can be established with regard to cases touching upon discrimination and unequal treatment under Article 14 ECHR, in which the Court usually demands very weighty reasons for justifying such an interference.[18] Furthermore, in cases touching upon the right to family life under Article 8 ECHR, the best interest of the child plays a crucial role in determining the weight of an interest.[19] The same holds true if a case touches upon 'a most intimate aspect of private life'.[20]

Just like the suggestion in literature that a distinction needs to be made between abstract and concrete weights of an interest, also the ECtHR holds that the weight may vary according to the specific circumstances of the case.[21] The Court usually scrutinises the quality of domestic decisions in a specific case, eg whether a proper balancing exercise has been conducted by the national authorities or whether a legislative act was preceded by extensive public deliberation.[22] This is a typical factor, which ties the determination of the weight to the concrete circumstances of a case.

Human Rights: The European Perspective: Studies in Memory of Rolv Ryssdal (Cologne, Heymanns, 2000) 53.

[14] Janneke H Gerards, *General Principles of the European Convention on Human Rights* (Cambridge, Cambridge University Press, 2019) 246; in the Court's case law see, eg, *A, B and C v Ireland* [GC] EHRR 2010-VI para 229.

[15] Gerards (n 14) 245; see also *Connors v UK* (2004) no 66746/01 para 82; *Dubská and Krejzová v the Czech Republic* [GC] EHRR 2016 para 92.

[16] Gerards (n 14) 245; *Evans v UK* [GC] EHRR 2007-I para 77; *A, B and C v Ireland* (n 14) paras 232 and 234.

[17] *Evans v UK*(n 16) para 77; *A, B and C v Ireland* (n 14) para 232.

[18] Gerards (n 14) 244; in the Court's case law see, eg, *Schalk und Kopf v Austria* EHRR 2010-IV 409 para 97; *Biao v Denmark* EHRR 2016 para 93.

[19] Gerards (n 14) 249; see also *Sommerfeld v Germany* [GC] EHRR 2003-VIII para 64; *Jansen v Norway* (2018) no 2822/16 paras 90, 91.

[20] *Dudgeon v UK* Series A no 45 (1981) para 52; *Mosley v UK* (2011) no 48009/08 para 109.

[21] Gerards (n 14) 246.

[22] ibid 256–60; see also *Hatton and others v UK* [GC] EHRR 2003-VIII para 99.

II. WEIGHTING RULES IN THE TIME DIMENSION OF INTERPRETATION

Chapter 7 has demonstrated that the core agenda of the CoE is the commitment to the three foundational concepts of human rights, democracy, and the rule of law. I have shown that all three elements of the Convention's constitutional core may provide a source for static and evolutive interpretation, which means that the reference to democracy, rule of law, and human rights alone is too vague to justify one interpretive approach or the other. However, the analysis of the three constitutional pillars has revealed that they unite more specific formal and substantive values, which can be attributed to evolutive and static interpretation. They constitute constitutional principles of the ECHR. If an interpretation seeks to protect one of these core principles of the ECHR, its importance as an interpretive approach increases. This can be expressed in the following, general weighting rule:

> The more an interpretation is able to foster the constitutional principles of the ECHR, the more weight it gains.
>
> *Basic Rule 1*

This general formulation applies to both interpretive approaches. We have seen that static as well as evolutive interpretation principally foster constitutional principles of the ECHR. Yet, they advance competing constitutional principles. Hence, Basic Rule 1 alone does not yet contribute to more clarity with regard to the determination of which constitutional principle is more important in a concrete case. For this purpose, we need weighting rules, which are more specific to either static or evolutive constitutional principles. These rules then allow us to determine the concrete preference relation among the constitutional principles. These rules ultimately allow us to take a choice between evolutive and static interpretation in a concrete case.

I will now explore in more detail how we can draw specific weighting rules from the constitutional fundaments of the ECHR.

A. Weighting Factors for the Intensity of the Interference With Static Principles

The factors determining the weight of static interpretation are rooted in the fundamental constitutional values of the ECHR. More specifically, it is the formal or procedural aspects of those principles which determine the weight of static interpretation.

Most importantly, under the umbrella of legal certainty as a vital aspect of the rule of law, several factors are relevant. First, if the wording of the Convention text or the intentions of the drafters are unambiguous, any departure from it needs to be justified by very weighty reasons. The following rule applies:

> The intensity of an interference with the static principles of the real dimension is higher the more an evolutive interpretation departs from the clear wording of the text or the intentions of the drafters.
>
> *Static Rule 1: Rule of Literal Meaning*

In the Court's case law, the literal meaning of the Convention text constituted a weighty argument against evolutive interpretation in the cases of *Soering v UK*[23] and *Johnston and others v Ireland*,[24] the interpretation of which was reiterated in the case of *Babiarz v Poland*.[25] While very weighty reasons may override Static Rule 1, there is also another factor which reduces the weight of the drafters' intentions. In the context of constitutional interpretation, Barak argues that the relevance of the drafters' intentions diminishes with the increasing age of the constitution.[26] I support the view that the weight gradually decreases but never becomes completely obsolete.

Second, if there is a precedent in the case law of the ECtHR, it is an established principle that the Court should not depart from it without good reason.[27] It is a generally accepted formal principle of legal argumentation that one should not depart from established practice without good reason.[28] The consistent application of the ECHR is a necessary precondition for legal certainty. In the case law of the ECtHR, again the case of *Babiarz v Poland*[29] provides a good example as the Court rejected a right to divorce under Article 12 ECHR with reference to the case of *Johnston and others v Ireland*.[30] Similarly, in the case of *Scoppola v Italy*[31] the ECtHR upheld the principles on prisoner voting rights established in *Hirst v UK*.[32] The relevance of precedence as a weighting factor can be expressed in the following rule:

> The intensity of an interference with the static principles of the real dimension is higher the more an evolutive interpretation departs from relevant precedents in the case law of the ECtHR.
>
> *Static Rule 2: Rule of Precedents*

[23] *Soering v UK* Series A no 161 (1989) para 103.
[24] *Johnston and Others v Ireland* Series A no 112 (1986) para 52.
[25] *Babiarz v Poland* (2017) no 1955/10 para 49.
[26] Aharon Barak, *The Judge in a Democracy* (Princeton, NJ, Princeton University Press, 2006) 131.
[27] See, eg, *Chapman v UK* [GC] (2001) EHRR 2001-I para 70; *I v UK* [GC] (2002) no 25680/94 para 54.
[28] Alexy, *A Theory of Constitutional Rights* (n 7) 58.
[29] *Babiarz v Poland* (n 25) para 49.
[30] *Johnston and Others v Ireland* (n 24).
[31] *Scoppola v Italy (No 2)* (2009) no 10249/03 paras 94f and 110.
[32] *Hirst v UK (No 2)* [GC] EHRR 2005-IX.

In a more general manner, the principle of subsidiarity supports static interpretation. As it holds that the member states have the primary obligation to protect the rights and freedoms protected by the ECHR, it seeks to prevent the Court from overruling domestic interpretations of the Convention too hastily.[33] The relevance of the subsidiarity principle has now been reinforced by Additional Protocol No 15 to the ECHR, which adds an explicit reference to this principle in the Convention's Preamble.[34] Likewise, the democratic legitimacy of a domestic interpretation of the Convention is a determining factor for the importance of static interpretation. If a static understanding of the Convention in a member state is preceded by an extensive democratic deliberation, this will be a strong incentive for the Court to follow the static approach. The factors of subsidiarity and democratic legitimacy of domestic decisions can be combined in the following rule:

> The interference with the static principles of the real dimension is higher the more an evolutive interpretation departs from a decision backed by a comprehensive democratic decision-making process at national level.
>
> *Static Rule 3: Rule of Democratic Legitimacy*

Democratic legitimacy and the principle of subsidiarity usually play a crucial role in the Court's case law when it comes to proportionality analysis and, more concretely, to the width of the margin of appreciation accorded to the member states. This was the case in *Hatton and others v UK* for example.[35] However, also in cases which raise questions of temporal interpretation, the Court sometimes resorts to its subsidiary role. This can be demonstrated by the case of *Schalk and Kopf v Austria*, in which the ECtHR sought to avoid an evolutive interpretation of the right to marry in order for it to apply to partners of different sex.[36] Apart from the lack of consensus, the Court also resorted to the argument that it should not replace the domestic decisions in such delicate societal questions as the national legislators were better placed to take into account national particularities.[37]

B. Weighting Factors for the Importance of Evolutive Principles

The values which underpin evolutive interpretations can be accorded to the categories of material rule of law, substantive aspects of democratic society, and the Convention's commitment to human rights.

[33] *Hatton and others v UK* (n 22) para 97.

[34] Protocol No 15 amending the Convention for the Protection of Human Rights and Fundamental Freedoms (Strasbourg, 24 June 2013) CETS No 213.

[35] *Hatton and others v UK* (n 22) paras 97 and 103f; see also *Dubská and Krejzová v the Czech Republic* (n 15) paras 175f.

[36] *Schalk und Kopf v Austria* (n 18) para 62.

[37] ibid.

The respect and protection of human dignity is one of the most important objectives of the Convention and an inherent element of its constitutional core.[38] Its maintenance creates a decisive justifying argument for evolutive interpretation, which can be expressed in the following rule:

> The importance of the evolutive principles of the ideal dimension is higher the more an evolutive interpretation protects human dignity.
>
> *Evolutive Rule 1: Rule of Human Dignity*

The ECtHR referred to human dignity in order to strengthen its evolutive interpretation in the cases of *Tyrer v UK*[39] in which the Court interpreted the corporal punishment of juvenile offenders as 'degrading treatment' and hence as being prohibited under Article 3 ECHR. Furthermore, in the twin cases of *Christine Goodwin v UK*[40] and *I v UK*[41] the argument of dignity came up concerning the rights of transgender people to have their new sex officially registered in their birth certificate.

Similarly, the protection of justice and peace are core objectives of the Convention, to which the Preamble refers.[42] Although references to those principles are very rare in the Court's practice, there are cases in which they formed a core element of the Court's reasoning.[43] The ideas of justice and peace are intimately connected to the founding ideals of the CoE as a system for the protection of human rights.[44] These principles should thus provide a compelling justification for evolutive interpretation. They lead to the following weighting rules:

> The importance of the evolutive principles of the ideal dimension is higher the more an evolutive interpretation protects justice.
>
> *Evolutive Rule 2: Rule of Justice*
>
> The importance of the evolutive principles of the ideal dimension is higher the more an evolutive interpretation protects peace.
>
> *Evolutive Rule 3: Rule of Peace*

Equality and the prohibition of discrimination are fundamental elements of the ECHR.[45] The value of equality is particularly supportive of evolutive

[38] Anthony Lester, 'The European Court of Human Rights After 50 Years' in Jonas Christoffersen and Mikael R Madsen (eds), *The European Court of Human Rights Between Law and Politics* (Oxford, Oxford University Press, 2011) 102.

[39] *Tyrer v UK* Series A no 26 (1978) paras 33 and 35.

[40] *Christine Goodwin v UK* [GC] EHRR 2002-VI para 90.

[41] *I v UK* (n 27) para 70.

[42] Convention for the Protection of Human Rights and Fundamental Freedoms (Rome, 4 November 1950) (Council of Europe) recital 4 of the Preamble.

[43] *Streletz, Kessler and Krenz v Germany* [GC] EHRR 2001-II para 83; see also *K.-H. W. v Germany* [GC] EHRR 2001-II para 86.

[44] Thorbjorn Jagland, 'Deep Security: Building a European Community of Values' (2011) 33(1) *Harvard International Review* 12, 13. See also Aline Royer, *The Council of Europe* (Strasbourg, Council of Europe Publishing, 2010) 3.

[45] Alkema (n 13) 53.

interpretation. Discriminatory practices are often rooted in long-established traditions and convictions at domestic level. Judicial review by external bodies is often in a more objective position to detect and overcome such a national bias. This can be expressed in the following rule:

> The importance of the evolutive principles of the ideal dimension is higher the more an evolutive interpretation protects the fundamental guarantees of equality.
>
> *Evolutive Rule 4: Rule of Equality*

The fact that the Court applies evolutive interpretation particularly in cases touching upon equality rights has already been demonstrated in Chapter 3. Some of the most important cases are *Marckx v Belgium*,[46] *I v UK*[47] and *Christine Goodwin v UK*.[48]

Similarly, the protection of a pluralist society as a substantive aspect of the democratic principle provides justification for an evolutive interpretation. Especially if a case touches upon the rights of marginalised and vulnerable groups such as non-citizens, Roma[49] or LGBTI people,[50] the Court is called upon to strengthen the protection of these groups because democratic majority votes in the member states run the risk of not according an adequate level of protection. This holds even more true if the affected persons themselves are excluded from the democratic decision-making process at domestic level. This leads to the following weighting rule:

> The importance of the dynamic principles of the ideal dimension is higher the more an evolutive interpretation protects the fundamental rights of vulnerable groups in order to maintain a pluralist society.
>
> *Evolutive Rule 5: Rule of Pluralism*

The argument of pluralism has not played a relevant role in cases of evolutive interpretation at the ECtHR so far. Rather, this line of argument is typically connected to the Court's assessment in proportionality analysis, when it comes to the 'necessary in a democratic society' criterion of Articles 8–10 ECHR, and when the Court has to determine the width of the margin of appreciation.[51] However, the argument should also be considered in cases of evolutive interpretation as it constitutes a fundamental constitutional principle of the Convention, and hence a relevant indicator for the weight of the evolutive argument.

[46] *Marckx v Belgium* Series A no 31 (1979) para 58.

[47] *I v UK* (n 27) para 70.

[48] *Christine Goodwin v UK* (n 40) para 90.

[49] *D.H. and others v the Czech Republic* [GC] EHRR 2007-IV paras 176 and 182f.

[50] *Identoba and Others v Georgia* (2015) no 73235/12 paras 93f.

[51] See, eg, *Bayatyan v Armenia* [GC] EHRR 2011-IV paras 118 and 122; *D.H. and others v the Czech Republic* (n 49) para 176.

Another constitutional principle of the Convention is the protection of personal freedom or self-determination.[52] The ECHR primarily protects freedom rights. It is thus a vital objective of the Convention to maintain personal integrity and self-determination. An evolutive interpretation of the Convention freedoms with regard to self-determination is indispensable in order to maintain the high level of human rights protection. The corresponding weighting rule reads as follows:

> The importance of the evolutive principles of the ideal dimension is higher the more an evolutive interpretation protects self-determination.
>
> *Evolutive Rule 6: Rule of Self-Determination*

The factor of self-determination has played a crucial role in justifying the interpretations in the cases of *Y.Y. v Turkey*[53] on the rights of transgender people or *Pretty v UK*[54] on the request of a patient to allow her husband to assist her in committing suicide as she was physically not able to end her life without assistance.

The principle of effectiveness is another vital guarantee of the ECHR which may serve as a justification for evolutive interpretation. It guarantees that the rights and freedoms protected by the Convention remain 'practical and effective' in an ever-changing societal context which creates new challenges for the protection of human rights.[55] Consequently, the following weighting rule applies:

> The importance of the evolutive principles of the ideal dimension is higher the more an evolutive interpretation fosters the effective protection of human rights under the ECHR.
>
> *Evolutive Rule 7: Rule of Effectiveness*

The nature of the rule of effectiveness differs from those of the other weighting rules. Whereas Evolutive Rules 1 to 6 refer to arguments about the kind of values that are protected by the ECHR, Rule 7 relates to the kind of protection that the Convention rights enjoy, namely an effective protection. It can thus be argued that Evolutive Rule 7 possesses a meta-status with regard to the other rules as it constitutes a further qualification to all of them. The argument of effectiveness has been widely used by the ECtHR in its cases of evolutive interpretation. For example, effectiveness constituted a considerably weighty reason in the cases of *Demir and Baykara v Turkey*,[56] *Sergey Zolotukhin v Russia*[57] and *Hirsi Jamaa and others v Italy*.[58]

[52] *Pretty v UK* EHRR 2002-III para 61; *Y.Y. v Turkey* EHRR 2015-I para 57.

[53] *Y.Y. v Turkey* (n 52) para 57.

[54] *Pretty v UK* (n 52) para 61.

[55] A. Mowbray, 'The Creativity of the European Court of Human Rights' (2005) 5(1) *Human Rights Law Review* 57, 72.

[56] *Demir and Baykara v Turkey* [GC] EHRR 2008-V paras 66, 70 and 146.

[57] *Sergey Zolotukhin v Russia* [GC] EHRR 2009-I para 80.

[58] *Hirsi Jamaa and others v Italy* EHRR 2012-II paras 175, 177 and 179.

C. The Weight of Consensus

Apart from the factors discussed so far, which can clearly be attributed to one or the other approach of interpretation, there is one factor which might be decisive on either side of the balancing exercise. It is the existence of a European consensus, which may support the choice of both approaches to interpretation equally. The argument of consensus relies on an empirical study of the legislative realities in the member states.[59] If the majority of the member states have developed their laws beyond the established level of protection in the ECHR with regard to a specific legal question, this consensus would support an evolutive interpretation. The same holds true for static interpretation if the member states have not adapted their respective legal systems. The special status of the consensus argument relating to time-sensitive interpretations is shown very well in the Court's case law, where consensus is more often than not the decisive argument in interpreting evolutively or statically. Consequently, two weighting rules can be established, which apply to both sides of the balancing exercise:

> The interference with the static principles of the real dimension is higher the more an evolutive interpretation departs from an established European consensus.
>
> *Static Rule 4: Rule of Consensus*
>
> The importance of the evolutive principles of the ideal dimension is higher the more an evolutive interpretation corresponds to an established European consensus.
>
> *Evolutive Rule 8: Rule of Consensus*

The argument of consensus plays a crucial role in the Court's case law when arguing in favour of or against evolutive interpretation. The static rule of consensus was the determining argument in the cases of *B v France*[60] or *Sheffield and Horsham v UK*,[61] while the evolutive rule of consensus was decisive in cases such as *Tyrer v UK*[62] or *Bayatyan v Armenia*.[63]

The suggestion of a weighting rule of consensus stands in contrast to my argumentation in Chapter 3, where I have dismissed the argument of consensus as the determining factor in justifying intertemporal interpretations. There, I have discussed in more detail that the use of a consensus argument bears the risk of an is-ought fallacy.[64] The fact that the majority of the member states of the CoE follow a legal practice must not be confused with the normative command that it is right to follow this legal practice. However, I do believe that we should not completely ban the consensus argument from the argumentative process for several reasons. Based on a more political consideration, one can

[59] For a critical discussion of the consensus argument see Chapter 3, Section IA.
[60] *B. v France* Series A no 232-C (1992) para 48.
[61] *Sheffield and Horsham v UK* [GC] (1998) EHRR 1998-V paras 55, 57 and 58.
[62] *Tyrer v UK* (n 39) para 31.
[63] *Bayatyan v Armenia* (n 51) paras 102–09.
[64] See Chapter 3, Section IA.

argue that the success of human rights protection mechanisms practically also depends to a certain extent on the willingness of states to back the decisions of a human rights court such as the ECtHR. The weighting rule of consensus is an attempt to acknowledge this political complexity of human rights practice. Yet, comparative arguments such as the consensus argument might also have positive effects on legal reasoning. Comparative arguments, contingent as they might be, may serve as an eye-opener to the fundamental values of a legal community.[65] They might also be useful to overcome a possible personal bias of a judge, which could be of even greater relevance at an international court such as the ECtHR, which groups judges with very diverse legal backgrounds.[66]

However, in order to reduce the potential detriments of an empirical consensus argument for normative reasoning, I argue that the weighting rule of consensus can only have an ancillary function. It can only support a tendency regarding the weight of static and evolutive constitutional principles, achieved by normative arguments, but never serve as the sole argument for justifying an evolutive or static approach to interpretation.

III. THE EPISTEMIC RELIABILITY OF THE UNDERLYING PREMISES

According to Alexy, 'epistemic discretion arises whenever knowledge of what is commanded, prohibited, or left free by constitutional rights is uncertain'.[67] He distinguishes between empirical and normative epistemic uncertainties. The former relates to the reliability of the 'knowledge of relevant facts'.[68] Klatt and Schmidt distinguish between two different scenarios of uncertainty of empirical premises, which influence the categorisation of the intensity of an interference: first, uncertainty about the premises underlying the interference, and second, uncertainty about the intensity of the interference itself.[69] Uncertainty with regard to normative premises arises in the process of categorising the intensity of an interference or the importance of a principle on a scale, eg from low to serious.[70] The general rule applies that 'The more refined the scale of classification, the more unreliable the normative classification'.[71]

[65] Arguing for the relevance of comparative arguments in constitutional interpretation, see Barak (n 26) 200–01.

[66] Compare Christopher A Ford, 'Judicial Discretion in International Jurisprudence: Article 38(1) (C) and "General Principles of Law"' (1994) 5 *Duke Journal of Comparative and International Law* 35, 78, arguing in the context of international courts more generally.

[67] Alexy, *A Theory of Constitutional Rights* (n 7) 414.

[68] ibid 414–15.

[69] Klatt and Schmidt, *Spielräume im öffentlichen Recht* (n 2) 19. See also Klatt and Schmidt, 'Epistemic Discretion in Constitutional Law' (n 3) 77–78.

[70] Alexy, *A Theory of Constitutional Rights* (n 7) 415; Klatt and Schmidt, *Spielräume im öffentlichen Recht* (n 2) 41, 46.

[71] Klatt and Schmidt, 'Epistemic Discretion in Constitutional Law' (n 3) 86.

Furthermore, it can be noted that the reliability of the normative premises is higher if the intensity is either very high or very low because it is more difficult to differentiate between more subtle normative nuances than between stronger nuances.[72] The epistemic reliability of premises thus affects the weighting of the colliding principles. They are determined according to the concrete circumstances of the case and thus contribute to the concrete weight of a principle in a specific case.[73]

Which kind of premises could be relevant when according weight to static and evolutive interpretation? On the static side of the scale, empirical epistemic premises play a crucial role in the Court's case law. First, premises of the historical legislator, the drafters of the ECHR, are relevant if the static interpretation refers to an interpretation which goes back to the intentions of the drafters.[74] The *travaux préparatoires* of the Convention's drafting process can provide vital insights into these intentions but they need to be treated with caution because very often the statements in the *travaux préparatoires* just express the intentions of single countries and are not representative of the rest of the member states.[75] Second, the premises of the ECtHR itself in interpreting a Convention right may become relevant if the static interpretation refers to an earlier case of the Court. The more plausible the earlier premises of the Court were, the more they add to the weight of the static interpretation. In the case of *Christine Goodwin v UK*, the ECtHR scrutinised the reliability of the empirical premises with regard to the situation of transsexuals in the United Kingdom, the medical and scientific considerations, the state of a European consensus, and the impact on the birth registration system,[76] all of which were decisive arguments in the preceding cases of *Cossey v UK*,[77] *Rees v UK*[78] and *Sheffield and Horsham v UK*.[79] Likewise, other empirical premises, such as those referring to a European consensus, a domestic democratic decision and the like, need to be scrutinised to determine their reliability.

On the evolutive side of the scale, all empirical premises relating to the development of European society are of pivotal interest. These may relate to a European consensus among domestic legislation as well as to societal developments at a lower level.[80] The more reliable these premises are, the higher will be the factor of the reliability of the empirical premises in the balancing exercise.

Besides, normative premises with regard to the importance of a principle as such are crucial for both the static and evolutive sides of the scale. Normative

[72] ibid.

[73] ibid 88, 89 and 103.

[74] *Johnston and Others v Ireland* (n 24) para 52; *Babiarz v Poland* (n 25) para 49.

[75] Humphrey Waldock, Third Report on the Law of Treaties Document A/CN.4/167, Vol II (1964) (Special Rapporteur, International Law Commission) 58.

[76] *Christine Goodwin v UK* (n 40) paras 76–88.

[77] *Cossey v UK* (1990) Series A no 184 (1990).

[78] *Rees v UK* Series A no 106 (1986).

[79] *Sheffield and Horsham v UK* (n 61).

[80] See, eg, *Marckx v Belgium* (n 46) para 41.

premises are relevant for categorising the intensity of the interference and the weight of a principle on a scale with more than one value.[81] For the purpose of balancing in the time dimension of interpretation, the categorisation of the concrete weight can be mitigated or strengthened according to the concrete circumstances of the case and needs to be based on reliable premises.

The ECtHR is cautious about according the weights of a principle in cases of evolutive or static interpretation to concrete values on a scale. It usually confines itself to stating that a principle is 'important'.[82] It is difficult to tell whether the categorisation of a principle as constituting 'the essence of the Convention'[83] in the Court's case law signals a higher weight than the categorisation as an important principle. Yet, case law with regard to proportionality analysis reveals that the Court does differentiate between different levels of intensity of interference. For example, in the case of *B. v France*,[84] one of the early cases on the right of transgender people to the legal recognition of their post-operative gender, the Court concluded that the applicant

> finds herself daily in a situation which, taken as a whole, is not compatible with the respect due to her private life. Consequently, ... the fair balance ... has not been attained and there has thus been a violation of Article 8 (art.8).[85]

In the later case of *Christine Goodwin v UK*, the ECtHR referred to this categorisation and held 'that the level of daily interference suffered by the applicant in B. v France ... has not been attained in this case'.[86]

One could interpret these findings as categorisations of a serious interference in the case of *B. v France* and of an intermediate interference in the case of *Christine Goodwin v UK*. There is no indication that the Court makes use of a more fine-tuned scale of intensity in proportionality analysis. This seems reasonable with regard to the above-mentioned analysis that more fine-tuned scales contribute to a higher level of uncertainty of normative premises. It would thus be advisable for the Court to adopt a similar scale for the importance of principles supporting static or evolutive interpretation.

[81] Klatt and Schmidt, 'Epistemic Discretion in Constitutional Law' (n 3) 86.

[82] See, eg, *Christine Goodwin v UK* (n 40) para 90, in which the Court categorised personal autonomy as important.

[83] ibid, where the Court classified human dignity and human freedom as being the very essence of the Convention.

[84] *B. v France* (n 60).

[85] ibid para 63.

[86] *Christine Goodwin v UK* (n 40) para 89.

Part IV

The Balanced Legitimacy Model Applied

THIS CHAPTER ILLUSTRATES the practicability of my balancing model for static and evolutive interpretation by applying it to selected cases of the ECtHR. These exemplifications demonstrate that the balancing model increases the rationality of the interpretation tremendously by providing a clear and reasonable argumentative structure. Especially the weighting rules, which I have defined in Chapter 10, provide guidance for the interpreter to consider all relevant factors for the interpretation in a concrete case. The balancing model allows for precise conclusions, whether the better arguments in a case speak in favour of static or evolutive constitutional principles. The weighting of all relevant factors leads to the definition of concrete weights for both sides of the scales. This results in the immediate visibility of the interpretive approach, which is supported by the weightier arguments in a concrete case. It thus facilitates a rational choice between static and evolutive interpretation, which is in full accordance with the constitutional principles of the ECHR.

I have selected cases raising intertemporal legal questions on which the ECtHR has already decided. Each case analysis results in a rewriting of the Court's justification of its interpretive approach. Rewriting in this sense means that I will approach the legal question in the respective cases from the perspective of the time dimension of interpretation, regardless of whether the ECtHR even considered an evolutive interpretation in these cases. I will limit my analysis to the question whether an evolutive or static interpretation would have been justifiable based on the Convention's constitutional principles. I will demonstrate that the model proves to be as reliable for cases of evolutive interpretation as for cases of static interpretation. I will illustrate that static constitutional principles can outweigh evolutive constitutional principles, and vice versa. We will further see that my model also clearly indicates cases of stalemate, meaning that both interpretive approaches are supported by arguments of equal weight.

I have selected the cases on the basis of the following three considerations. First, a case had to touch upon subject matter of which the societal perception had changed since the entry into force of the ECHR. This was primarily measured by the fact that the respective legal question had been omitted, either implicitly or explicitly, in the drafting of the original Convention text, but had been increasingly raised by parties before the Court since the entry into force of the Convention. Second, although all the selected cases are linked to Article 8 ECHR to a certain extent, the selected cases represent three different subjects of Article 8. On the one hand, this self-imposed restriction on case selection arises from the aspiration to demonstrate the diverse field of time-related interpretive questions to which my balancing model is applicable. On the other, I wanted to avoid a bias regarding matters of discrimination and unequal treatment. As has been demonstrated in Chapter 3, matters of discrimination, unequal treatment, and changing family constellations constitute the prior field of application for evolutive interpretation in the Court's case law. They thus seem to have a certain prima facie tendency to evolutive interpretation. Consequently, I have sought to present a greater variety of subject matter. The three selected cases relate to the right to divorce,[1] the right to assisted suicide,[2] and the right to the preservation of the environment.[3] Third, I have selected subject matter that the Court did not interpret evolutively. Although the cases date from different years (2002, 2010 and 2017), the Court has not yet changed its interpretation of any of the respective subject matter, even if some of the issues have been brought before the Court repeatedly ever since.

The three case studies that follow will all be subdivided into five sections. Section I will summarise the facts of the respective case. Section II will then demonstrate why the subject matter of those cases raises intertemporal questions. Subsequently, Section III will demonstrate the Court's reasoning in the cases. Section IV will apply my balancing model for the time dimension of interpretation to the respective case. Finally, Section V will present the outcome of the balancing in the interpretation stage. It will thus demonstrate which interpretive approach is normatively desirable in the concrete case.

[1] *Babiarz v Poland* (2017) no 1955/10.
[2] *Pretty v UK* EHRR 2002-III.
[3] *Ivan Atanasov v Bulgaria* (2010) no 12853/03.

11

The Right to Divorce

THE FIRST CASE illustrates a balancing result in favour of the evolutive theory of interpretation. The selected judgment of the ECtHR dates from January 2017 and deals with the question of whether Articles 8 and 12 of the ECHR grant a right to divorce.

I. FACTS OF THE CASE

The Polish applicant, Mr Artur Babiarz, married his wife R in 1997. In 2004 his wife received treatment to cure her infertility.[1] In the same year the applicant met his new partner AH and moved out in early 2005.[2] In October 2005 the applicant had a child with AH.[3] In September 2006 the applicant filed for divorce from R.[4] While he filed for a no-fault divorce at first,[5] he changed his claim to a fault-based divorce later in 2006.[6] His wife R refused to accept the divorce and claimed dismissal of the applicant's claim.[7] In its decision the Polish Lublin Regional Court accepted that there was 'a complete and irretrievable marriage breakdown',[8] which was due to the applicant's fault.[9] Yet, the claim of the applicant was dismissed for the reason that the Polish Family and Guardianship Code does not grant a possibility to divorce for the partner who is responsible for the marriage breakdown if the other partner does not consent to the divorce and if this refusal is not 'contrary to the reasonable principles of social coexistence'.[10] The Court stressed that the applicant's new relationship with AH, and the fact that they had a child together, was not sufficient to permit the applicant's request for divorce.[11]

[1] *Babiarz v Poland* (2017) no 1955/10 para 6.
[2] ibid para 7.
[3] ibid para 8.
[4] ibid para 9.
[5] ibid.
[6] ibid para 11.
[7] ibid paras 10 and 13.
[8] ibid para 16.
[9] ibid paras 14–15.
[10] ibid para 17.
[11] ibid para 19.

The subsequent appeal on behalf of the applicant was dismissed by the Lublin Court of Appeal in June 2009,[12] and no further remedy was possible.[13]

In December 2009 the applicant filed his application against the Republic of Poland at the ECtHR, claiming that the denial of his petition for divorce by the Polish authorities was in breach of his Convention right to private and family life under Article 8 and his right to marry under Article 12.[14]

II. TIME DIMENSION OF INTERPRETATION

The case required an interpretation of Articles 8 (right to respect for private and family life) and 12 (right to marry) ECHR regarding the question whether they grant a right to divorce for the applicant.

A brief analysis of the history of the right to divorce in the ECHR reveals why the central question in *Babiarz v Poland* opens the field of intertemporal interpretation. Regarding Article 12 ECHR, the *travaux préparatoires* of the Convention's drafting process indicate the intention of the drafters to exclude a right to divorce from the Convention.[15] Article 12 ECHR was originally based on Article 16 of the Universal Declaration of Human Rights (UDHR), which reads as follows:

> Men and women of full age, without any limitation due to race, nationality or religion, have the right to marry and to found a family. They are entitled to equal rights as to marriage, during marriage and at its dissolution.[16]

The UDHR thus explicitly refers to rights with regard to the dissolution of marriage.

The drafters of the ECHR decided to omit the last phrase of the UDHR's text, which was expressed in the words of Monsieur Henri Teitgen:

> In mentioning the particular Article [of the UDHR], we have used only that part of the paragraph of the Article which affirms the right to marry and to found a family; but not the subsequent provisions of the Article concerning equal rights after marriage, since we only guarantee the right to marry.[17]

The will of the legislators not to grant a right to divorce under the ECHR is thus unmistakeably clear.

Furthermore, there is a precedent in the case law of the ECtHR in which the Plenary Chamber had denied the right to divorce under Articles 8 and 12 of the

[12] ibid para 21.

[13] ibid para 23.

[14] ibid paras 1 and 3.

[15] *Collected Edition of the 'Travaux Préparatoires'* Volume I (The Hague, Martinus Nijhoff, 1975) 268; this was also discussed in *Babiarz v Poland* (n 1) para 49.

[16] Universal Declaration of Human Rights (Paris, 10 December 1948) UN General Assembly Resolution 217 A (III) Art 16.

[17] *Collected Edition of the 'Travaux Préparatoires'* Volume I (n 15) 268.

Convention. In the case of *Johnston and others v Ireland*,[18] dating from 1986, the Plenary Chamber dealt with a blanket ban on divorces in Ireland, which was held to be in accordance with Ireland's obligations under the Convention. The reasoning of the Plenary Chamber in *Johnston and others v Ireland* relied heavily on the clear intentions of the drafters in the *travaux préparatoires*.[19] The Court in *Johnston and others* considered an evolutive interpretation of Article 12, but concluded that 'the Court cannot, by means of an evolutive interpretation, derive from these instruments a right that was not included therein at the outset. This is particularly so here, where the omission was deliberate'.[20]

The Court further stressed that the right to divorce was also deliberately omitted in the later Protocol No 7 to the ECHR,[21] of which Article 5 grants additional rights to spouses in the case of dissolution of marriage. The protection of these additional rights did not, however, go hand in hand with the intention also to introduce a right to divorce into the Protocol. The Court thus concluded that the Convention did not oblige the member states to provide for a right to divorce in their domestic legal systems.[22] The Court also denied that such a right could be derived from the right to respect for family life in Article 8.[23]

The right to divorce is a good illustration of a possible conflict in the time dimension of interpretation. The intentions of the Convention's drafters and the case law of the ECtHR clearly support a static reading of the Convention, which upholds the traditional value of marriage as being a life-long bond without dissolution. A reading that departs from this interpretive approach would thus amount to an evolutive interpretation of the ECHR. The next section will shed light on how the ECtHR approached this question in its decision in *Babiarz v Poland*.

III. THE ECtHR'S REASONING

In its assessment of the merits, the Court decided to treat the questions arising from Articles 8 and 12 jointly.[24] It reiterated the principle established in *Johnston and others v Ireland* that the member states enjoy a wide margin of appreciation regarding the framing and implementation of divorce law.[25] The Court reiterated 'that the Convention is a living instrument to be interpreted in the light of present-day conditions'.[26] At the same time it referred to the

[18] *Johnston and Others v Ireland* Series A no 112 (1986).
[19] ibid para 52.
[20] ibid para 53.
[21] Protocol No 7 to the Convention for the Protection of Human Rights and Fundamental Freedoms (Strasbourg, 22 November 1984) ETS No 117.
[22] *Johnston and Others v Ireland* (n 18) para 53.
[23] ibid para 57.
[24] *Babiarz v Poland* (n 1) para 46.
[25] ibid para 47.
[26] ibid para 49.

clearly expressed intentions of the drafters not to grant a Convention right to divorce.[27] The Court further emphasised the fact that Polish law did not ban divorce completely so that the applicant still had a possibility to divorce if his wife consented to it.[28] The applicant thus merely faced a situation in which his petition for divorce was dismissed by a court due to 'substantive and procedural rules' of Polish divorce law.[29] The Court highlighted the fact that Polish law would not prevent the applicant from filing a new petition for divorce once 'circumstances change'.[30] The fact that the applicant has formed a new family, consisting of his new partner and his daughter, did not lead to a right to have his claim to divorce granted.[31] The Court highlighted that 'While under Article 8, de facto families and relationships are protected, such protection does not mean that particular legal recognition has to be accorded to them'.[32] Moreover, not being granted a divorce did not hinder the applicant from having a legal bond with this child.[33]

For these reasons the Court decided by five votes to two that there had been no violation of Articles 8 and 12 ECHR.[34] Two Judges András Sajó and Paulo Pinto de Albuquerque dissented from the majority's vote and voted in favour of a right to divorce under both Articles 8 and 12 ECHR. I will shed more light on some of their arguments in the following section, which will demonstrate the justification of an evolutive interpretation in this case.

IV. THE BALANCING OF STATIC AND EVOLUTIVE INTERPRETATION

While the moral climate at the time of the Convention's birth was dominated by a traditional picture of marital family life, in which divorce was unusual and taboo, this picture has certainly changed today. Marriage now is first and foremost a civil bond, which is detached from its religious origins, and which can be terminated by either partner. Individual self-determination and the right not only to choose one's partner deliberately, but also to change the partner, have gained importance since the entry into force of the Convention. This section illustrates how a normative theory of interpretation can do justice to these societal changes.

To begin with, the evolutive interpretation in the case of *Babiarz v Poland* amounts to granting a right to divorce under Convention Articles 8 and 12, whereas the static interpretation amounts to repudiating such a right. In more

[27] ibid para 49.
[28] ibid para 51.
[29] ibid para 52
[30] ibid para 56.
[31] ibid para 54.
[32] ibid.
[33] ibid para 54.
[34] ibid paras 57–58.

concrete terms, the conflict between evolutive interpretation and static interpretation amounts to a conflict between the principles of self-determination, effectiveness, pluralist democracy, and consensus on the one hand, and legal certainty, the intentions of the drafters and respect for democratic decisions on the other. As I have demonstrated in Chapter 7, these principles can be accorded to the ideal dimension of law on the one hand and the real dimension of law on the other. I have further demonstrated that these principles carry equal abstract weight in the balancing process.[35] It thus remains to be answered how heavily these arguments weigh in the concrete case of *Babiarz v Poland*.

Following the internal structure of the suggested balancing model, which I have developed in Chapter 9, I have to determine the intensity of the interference of an evolutive interpretation with the static principles of the real dimension first. Then I have to establish the importance of the evolutive principles, which support the evolutive interpretation. Finally, I must determine whether the importance of the evolutive principles justifies the interference with the static principles.[36] In order to establish the intensity of the interference with the static principles on the one hand and the importance of the evolutive principles on the other, I have to accord weight to each of them respectively.

I will start with the first step of determining the intensity of interference with static constitutional principles. I will argue that the intensity of the interference of an evolutive interpretation with the real dimension is moderate. Certainly, the aspects of legal certainty and the respect for democratic decisions of member states in morally debatable religious matters weigh heavily in abstract terms. If one sheds light on these values in the concrete circumstances of the case, however, the arguments lose power. The relevant factors which need to be taken into consideration are the departure from the literal meaning and the drafters' intentions (Static Rule 1), from precedents (Static Rule 2), as well as from the democratically enacted Polish divorce law (Static Rule 3).[37]

As far as Static Rule 1 is concerned, the historical legislator has clearly expressed its intention to exclude the right to divorce from the ECHR. An evolutive interpretation would thus clearly depart from these express intentions. As far as Static Rule 2 is concerned, there is a precedent by the Plenary Chamber, which has denied this right even in the more extreme case of a blanket ban on divorce rights.[38] An evolutive interpretation would thus depart from this precedent. Each of these arguments contributes to a more fundamental principle, which is deeply embedded in the constitutional core of the Convention. It is the aspect of legal certainty, which connects to the Convention's constitutional principle of the rule of law, and which is said to be inherent in all Convention rights.[39]

[35] See Chapter 9.
[36] ibid.
[37] On the weighting rules see Chapter 10.
[38] *Johnston and Others v Ireland* (n 18).
[39] This follows from the analysis of the rule-of-law principle in the ECHR in Chapter 7, Section I.

One could also call it 'security of legal expectations'.[40] Opting for a static interpretation in the sense of not granting a right to divorce thus contributes considerably to legal certainty. It preserves the traditional view that marriage creates a legal bond for eternity, which protects the partner as well as any child stemming from the marriage. This goes hand in hand with a concern for financial security as provided by a stable marital life. It thus protects people's expectations that a marital bond is protected under the Convention as an eternal legal bond in accordance with the religious family tradition of European societies. Yet, what kind of family tradition is protected in the case of the applicant and his wife in *Babiarz v Poland*? De facto, their marital relationship had ended over a decade earlier, which reduces the notion of protected family life with his spouse to mere fiction. A static interpretation does more to harm the traditional values of family life than it does to protect them. It accepts that the applicant has to live with his new partner and child in mere cohabitation, de facto living the life of a traditional family, but without any chance of achieving the legal status of a family in the traditional sense. We can thus come to an interim conclusion with regard to Static Rules 1 and 2. Although an evolutive interpretation would lead to a significant departure from the intentions of the drafters and the case law of the ECtHR, it would not depart as significantly from the traditional picture of a family, which the drafters and the Court sought to protect.

It should be added that as far as the certainty of legal expectations of the applicant's wife relate to financial aspects of, eg, alimony payments, this certainty can be upheld even when granting a right to divorce to the applicant. The facts of the case reveal that the applicant willingly acknowledged that the marital breakdown was his fault and that this failure might lead to financial consequences of one kind or another.

Besides legal certainty, the argument not to grant a right to divorce should also be considered with regard to Static Rule 3, protecting decisions that have been reached in a democratic process. The question of whether or not to grant a right to divorce is deeply connected to religious moral values. It protects the traditional Catholic understanding of family, which amounts to a relationship between a man and a woman, and any child born in marriage. Matters which relate to religious morality usually lead to a wide margin of appreciation of the member states in how to regulate and implement them, as they are usually controversial among the different CoE states.[41] One could thus argue that it is a question of legitimate moral disagreement. If Poland has a society with a more conservative religious tradition, the Convention's principle of subsidiarity requires that it provides for laws which correspond best to the traditions

[40] Jerzy Wróblewski and Neil MaCcormick, 'On Justification and Interpretation' (1994) 53 *ARSP Beiheft* 255, 265.

[41] See, eg, the Court's statement on abortion laws in Ireland: *A, B and C v Ireland* [GC] EHRR 2010-VI 233.

of Polish society. This connects to the democratic principle in the Convention, which demands respect for the democratic decisions of the domestic legislator. Yet, evolutive interpretation in this case would depart from the moral values in Poland only to a moderate degree. Given the fact that Poland allows for divorce in other circumstances, there seems to be a certain agreement on the legitimacy of divorce. An evolutive interpretation with regard to opening a further possibility of divorce under Polish law would thus not amount to a complete overturning of the publicly held views in Poland.

Consequently, the considerations concerning the three static rules amount to a moderate interference with the principles of the real dimension in the ECHR.

The second step of the balancing exercise requires the determination of the importance of the competing evolutive constitutional principles. I will argue that the importance of the right of the applicant to have a divorce, which is rooted in the principles of the ideal dimension of law in the ECHR, needs to be weighted as serious. When shedding light on the weight of the evolutive principles in the concrete circumstances of the case, the following considerations are relevant in the case of *Babiarz v Poland*: to what extent evolutive interpretation fosters the principles of pluralism (Evolutive Rule 5), self-determination (Evolutive Rule 6), effectiveness (Evolutive Rule 7) and whether it corresponds to a European consensus (Evolutive Rule 8).[42]

With regard to Evolutive Rule 7 protecting the principle of effectiveness, it must be noted that the right to divorce is a necessary precondition for the full enjoyment of family life with the applicant's new family. Not to grant a right to divorce actually hinders the effective implementation of the right to marry in Article 12 ECHR. In order to be able to remarry, a divorce seems to be an indispensable prerequisite.[43] The ECtHR has acknowledged that the right to remarry is covered by the Convention,[44] but without a right to divorce, the possibility of remarrying is downgraded to a fictitious right.[45] A denial of the right to divorce also hinders the effective protection of the right to private and family life in Article 8 as it leads to a situation of lack of respect for any family formed after the breakdown of a previous marital family. The Court even stated in *Babiarz* that such 'de facto families' do enjoy the protection of the ECHR.[46] Respect for these families amounts to an illusion without the right to divorce, however. Without the possibility for divorce, the applicant's relationship with his new partner is downgraded to a simple cohabitation, which is not 'socially and legally equivalent to living in marriage'.[47] Hence, his new de facto family is unable to enjoy the same rights as any other married family. This not only interferes with his and his new family's rights under Article 8 ECHR, but also

[42] For a list of the evolutive weighting rules see Chapter 10, Section IIB.
[43] *Babiarz v Poland* (n 1) dissenting opinion of Judge Sajó, para 1.
[44] *F. v Switzerland* Series A no 128 (1987) para 38.
[45] *Babiarz v Poland* (n 1) dissenting opinion of Judge Pinto de Albuquerque, para 35.
[46] ibid para 54.
[47] ibid, dissenting opinion of Judge Sajó, para 12.

puts an unjustified restriction on the right to marry of his new partner, who is unable to marry her partner as long as he is still married to his former spouse. Furthermore, the best interest of the applicant's child seems to be a weighty argument in this case. Although the legal bonds to the applicant's child are not diminished by the lack of possibility of marriage, due to the possibility of legal recognition of his paternity,[48] there is certainly an interest of the child in growing up in a family which is also legally registered. The best interest of the child as well as the interests of the new partner are certainly factors which should have been considered by the ECtHR in its decision in *Babiarz v Poland*, at least with regard to the fact that the domestic courts should have taken these interests into account.[49] The fact that such considerations have been completely left aside by the ECtHR gives the decision a touch of one-sidedness.

Concerning the importance of self-determination (Evolutive Rule 6), it must be noted that the protection of freedom lies at the very core of the Convention[50] and forms an essential part of the constitutional principle of human rights.[51] Personal freedom and self-determination are also vital aspects of the right to private and family life, which covers the freedom not to be forced to live with someone or to be tied to a personal relationship with someone. If a marital relationship breaks down, it is questionable whether the upholding of a fictitious bond is able to contribute to the respect for private and family life at all. This is because there are human costs involved if a person is forced to remain in a personal relationship with someone against his or her will.[52] This is not to say that there are no legal bonds whatsoever after a divorce as any divorce might lead to alimony payments or other benefits or caring obligations owed to children or the former spouse. But these consequences need to be clearly distinguished from the possibility of divorce as a legal separation of the personal relationship between two spouses.[53] There is no right to be loved by a specific person against his or her will, nor does the state have any authorisation to enforce family life.[54] As Judge Sajó rightly stated in his dissenting opinion, 'It might be morally reprehensible that the applicant left his wife after all that she had had to undergo and the conditions under which he left her, but denial of divorce cannot be a punishment for immorality'.[55] The Court merely states that the Polish law does not prevent the applicant from resubmitting his petition for divorce as soon as his circumstances change.[56] However, what else could change in the applicant's life?

[48] ibid para 13.
[49] ibid.
[50] Janneke H Gerards, *General Principles of the European Convention on Human Rights* (Cambridge, Cambridge University Press, 2019) 62f.
[51] For a discussion of the human rights principle see Chapter 7, Section IC.
[52] *Babiarz v Poland* (n 1) dissenting opinion of Judge Pinto de Albuquerque, para 35.
[53] ibid, dissenting opinion of Judge Sajó, para 10.
[54] ibid, dissenting opinion of Judge Sajó, para 22.
[55] ibid, dissenting opinion of Judge Sajó, para 10.
[56] ibid para 55.

He had already been with his new partner and had their child for more than 11 years at the time of the Court's decision. He had even been separated from his former partner for a period of 12 years at the time of the decision. The Court's argument thus seems to be far removed from the applicant's reality when it states that the applicant's request for divorce simply did not meet the 'substantive and procedural rules' of Polish divorce law.[57] These procedural and substantive rules can be reduced to one single requirement. The fate of the divorce petition depends solely on the will of the former spouse, hence on whether she changes her opinion on the divorce or not. Under such conditions, the rights to divorce and to remarry in Polish law amount to nothing more than a mere illusion.[58]

Concerning Evolutive Rule 5, the imposition of traditional religious values by the state through restrictive divorce laws is in conflict with the democratic constitutional principle in the Convention. This principle is based on a pluralist society and consequently does not foster a specific religion but respects the various life choices of people.[59] Just like the security of legal expectations, one could also ask for the security of 'social expectations'[60] in this regard. These social expectations refer to a society which has changed towards a more open-minded approach to divorce. The civil legal bond of marriage is more dominant than its religious meaning today, and people expect to be able to leave this civil contract in the event of marriage breakdown.

Finally, regarding Evolutive Rule 8, it is essential to shed light on the broad consensus on divorce laws which exists among the contracting states to the Convention. As ECtHR Judge Pinto de Albuquerque stated in his dissenting opinion in *Babiarz v Poland*, no member state of the CoE holds retains a blanket ban on divorce today.[61] Furthermore, in European Union countries it is commonly accepted that the fact that spouses live in separate households for a certain amount of time constitutes a rebuttable presumption of marital breakdown, independent of mutual consent.[62] The requirement of consent of the respondent spouse to a petition for divorce still exists, for example, in the United Kingdom if the couple live separately for less than five years. However, in the case of separation of the spouses beyond the five-year period, divorce can be requested by one spouse only.[63] Consequently, more than half of the member states of the CoE allow for divorce in the situation of the applicant in *Babiarz v Poland*. Accordingly, if there is a margin of appreciation for the member states in framing their divorce laws, it must be a narrow one.

[57] ibid paras 52 and 54.

[58] ibid, dissenting opinion of Judge Pinto de Albuquerque, para 35.

[59] ibid, dissenting opinion of Judge Pinto de Albuquerque, para 33.

[60] Wróblewski and MacCormick (n 40) 265.

[61] *Babiarz v Poland* (n 1) dissenting opinion of Judge Pinto de Albuquerque, para 17, especially at fn 39.

[62] European Judicial Network, 'European e-Justice', https://e-justice.europa.eu/content_divorce-45-en.do on divorce laws in all EU Member States.

[63] European Judicial Network, 'European e-Justice, Divorce – England and Wales', https://e-justice.europa.eu/content_divorce-45-ew-en.do?member=1#toc_1.

All these considerations relating to Evolutive Rules 5, 6, 7 and 8 contribute to the result that the importance of the evolutive principles, which foster an evolutive interpretation of the right to divorce under the ECHR, must be rated as serious. Not granting a right to divorce interferes heavily with the constitutional principles of effectiveness, self-determination and pluralism. It further stands in contrast to an existing European consensus on divorce laws.

V. THE LEGITIMACY OF THE EVOLUTIVE APPROACH TO INTERPRETATION

Consequently, the principles of the real dimension as being just moderate have to yield to the principles of the ideal dimension in this case. The fact that the drafters of the Convention clearly intended not to grant a right to divorce turned out to be of moderate importance only. Contrary to that, interference with the evolutive principles would lead to a highly unjust situation in the lives of the applicant and his new partner and child, which leaves them with no legal recognition of their familial ties.

Hence, the legitimate interpretive approach to this question is an evolutive one, not a static one. The decision of the ECtHR in *Babiarz v Poland* is thus not responsive to the constitutional commands of the ECHR. The evolutive principles clearly require the choice of an evolutive interpretation.

on the outcome at the interpretation phase presented here does not preclude a different outcome at the subsequent proportionality stage. At this stage, one could still examine whether the interference of not granting the right to divorce as protected by the ECHR according to an evolutive interpretation was justified by any of the reasons provided in Article 8(2) ECHR. Consequently, balancing at the interpretation stage does not anticipate or replace the subsequent proportionality analysis.

12

The Right to Assisted Suicide

THE SECOND CASE exemplifies an argument in favour of static interpretation. The selected judgment dates from 2002 and deals with the question of whether Articles 2 and 8 ECHR grant a negative right to assisted suicide.

I. FACTS OF THE CASE

The applicant, a woman of 43 years, suffered from motor neurone disease (MND), a severe disease within the central nervous system.[1] MND affects the muscles of the body and is incurable. The lethal effect of the disease usually results from the inability to breathe or swallow due to the weakening of the respective muscles.[2] The applicant was in an advanced stage of MND, which left her paralysed from the neck downwards and unable to speak and eat. The disease did not, however, affect her brain functions and intellectual capacity. The applicant wished not to await the undignified death caused by MND, but to decide herself when and how to put an end to her life.[3] However, the disease left the applicant unable to commit suicide herself, which is why she was dependent on the assistance of someone else.[4] Although her husband was willing to assist her, UK law prevented him from doing so, as the assistance to suicide constituted a crime under the British Suicide Act.[5] Consequently, the applicant's solicitor wrote a letter to the Director of Public Prosecutions requesting that the applicant's husband not be prosecuted if he assisted her in her suicide.[6] Her request and also the subsequent appeals to the Divisional Court and the House of Lords were dismissed.[7] The applicant argued that the UK legislation interfered with her protected Convention rights. The UK authorities argued that the Director of Public Prosecutions did not have the power to guarantee the non-prosecution of a future crime and that the prohibition of assisted suicide in the British Suicide Act was not in breach of the rights and freedoms set forth in the ECHR.[8]

[1] *Pretty v UK* EHRR 2002-III para 7.
[2] ibid.
[3] ibid para 8.
[4] ibid para 9.
[5] ibid paras 9–10.
[6] ibid para 10.
[7] ibid paras 11–14.
[8] ibid paras 11, 13 and 14.

II. TIME DIMENSION OF INTERPRETATION

Pretty v the United Kingdom was the first case brought to the ECtHR to raise the issue of protection for the decision to end one's life. The question of whether the Convention protects a right to assisted suicide clearly constitutes a conflict between static and evolutive interpretation. Such a right was not at all intended by the drafters and was largely taboo at the time of the Convention's drafting. It is deeply connected to ethical, moral and religious questions arising in the context of suicide committed by oneself or with the help of a second person. The wording of the ECHR omits any reference to end-of-life-rights but protects the right to life on the one hand, as well as the right to self-determination on the other. The two articles that play a role in this context are Article 2 (right to life) and Article 8 (right to respect for private and family life).

Both Articles have undergone relevant developments since the entry into force of the Convention in 1953. The exception of the right to life with regard to the execution of a sentence of a court is no longer effective as Protocols 6 and 13 to the Convention have incrementally introduced a total ban on the death penalty, including in times of war.[9] In the Court's case law, the right to life has further been developed with regard to positive obligations of the state to protect individuals from any life-endangering circumstances in public institutions and from ineffective investigations of deaths caused by public officials in the lawful fulfilment of their duties.[10] The jurisprudence of the ECtHR has thus enhanced the protection of the right to life so far. The question arising in *Pretty* points to a very different direction, however. It asks whether the protection of the right to life includes a right of the individual to decide freely whether to live, and whether the state has a positive obligation to provide its citizens with the necessary facilities to enjoy their freedom. As this right to self-determination in matters of life and death touches upon the intimate private sphere of individuals, it also raises questions under the right to private and family life under Article 8. With regard to the ending of life, this right so far has played a role in the context of the right to abortion, which the Court has not yet explicitly recognised, but which it has at least acknowledged to fall under the scope of Article 8.[11]

Since the decision in the case of *Pretty v the United Kingdom* an increasing number of cases concerning end-of-life decision have been brought to the ECtHR. The cases of *Haas v Switzerland*[12] and *Gross v Switzerland*[13] turned on

[9] Protocol No 6 to the Convention for the Protection of Human Rights and Fundamental Freedoms concerning the Abolition of the Death Penalty (Strasbourg, 28 April 1983) ETS No 114 which abolished the death penalty in Art 1, but still allowed it in times of war, according to Art 2; Additional Protocol No 13 finally introduced a total ban on death penalty: Protocol No 13 to the Convention for the Protection of Human Rights and Fundamental Freedoms concerning the Abolition of the Death Penalty in all circumstances (Strasbourg, 3 May 2003) ETS No 187.

[10] *Mahmut Kaya v Turkey* (2000) EHRR 2000-III para 102; *McCann and Others v UK* [GC] Series A no 324 (1997) para 161.

[11] *A, B and C v Ireland* [GC] EHRR 2010-VI 214.

[12] *Haas v Switzerland* EHRR 2011-I.

[13] *Gross v Switzerland* [GC] EHRR 2014-IV.

the specificities of the Swiss legislation, which allowed for publicly controlled suicide of individuals. They both raised the question whether the Swiss requirement of a medical prescription for receiving a lethal drug constituted a disproportionate interference with their right to self-determination under Article 8 ECHR.[14] In the subsequent case of *Koch v Germany*, the applicant complained that the German authorities did not even substantively examine his request for obtaining a lethal drug in order to assist in the suicide of his terminally ill wife.[15] The Grand Chamber case of *Lambert and others v France* raised the question of whether the medical decision to end life-prolonging treatment was in breach of the state's positive obligation to protect the right to life under Article 2 ECHR and whether it amounted to ill-treatment as prohibited by Article 3 ECHR.[16] There has also been an application pending since 2017 against Belgium, which deals with the euthanasia of a patient without the knowledge of her family.[17]

The laws in CoE member states on active or passive assistance in suicide are still highly divergent. Most of the CoE member states prohibit any form of assisted suicide.[18] So far only the Netherlands, Belgium and Luxembourg allow for assisted suicide conducted by a physician.[19] Other countries such as Switzerland, Germany, Spain and France allow for suicide by the affected person him- or herself upon prescription of a lethal drug by a physician or other means.[20] Several other countries in the CoE do allow for the termination of life-prolonging medical treatment if the patient so requires or under further specific circumstances.[21] However, the Court clearly distinguishes between these two forms of end-of-life decisions, taking the former – euthanasia – to be the more contested form in Europe.[22] Studies show that there is a sharp divide between Eastern and Western Europe concerning public acceptance of assisted suicide, Western Europe being more open to it.[23]

There is thus a noticeable development in the societies of some member states of the CoE regarding end-of-life decisions.

III. THE ECTHR'S REASONING

Although the applicant alleged violations of Articles 2, 3, 8, 9 and 14 of the Convention, the analysis of the Court's reasoning will be reduced to

[14] *Haas v Switzerland* (n 12) para 32; *Gross v Switzerland* (n 13) para 14.
[15] *Koch v Germany* (2012) no 497/09 para 27.
[16] *Lambert and others v France* [GC] EHRR 2015-III para 80.
[17] European Court of Human Rights, *Factsheet – End of Life and the ECHR (European Court of Human Rights)* (Strasbourg, Press Unit of the European Court of Human Rights, 2019) 6.
[18] See, eg, the comparative analysis by the ECtHR in *Koch v Germany* (n 15) para 28.
[19] Arend C Hendriks, 'End-of-life Decisions. Recent Jurisprudence of the European Court of Human Rights' (2019) 19(4) *ERA Forum* 561, 562.
[20] ibid 562.
[21] See, eg, the comparative analysis by the ECtHR in *Lambert and others v France* (n 16) para 72.
[22] ibid paras 124 and 141.
[23] Joachim Cohen, Paul van Landeghem, Nico Carpentier and Luc Deliens, 'Public Acceptance of Euthanasia in Europe: A Survey Study in 47 Countries' (2014) 59(1) *International Journal of Public Health* 143, 153.

Articles 2 and 8 only as they seem to be more intimately connected to a possible right of assisted suicide.

With regard to Article 2, the Court stressed that the case law so far put the emphasis on the aspect of the protection of life by the state, rather than on the negative aspect of a right to die.[24] The phrasing of the Article implies that the right to life 'is unconcerned with issues to do with the quality of living or what a person chooses to do with his or her life'.[25]

The Court went on to argue that

> Article 2 cannot, without a distortion of language, be interpreted as conferring the diametrically opposite right, namely a right to die; nor can it create a right to self-determination in the sense of conferring on an individual the entitlement to choose death rather than life.[26]

Although the Court recalled that the Convention had to be interpreted as a living instrument and in the light of present-day conditions, it also stressed that the clear object of Article 2 was to protect the lives of individuals against the use of lethal force on the part of the state rather than to oblige public authorities to employ such force.[27] Consequently, the Court did not find a violation of Article 2 ECHR in this case.[28]

Regarding Article 8, the Court recalled that matters of physical integrity clearly fall within the ambit of the right to private life.[29] The Court acknowledged for the first time that also the right to self-determination of individuals is a vital guarantee underlying the interpretation of Article 8.[30] While it denied that quality of life played a role under Article 2, it acknowledged that it

> is under Article 8 that notions of the quality of life take on significance. In an era of growing medical sophistication combined with longer life expectancies, many people are concerned that they should not be forced to linger on in old age or in states of advanced physical or mental decrepitude which conflict with strongly held ideas of self and personal identity.[31]
>
> The applicant in this case is prevented by law from exercising her choice to avoid what she considers will be an undignified and distressing end to her life. The Court is not prepared to exclude that this constitutes an interference with her right to respect for private life as guaranteed under Article 8 § 1 of the Convention.[32]

Consequently, the Court accepted that the case of the applicant fell under the ambit of the right to respect for private life. Yet, in its further assessment the

[24] *Pretty v UK* (n 1) para 39.
[25] ibid para 39.
[26] ibid.
[27] ibid para 54.
[28] ibid para 42.
[29] ibid para 61.
[30] ibid para 61.
[31] ibid para 65.
[32] ibid para 67.

Court concluded that the interference was justified according to Article 8(2) ECHR, as considerations of public health and safety as well as the protection of vulnerable groups carried greater weight than the interest of self-determination in this case.[33] It thus found that there had been no violation of Article 8 ECHR in this case.[34]

To conclude, the ECtHR in the case of *Pretty* did not establish a right to die under Article 2 of the Convention. It acknowledged, however, that the factual and legal impossibility of suicide in this case interfered with the applicant's right to respect for private life.

IV. THE BALANCING OF STATIC AND EVOLUTIVE INTERPRETATION

Pretty v UK touches upon a core right of the Convention – the right to life. It asks whether this right protects also the negative aspect of the choice to die as being intimately connected to an individual's right to self-determination. While such a protection was clearly not intended by the drafters of the Convention, it is beyond doubt that society – at least in some parts of Europe – has developed an increased appreciation and acceptance of life-ending decisions. This raises the question of whether an evolutive interpretation of the Convention in favour of a right to assisted suicide would have been the normatively favourable approach in the case of *Pretty v UK*. An evolutive interpretation would amount to reading a right to assisted suicide into Articles 2 and 8 ECHR, whereas a static interpretation would amount to repudiating such a right.

The competing principles in this case are the principles of human dignity and self-determination on the evolutive side of the scales, and the principles of legal certainty and democratic legitimacy on the static side. Again, regarding the arguments put forward in Chapter 9, we can accept that the principles of both sides display the same abstract weight, which leaves us to determine the concrete weights with regard to the specific circumstances of the case only.

The first step of the balancing exercise requires the determination of the intensity of interference with static constitutional principles. I will argue that the intensity of the interference of an evolutive interpretation with the principles of the real dimension should be categorised as serious. The following weighting rules apply: the rule of literal meaning (Static Rule 1), the rule of precedents (Static Rule 2), and the rule of consensus (Static Rule 4).

I will first consider arguments relating to Static Rule 1. First, there is the clear wording of Article 2 ECHR that human life is inviolable, the object of which is to protect life, not death. Second, there is intention whatsoever by the drafters to include the protection of end-of-life decisions into the guarantees

[33] ibid para 74.
[34] ibid para 78.

of the ECHR. The topic has been completely omitted in the drafting process.[35] Consequently, an evolutive interpretation would amount to a clear departure from the text and the intentions of the drafters. Regarding Static Rule 2, it needs to be noted that the analysis in Section II above has demonstrated that there is established case law which denies the right to end one's life under Article 2 ECHR.[36] These aspects all relate to legal certainty and speak against a right to assisted suicide.

As far as Static Rule 4 is concerned, consensus among the domestic legal systems on end-of-life decisions is almost non-existent. Admittedly, many countries have developed an acceptance of the patient's autonomy to predetermine the termination of life-prolonging treatment in the form of a living will. Yet, quite the opposite holds true for any form of active contribution on the part of the state to the desired suicide of a person. The difference between these two forms of end-of-life decisions is that the former alternative deals with patients in the very final stage of life, in which the continuation of life depends solely on life-sustaining machines without any remaining mental capability of the patient to still take an informed decision, whereas the latter alternative deals with patients in an earlier stage, in which their (expectancy of) suffering due to an incurable disease triggers their desire to anticipate death. This amounts to a desire to die in dignity by means of a self-induced death, caused by a prescribed lethal drug. So far, this form of ending one's life is accepted in very few Western countries within the CoE.[37] However, exactly this form of end-of-life decision is the one on which the case of *Pretty v UK* turns. Consequently, the CoE member states are far away from a common European approach to the matter of publicly assisted suicide. An evolutive interpretation would thus depart from the current consensus in Europe.

Besides, the finality of the decision to die, and hence the seriousness of the consequence, adds further weight to a more cautious interpretation of the right to life under the Convention. Even if assisted suicide were accepted, the requirements regarding procedural standards need to be very high in order to avoid any risk of abuse or any kind of pressure on patients to end the burden they place on their families or other caregivers.

Lastly, the premises underlying the plurality of arguments which have just been presented display a high level of certainty and hence add weight to static interpretation.[38] There was no intention of the drafters to protect the right to die, but rather a clear commitment in the drafting process as well as in the case law of the Court to oblige the state to protect life in all its facets. Also, the UK

[35] There is no indication in the *travaux préparatoires* that the member states even thought of the option to include a right to end one's life: *Collected Edition of the 'Travaux Préparatoires'* Volume I (The Hague, Martinus Nijhoff, 1975).

[36] *Koch v Germany* (n 15); *Haas v Switzerland* (n 12); *Gross v Switzerland* (n 13).

[37] See Section II above.

[38] For the criterion of the epistemic reliability of the underlying premises see Chapter 10, Section III.

classification of assisted suicide as a crime is explicit and not just a gap in the legal system. It thus reflects a deliberate decision by the drafters backed by a democratic decision-making process.

The second step of the balancing exercise requires the determination of the importance of the competing evolutive principles. Weighty arguments also support the alternative interpretation of a right to die. Most importantly, the fundamental values of human dignity and self-determination weigh in favour of a right to assisted suicide. Both constitute core values of the ECHR.[39] Thus, the weighting rules of human dignity (Evolutive Rule 1), self-determination (Evolutive Rule 6) and consensus (Evolutive Rule 8) apply in the current case of *Pretty v UK*.

Concerning Evolutive Rule 6 relating to the principle of self-determination, the question arises as to why some autonomous personal decisions are more accepted by law than others. The first question turns on the distinction which the current legal situation draws between committing suicide in a publicly controlled way and committing suicide all alone. Both amount to deliberate decisions as expressed in the principle of self-determination. Still, the only commonly accepted end-of-life choice is the suicide of a person, which today no longer constitutes a criminal offence. However, suicide in a publicly controlled way would ensure that a person harms only him- or herself and does not endanger others with the suicide act. Suicide by a medically prescribed lethal drug further minimises the risk of trauma of relatives and third parties witnessing the suicide of a person directly or indirectly. It further enables patients to die in dignity and peace in the company of their families instead of being pushed into concealment of their suicide plans. Or, as in the case of the applicant, who was physically unable to commit suicide without the help of others, not allowing publicly assisted suicide amounts to an overall impossibility of committing suicide at all.

The second question turns on the distinction which the current legal situation draws between passive and active euthanasia. In the latter case, patients consciously face the fate of suffering and death and take an informed decision in the particular situation. Why is it more acceptable to anticipate this decision by means of a living will than to take it in the very moment when in possession of one's full mental capabilities? The current acceptance of the former but not the latter gives the impression that at a certain point of their suffering patients lose their right to self-determination.

Similar arguments can be raised with regard to Evolutive Rule 1. It appears that the current situation deprives patients not only of their right to self-determination, but also of parts of their dignity. The applicant expressed a clear and informed decision, which was not accepted. This was aggravated by the fact

[39] Janneke H Gerards, *General Principles of the European Convention on Human Rights* (Cambridge, Cambridge University Press, 2019) 61–64.

that she was physically dependent on the assistance of a second person. These considerations raise the question whether it is really justifiable for a state to force people to bear their suffering.

Notwithstanding these weighty arguments, one needs to be careful in concluding that they justify more than a negative obligation of the state to simply accept the end-of-life choices of people, thus extending it to a positive obligation of the state to facilitate the implementation of these choices. Although an evolutive interpretation in this matter would foster self-determination and human dignity, there is still a risk that the acceptance of a right to die under the ECHR would also have the opposite effect of pressurising people to opt for an early death rather than a longer burdensome life for their families. This holds particularly true with regard to the facts of the case in *Pretty v UK*, where the applicant claimed a right for her husband not to be prosecuted for assisting her in her suicide. Such a guarantee of non-prosecution is prone to abuse. A right to assisted suicide would need to follow a strict procedure involving medical and psychological expertise, as is the case in Switzerland, for example. Consequently, it is indeed questionable to what extent an evolutive interpretation in this case would lead to enhanced protection of the rights to self-determination and human dignity.

Finally, regard must be had to Evolutive Rule 8 and the role of consensus. As has been demonstrated above, there is not yet a clear societal trend in favour of accepting publicly assisted suicide. The increased case law before the ECtHR touching on the protection of assisted suicide mirrors an emerging trend in society, which is not yet reflected in a legal consensus in Europe. While the importance of human dignity and the right to self-determination is more than just *light*, it is difficult to argue that they are of *serious* importance in light of the above considerations. I thus conclude that the principles of the ideal dimension cannot be categorised as being of more than moderate importance in the case of *Pretty v UK*.

V. THE LEGITIMACY OF THE STATIC APPROACH TO INTERPRETATION

As a consequence, the principles of the ideal dimension with the categorisation of 'moderate' have to give way to the principles of the real dimension, interference with which has been weighted as serious. Although the protection of human dignity and self-determination lies at the core of the Convention, it could not be established that an evolutive interpretation of the right to life in order also to cover a right to die would really contribute to an undistorted protection of these principles. Hence, a static approach to the interpretation in this case is backed by a better normative justification.

The decision of the ECtHR is thus reasonably justifiable by reference to the constitutional principles of the ECHR. Yet, my case analysis has demonstrated that the justification of the static approach to interpretation could be improved considerably by making use of the balancing model.

13

The Right to Preservation of the Environment

THE THIRD CASE reveals a stalemate position between static and evolutive constitutional principles, thus leading to an interpretive margin of appreciation. The selected judgment by the ECtHR dates from December 2010 and deals with the extent to which environmental claims can be interpreted under the right to respect for private and family life in Article 8 ECHR.

I. FACTS OF THE CASE

The applicant lived in the Bulgarian village of Elshitsa, in a house which was located at a distance of one kilometre from the tailings pond and the flotation plant of a former copper-ore mine. The applicant further owned agricultural land in an area located about four kilometres away from the pond.[1] The pond was in operation until 1991 and it was always part of a state-owned company.[2] Afterwards, a years-long process of finding alternative reclamation schemes for the pond started.[3] In January 1999 a scheme which sought to put earth, soil and new vegetation on the pond started to be implemented, after an environmental impact assessment had led to a positive result. However, the implementation was stopped in April 1999.[4] In May 1999 a new scheme had been suggested to the Ministry of Industry by a sole trader, which sought to cap the pond's surface temporarily with soil cement in order to avoid the spread of dust, and in order to use the sludge of a close waste-water treatment plant for biological reclamation.[5] Subsequently, the Regional Inspectorate of Environment and Water, as well as the mayor, gave a negative opinion on the suggested scheme for two major reasons. First, the sustainability and stability of the soil cement as well as the full reclamation of the pond were questionable. Second, the sludge

[1] *Ivan Atanasov v Bulgaria* (2010) no 12853/03 para 7.
[2] ibid paras 8 and 14.
[3] ibid para 8.
[4] ibid.
[5] ibid para 9.

from the waste-water treatment plant partly contained heavy metals as the plant treated both domestic and industrial waste, the latter constituting hazardous waste.[6] Consequently, the Ministry of Industry entrusted a board of experts with the assessment of the two competing schemes, which came to the result that the second scheme from May 1999 should be implemented.[7] The implementation of the new scheme thus started in October 1999.[8] It was licensed to transport up to 400 tons of domestic waste-water sludge per day from the waste-water treatment plant to the pond, to lay it on the pond and to use it for fertilising soils or improving the environment. Chemical analyses had to be provided quarterly.[9]

The applicant applied to the Supreme Administrative Court for review of the Minister's approval of the scheme. He argued that the sludge could have a detrimental impact on health and the environment as it was not possible to guarantee that only domestic sludge and not industrial sludge was transported from the waste-water plant to the pond. Hence, it could not be guaranteed that hazardous waste was transported to the pond.[10] The applicant claimed that the approval impaired the right of the inhabitants to a safe and healthy environment.[11] His initial application and subsequent appeals were unsuccessful.[12]

Subsequently, the Municipal Council sent a request to the Ministry of Health and the National Centre for Hygiene, Medical Ecology and Nutrition for an expert opinion on whether the new scheme constituted a health risk for people living in the surroundings of the pond.[13] After having examined samples from the pond, the Centre came to the conclusion that there was an increased health risk due to heavy-metal contamination within 10 kilometres of the pond. The samples of the sludge on the pond displayed a heavy-metal content which was above the maximum. There was thus an increased risk of air pollution stemming from the dust of the sludge, and of underground water pollution stemming from the migration of heavy metals through the surface.[14] The report specified that such contamination could affect the peripheral and central nervous systems, the production of blood, and the liver and the kidneys, as well as leading to carcinogenic and allergenic effects.[15] Further samples, which had been taken by a commission appointed by the mayor, also displayed a contamination of lead, cadmium, copper, zinc, chrome and nickel above the maximum. It further questioned whether the soil cement cover was sufficient to prevent the contamination of the pond with those heavy metals.[16]

[6] ibid paras 10–11.
[7] ibid para 16.
[8] ibid para 19.
[9] ibid para 21.
[10] ibid para 22.
[11] ibid para 23.
[12] ibid paras 24–30.
[13] ibid para 31.
[14] ibid para 32.
[15] ibid para 34.
[16] ibid.

Due to public pressure, an environmental impact assessment was ordered in 2001 by the Minister for the Environment and Water.[17] However, the Minister did not accept the outcome of this assessment and ordered its revision.[18] Even after a further examination had been carried out, the Minister decided that she was unable to draw any reliable conclusions with regard to the impact of the scheme on the health of the people and the environment. The environmental impact assessment was thus stopped by the Ministry.[19] A subsequent order of the Minister of Health for a new assessment of the environmental and health effects failed due to a lack of funding and was thus never carried out.[20] In 2007, after the contested reclamation scheme for the pond had been finished, and thus the whole surface of the pond had been covered with sludge, Eco Elshitsa EOOD, which had implemented the scheme, presented a self-monitoring report on the contamination of the environment with heavy metals. The examined samples demonstrated heavy pollution of the pond's drainage water.[21]

The applicant thus claimed that the Bulgarian authorities had violated his right to private and family life under Article 8 ECHR as they had allowed a reclamation scheme of the pond, which put his health at risk.[22] The applicant argued that long-term effects on his health were very likely and that the risk of such effects constituted a violation of Article 8 ECHR.[23]

II. TIME DIMENSION OF INTERPRETATION

The case of *Ivan Atanasov v Bulgaria* raises the issue of whether the ECHR grants a right to the preservation of a healthy environment. The relevant article under scrutiny is again the right to respect for private and family life in Article 8 ECHR.

The wording of Article 8 ECHR clearly does not address environmental matters at all. The same holds true for all other articles of the Convention, which remain silent on environmental protection. Yet, a certain evolution of the Convention has taken place regarding environmental claims, which have increasingly been brought before the ECtHR since the entry into force of the ECHR.[24] So far, the Court has acknowledged protection of the Convention for direct adverse effects of environmental pollution on the life and health of individuals[25]

[17] ibid para 39.
[18] ibid para 42.
[19] ibid para 43.
[20] ibid para 44.
[21] ibid para 45.
[22] ibid para 58.
[23] ibid para 62.
[24] For a good overview of early environmental cases, see Richard Desgagné, 'Integrating Environmental Values into the European Convention on Human Rights' (1995) 89(2) *American Journal of International Law* 263, 265f.
[25] ibid 266–77. See also Council of Europe, *Manual on Human Rights and the Environment* (Strasbourg, Council of Europe Publishing, 2012) 45f.

and for procedural rights of individuals regarding decision-making processes in environmental matters.[26] Furthermore, the Court has held that property rights of individuals may legitimately be interfered with for the purpose of environmental protection.[27]

For the case of *Ivan Atanasov v Bulgaria*, the first limb of these developments is the most relevant one, as the case also touches on adverse effects of environmental pollution on the health and well-being of individuals. In order to distinguish the case of *Ivan Atanasov v Bulgaria* from previous case law in that limb, I need to dig deeper into the established principles for the protection of health from detrimental environmental impacts under Article 8 ECHR. In order for Article 8 to be applicable, environmental effects have to have a direct and severe impact on the private life or home of an individual.[28] There thus needs to be a direct causal link and a certain intensity of the harm caused by the environmental effects.[29] However, it is also established case law that 'Environmental degradation does not necessarily involve a violation of Article 8 as it does not include an express right to environmental protection or nature conservation'.[30] There is thus no right to a clean and quiet environment covered by the Convention.[31] In cases of environmental pollution, the Court requires an actual deterioration of the individual's health in order to accept a violation of Article 8 ECHR.[32] The mere risk of problems for the individual or public health is not sufficient to raise an issue under Article 8 ECHR.[33] As the next section will demonstrate, the case of *Ivan Atanasov v Bulgaria* exemplifies that this is so even if there is scientific proof of the health risk. This is exactly where the case of *Ivan Atanasov v Bulgaria* opens the discussion of an evolutive interpretation of Article 8 ECHR. Although the question of evolutive interpretation was not discussed at all in the judgment, the case should be looked at from this perspective. It implicitly asks the question whether it is reasonable to expect an individual to take the burden of actual detriment to his or her health in order to have a human right to protection against environmental pollution. This question needs to be discussed in light of the background that reliable scientific data on the long-term health impacts of environmental pollution have increased tremendously since the entry into force of the Convention. Whereas it is often difficult or even impossible to measure

[26] Ivana Krstić and Bojana Čučković, 'Procedural Aspects of Article 8 of the ECHR in Environmental Cases – The Greening of Human Rights Law' (2015) LXIII(3) *Belgrade Law Review* 170.

[27] Desgagné (n 24) 277–80; Council of Europe (n 25) 61f.

[28] Council of Europe (n 25) 19; *Fadeyeva v Russia* EHRR 2005-IV para 69.

[29] Council of Europe (n 25) 20; *Fadeyeva v Russia* (n 28) para 69.

[30] *Kyrtatos v Greece* EHRR 2003-VI para 52; *Fadeyeva v Russia* (n 28) para 68; *Dubetska and others v Ukraine* (2011) no 30499/03 para 105.

[31] *Leon and Agnieszka Kania v Poland* (2009) no 12605/03 paras 98–104.

[32] *Fadeyeva v Russia* (n 28) para 69.

[33] *Dubetska and others v Ukraine* (n 30) para 105. But see *Taskin and others v Turkey* EHRR 2004-X para 113.

immediate hazardous environmental harms for individuals,[34] it is at least feasible to collect data with regard to possible health detriments. Societal awareness of the correlation between environmental pollution and health problems is on the rise. Comparative analysis of CoE member states illustrates that since the entry into force of the Convention, the protection of a healthy environment has come under constitutional protection in several member states, among them Bulgaria.[35] Furthermore, the European Union has institutionalised the protection of the environment in Article 37 of the EU Charter of Fundamental Rights.

There is thus a considerable dynamic aspect in the relevant subject matter of the case. Yet, the other side of the coin is that the Convention – unlike other international instruments – remains silent on environmental rights, and the Court has already rejected the acceptance of a general right to a healthy environment. Hence, there are also considerable static arguments against an evolutive interpretation of the ECHR.

III. THE ECtHR'S REASONING

In its reasoning the Court acknowledged that environmental protection was of increased relevance today. It further stressed that the Convention did not provide for a general right to the preservation of nature, but that there needed to be a direct causal link between the pollution and the rights under Article 8 ECHR.[36] Finally, the Court concluded that it was 'not persuaded that the resulting pollution affected the applicant's private sphere to the extent necessary to trigger the application of Article 8'.[37]

The Court justified this with the arguments that the applicant's house was located about one kilometre away from the pond, that a 'sudden release of large amounts of toxic gases' was not expected, and that the applicant could not demonstrate any negative consequences for the population living in the surroundings of the pond.[38] The Court acknowledged that expert reports had proven the contamination of the sludge with heavy metals, which were

> capable of adversely affecting human health when spreading in the environment … However, there are no materials in the case file to show that the pollution in and around the pond has caused an increase in the morbidity rate of Elshitsa's residents …

[34] *Kyrtatos v Greece* (n 30) dissenting opinion of Judge Zagrebelsky, in which he points to this fact, even though he was arguing in favour of a Convention violation against the majority of the bench.

[35] *Ivan Atanasov v Bulgaria* (n 1) para 47, which recites Art 15 of the Bulgarian Constitution; other CoE member states with constitutional protection of a healthy environment are Greece, Spain, Portugal, the Netherlands, Hungary, Croatia, Slovenia, Macedonia, Czech Republic, Norway, Slovak Republic, Russia, Belgium, Moldova, Armenia, Azerbaijan, Finland, Georgia, Ukraine, Poland, Albania, Latvia, Romania, France, Serbia, Montenegro and Iceland.

[36] ibid para 66.

[37] ibid para 76.

[38] ibid.

> or has had a sufficiently adverse impact on the applicant's enjoyment of his home and the quality of his private and family life. Indeed, the applicant conceded that he could not show any actual harm to his health or even a short-term health risk, but merely feared negative consequences in the long term.[39]

The Court also stressed the fact that the ECHR was not intended to cover environmental rights. 'As already noted, neither Article 8 nor any of other provision of the Convention or its Protocols were specifically designed to provide protection of the environment; other international instruments and domestic legislation are better suited to address such issues'.[40] Consequently, the ECtHR did not find a violation of the applicant's right to respect for his private and family life.[41]

IV. THE BALANCING OF STATIC AND EVOLUTIVE INTERPRETATION

The protection of the environment through a human rights document such as the ECHR was not the intention of the drafters of the Convention. Yet, scientific progress and increased knowledge about the adverse effects of environmental pollution have demonstrated that individuals can suffer tremendously from exposure to pollution, in the short as well as in the long term. This raises the question of whether the given Convention rights oblige states to protect individuals from environmentally induced harm to their health. While such protection has been acknowledged in cases in which the applicants already suffered from a deterioration of their health condition, there is still no protection for mere exposure to a health risk. The case of *Ivan Atanasov v Bulgaria* is a good illustration of a case in which the existence of a health risk due to environmental pollution has been scientifically proven but has not yet led to a deterioration of the applicant's health condition.

An evolutive interpretation in this case would amount to accepting the mere risk of long-term health problems caused by environmental pollution as sufficient to constitute an infringement of the Convention rights under Article 8. Contrary to that, a static interpretation would stick to the requirement that the health problems must have occurred at the time of the application. The competing principles are the principle of effectiveness on the evolutive side of the scale and legal certainty on the static side. As the suggested balancing model assumes in Chapter 9 that the abstract weights of the competing constitutional principles are equal, it is the concrete weights of the colliding principles which remain to be determined in light of the circumstances of the case at hand.

[39] ibid.
[40] ibid para 77.
[41] ibid para 79.

I will, in a first step, determine the intensity of the interference with the static constitutional principles. In a second step I will then examine the importance of the evolutive principles involved. In a third step I will then demonstrate why this subject matter leads to a stalemate position between static and evolutive interpretation and the underlying constitutional principles.

As far as the intensity of the interference of an evolutive interpretation with static principles is concerned, the following weighting rules need to be taken into consideration. First, it is Static Rule 1 (Rule of Literal Meaning), which is relevant, as an evolutive approach would depart from the wording of the Convention text. Second, an evolutive interpretation would also depart from precedents, which triggers Static Rule 2 (Rule of Precedents).

Regarding Static Rule 1 it needs to be noted that granting the right to the preservation of a healthy environment would clearly depart from the literal meaning of the ECHR and the intentions of the drafters. Although the protection of the environment has not been explicitly excluded from the Convention's protection, the discussion of such a right has been completely omitted in the whole drafting process. Environmental protection was not on the agenda of the drafters, who rather aimed at the preservation of peace and security.[42] And there is still no tendency among the CoE to extend the Convention's protection to environmental matters today. Although the Parliamentary Assembly of the CoE has recommended twice to the Committee of Ministers to consider the drafting of an additional Protocol, which establishes an individual right to a healthy environment and procedural rights in environmental matters,[43] the Convention text has never been amended by an additional Protocol so far.

As far as Static Rule 2 is concerned, an evolutive interpretation in the case of *Ivan Atanasov v Bulgaria* would also depart from existing case law by the ECtHR in the field of environmentally induced health problems. As has been demonstrated in Section II, the Court's established case law requires that the health problems must already have occurred or at least that there must have been exposure to very dangerous environmental activities. Contrary to that, prior to the case of *Ivan Atanasov v Bulgaria*, the Court held that the mere destruction and pollution of the environment do not raise an issue under Article 8 ECHR. In *Kyrtatos v Greece* the ECtHR maintained that 'Neither Article 8 nor any of the other Articles of the Convention are specifically designed to provide general protection of the environment as such'.[44]

[42] Thorbjorn Jagland, 'Deep Security: Building a European Community of Values' (2011) 33(1) *Harvard International Review* 12, 13; Aline Royer, *The Council of Europe* (Strasbourg, Council of Europe Publishing, 2010) 3.

[43] Doc 8560, Future action to be taken by the Council of Europe in the field of environmental protection, Report, 5 October 1999, para 11, ii.b; Doc 9791, Environment and human rights, Report, 16 April 2003 (Parliamentary Assembly of the Council of Europe) para 10.a.

[44] *Kyrtatos v Greece* (n 30) para 52.

Unlike in the case of *Ivan Atanasov v Bulgaria*, however, the applicant in the case of *Kyrtatos v Greece* did not provide scientific proof of the possible health risks. The facts of the case in *Ivan Atanasov v Bulgaria* thus differ slightly from the relevant precedent.

As far as the two static rules are concerned, an evolutive interpretation would certainly interfere with the constitutional principle of legal certainty. In light of the above considerations, this interference should be classified as only moderate, however.

The second step of the balancing model requires the determination of the importance of the evolutive constitutional principles. It is Evolutive Rule 7 (Rule of Effectiveness) that lies at the core of the weighting considerations. One main purpose of Article 8 ECHR is to protect the personal integrity and well-being of individuals from unjustified interference by the state. If one excludes hazardous state activities leading to a deterioration or pollution of the environment from the scope of Article 8 ECHR, this affects the effectiveness of the intended protection. This assumption builds on the fact that scientific knowledge today has sufficiently demonstrated the impact of the environment on the human condition. As has been demonstrated in Section II, the Court already interprets the Convention so as to cover environmentally induced health problems. The open question is thus whether the principle of effectiveness also requires that the protection of the Convention is granted *ex ante* if an individual is exposed to a health risk in the long run but does not yet suffer from immediate health problems. Can a human rights instrument really ask an applicant to wait for a deterioration of his or her health before granting the full protection of the rights? This question is all the more pressing if one considers the fact that some of the effects of environmental pollution might only show after many years or even decades, when it is too late to fight the source of these effects. If the current interpretation of Article 8 ECHR is upheld, then individuals and families would be well advised to leave areas exposed to environmental pollution if they can do so, instead of fighting for the protection of their rights under Article 8 ECHR. This would certainly minimise the effectiveness of the right to respect for private and family life to a considerable extent.

Yet, the other side of the coin is that the real impact of environmental pollution on individual right bearers is very difficult to predict.[45] Certainly, the applicant in the case of *Ivan Atanasov v Bulgaria* could base his claim on the results of several examinations of the sludge, water and grass in and around the pond. Still, it was difficult to substantiate that the detected toxic substances had actually migrated through the air or the underground water and thus constituted an actual health risk for the applicant. Consequently, maybe other preventive measures such as the enhanced protection of procedural rights of individuals in public projects affecting the environment might also contribute to a more effective protection against adverse health effects in the first place.

[45] ibid; see dissenting opinion of Judge Zagrebelsky.

From the above considerations on Evolutive Rule 7, it follows that the evolutive interpretation in the case of *Ivan Atanasov v Bulgaria* would contribute to the effectiveness principle but that the importance of this evolutive principle in the concrete case is only moderate.

V. A STALEMATE CASE

The foregoing analysis of the static and evolutive principles guiding the interpretation in the case of *Ivan Atanasov v Bulgaria* has resulted in a stalemate as both sides of the scales have turned out to be of moderate weight. In accordance with the internal structure of the suggested balancing model in the interpretation stage, a stalemate case leads to the situation that it is for the member states to decide whether they want to opt for an evolutive or static theory of interpretation. It is thus a case which demonstrates a possible field of application for the interpretive margin of appreciation, which has been defined in Chapter 9. Bulgaria would have good reasons to opt for an evolutive approach to the protection of individuals against environmental pollution as the preservation of the environment is anchored in the country's Constitution.[46] Yet, as it is not for the ECtHR but for the Bulgarian authorities to evaluate this question, the outcome in the case of *Ivan Atanasov v Bulgaria* must be that Article 8 ECHR cannot be interpreted so as to grant a right to the preservation of the environment for the preventive protection of health.

Consequently, the decision of the Court to opt for a static interpretation conformed to the Convention's constitutional requirements as the interpretive question falls within the margin of appreciation of the member states. Still, the case analysis has also demonstrated that the balancing model improves the justification of the Court as it renders the outcome more transparent and reasonable.

[46] See Art 15 of the Bulgarian Constitution, which reads: 'The Republic of Bulgaria shall ensure the preservation and the reproduction of the environment, the conservation of the variety of living nature, and the reasonable utilisation of the country's natural and other resources'; see *Ivan Atanasov v Bulgaria* (n 1) para 47.

Conclusion

THE INTRODUCTION TO this book tracked a growing concern among scholars and politicians about the legitimacy of the ECtHR's evolutive interpretation of the ECHR. While many member states increasingly criticised the Court for disregarding its subsidiary role in human rights protection, academia disapproved of the level of justification in the Court's reasoning. Even within the Court there was disagreement on how to deal with cases raising intertemporal questions.

I have demonstrated that the most fundamental weakness of the current debate on intertemporal interpretation is its limitation to an either-or perspective on the legitimacy of evolutive and static interpretation. Absolute legitimacy theories supporting either evolutive interpretation or static interpretation are doomed to fail. They do not capture the inherent duality between formal and substantive principles in the ECHR's constitutional core. Theories striving for an absolute legitimacy of evolutive interpretation result in neglect of vital principles of the ECHR, such as legal certainty. Likewise, theories arguing for the absolute illegitimacy of evolutive interpretation neglect other vital principles, such as material justice or effective human rights protection.

Against this background, this book constructed a comprehensive legitimacy theory, which accounts for evolution as well as stability in the interpretation of the ECHR. It takes account of the 'maintenance' as well as the 'further realisation' of human rights, to which the Preamble of the ECHR refers. It respects sovereign democratic decisions on the evolution of human rights, but also takes the effective protection of human rights seriously. Based on the ideas of cosmopolitan and deliberative constitutionalism, it integrates constitutional arguments into the interpretation of the ECHR. It is the first model for the legitimacy of evolutive and static interpretation, which is not only sensitive to the constitutional principles of the ECHR, but which acknowledges the dual nature of the ECHR legal system.

At the heart of the legitimacy theory lies the construction of a constitutional framework for the ECHR. It is based on the three most fundamental principles to which the CoE commits itself, being human rights, democracy, and the rule of law. A thorough analysis of these three core principles of the Convention revealed that they all unfold in a multitude of sub-principles, uniting formal as well as substantive principles. This is justifiable from a normative-theoretical perspective, meaning that the dual nature of the ECHR legal system necessitates the pursuit of both formal and substantive aspects of these principles. Yet, it also holds true from a practical perspective regarding the perception of the constitutional principles in the political and judicial organs of the CoE. I have demonstrated that the judicial and political bodies of the CoE foster a substantive as well as a formal understanding of the three principles. The result of this analysis was surprising insofar as it showed that the political bodies of the CoE – consisting of representatives of all the member states – are more active than the ECtHR in promoting exactly those principles which call for evolutive interpretations. This reflects an arbitrary approach of the member states to the further development of the ECHR depending on whether they act on behalf of the CoE or on behalf of their respective nation states. In the latter function they accuse the ECtHR of being too activist. In the former function they push the further development of the Convention in manifold ways, most fundamentally by adopting a deeply substantive and broad understanding of the Convention's constitutional values of human rights, democracy, and the rule of law. The inherent duality in the Convention's constitutional core is the source of legitimacy for evolutive and static interpretation.

While the constitutional principles of the ECHR thus provide a relative legitimacy for both evolutive and static interpretation, the concrete legitimacy depends on a further, case-sensitive argumentation. This required a theory for the legitimate choice between evolutive and static interpretation based on the underlying constitutional principles. I reconstructed the conflict between evolutive and static interpretation as a conflict between evolutive (material) and static (formal) constitutional principles, and I resolved this conflict by means of balancing. It is not the possible interpretations in a case that are being balanced, but a balancing of the competing static and evolutive constitutional principles of the ECHR, which serve as arguments in the justification of the interpretation in a case. The balancing exercise requires the determination of the concrete weights of the competing evolutive and static constitutional principles in order to conclude which ones are more important in a concrete case. For this purpose, I have introduced weighting rules, which guide the determination of the concrete weights in the Court's reasoning.

The balancing model facilitates a thorough and reasonable justification of evolutive and static interpretations. It must be clear, however, that this procedure – in all its detail – does not 'dictate correct answers to legal problems'.[1] It is not a robotic mechanism, but rather a model which acknowledges the highly argumentative character of interpretation, and which seeks to achieve more transparency and rationality in the reason-giving process. Still, it is not an arbitrary model for the interpretation of the ECHR, which would lead to unpredictable applications of evolutive and static interpretation. The repeated application of the suggested balancing model by the ECtHR will, in the long run, lead to rules of preference, which will become an integral part of the Court's established principles

[1] Alec Stone Sweet and Jud Mathews, 'Proportionality, Judicial Review, and Global Constitutionalism' in Giorgio Bongiovanni, Giovanni Sartor and Chiara Valentini (eds), *Reasonableness and Law* (Dordrecht, Springer, 2009) 175.

of interpretation.[2] The balancing model enhances the argumentative burden of the ECtHR in the interpretation stage, while not sparing it from the argumentative burden which it faces in other stages of the application of law, such as, for example, proportionality analysis. As I have provided a detailed outline of the internal structure as well as the external justification of the balancing exercise, it can be immediately applied by legal practitioners and judges interpreting the Convention.

The research also leads to vital insights relating to the effects of Protocol No 15 to the ECHR. The introduction to this book picked up concerns that the reference to the subsidiarity principle and the margin of appreciation doctrine in the Preamble would reduce the legitimate field of application for evolutive interpretation. Yet, the study has demonstrated that these two principles form an integral part of the constitutional core of the ECHR. Subsidiarity and margin of appreciation are both formal or static constitutional principles of the Convention. They belong to a wider constitutional framework uniting a multitude of static and evolutive constitutional principles, which conflict with each other and which constantly have to be put in the correct proportion. The references to the margin of appreciation and the subsidiarity principle in the amended version of the Preamble might be a political signal. Legally, it is no more than a concrete manifestation of two static constitutional principles of the Convention, however. Likewise, the Preamble also contains explicit references to evolutive constitutional principles. The new version of the Preamble makes this conflict between static and evolutive principles in the constitutional core of the ECHR more visible instead of creating a new conflict affecting the interpretation of the Convention. The amendments introduced by Protocol No 15 will thus not 'shift the centres of gravity in human rights protection'[3] in Europe towards an enhanced role of nation states.

Finally, this book also opens a rich research agenda for the future. I have begun to explore the potential of constitutional arguments for the interpretation of the ECHR. Subsequent studies will show how my balancing model can account for the adaptation of the Convention rights to new societal contexts. While I have constructed a rational argumentative procedure for legitimising intertemporal interpretation, it is for legal practitioners to act on this model and to increase the level of rationality in the interpretation of the ECHR in the course of time. The study of this book paves the way for subsequent normative and empirical inquiries to explore the further possibilities of constitutional reasoning for the Convention's interpretation. At a certain level of abstraction, the idea of balancing at the interpretation stage also opens questions of transferability to other international human rights courts.

[2] Robert Alexy, *A Theory of Constitutional Rights* (Julian Rivers trans, Oxford, Oxford University Press, 2010 (repr)) 108.

[3] This expression is borrowed from Oddný Mjöll Arnardóttir and Antoine C Buyse (eds), *Shifting Centres of Gravity in Human Rights Protection: Rethinking Relations Between the ECHR, EU and National Legal Orders* (London, Routledge, 2016).

Bibliography

Alexy, R, 'On Balancing and Subsumption. A Structural Comparison' (2003) 16(4) *Ratio Juris* 433.

—— 'Menschenrechte ohne Metaphysik' (2004) 52(1) *Deutsche Zeitschrift für Philosophie* 15.

—— 'Balancing, Constitutional Review, and Representation' (2005) 3(4) *International Journal of Constitutional Law* 572.

—— 'Die Institutionalisierung der Menschenrechte im demokratischen Verfassungsstaat' in Stefan Gosepath and Georg Lohmann (eds), *Philosophie der Menschenrechte* (Frankfurt am Main, Suhrkamp, 2007).

—— *A Theory of Constitutional Rights* (Julian Rivers trans, Oxford, Oxford University Press, 2010 (repr)).

—— 'The Dual Nature of Law' (2010) 23(2) *Ratio Juris* 167.

—— *A Theory of Legal Argumentation: The Theory of Rational Discourse as Theory of Legal Justification* (Ruth Adler and Neil MacCormick trans, Oxford, Oxford University Press, 2011).

—— 'Rights and Liberties as Concepts' in Michel Rosenfeld (ed), *The Oxford Handbook of Comparative Constitutional Law* (Oxford, Oxford University Press, 2012).

—— 'Formal Principles: Some Replies to Critics' (2014) 12(3) *International Journal of Constitutional Law* 511.

Alkema EA, 'The European Convention as a Constitution and Its Court as a Constitutional Court' in Paul Mahoney, Franz Matscher, Herbert Petzold and Luzius Wildhaber (eds), *Protecting Human Rights: The European Perspective* (Cologne, Heymanns, 2000).

Allan TRS, 'Constitutional Rights and the Rule of Law' in Matthias Klatt (ed), *Institutionalized Reason: The Jurisprudence of Robert Alexy* (Oxford, Oxford University Press, 2012).

Aust A, *Handbook of International Law* (2nd edn, Cambridge, Cambridge University Press, 2014).

Baade B, *Der EGMR als Diskurswächter* (Berlin, Springer, 2016).

Balkin JM, *Living Originalism* (Cambridge, MA, Belknap Press of Harvard University Press, 2011).

Barak A, *The Judge in a Democracy* (Princeton, NJ, Princeton University Press, 2006).

Barber NW, Ekins R and Yowell P (eds), *Lord Sumption and the Limits of the Law* (Oxford, Hart Publishing, 2016).

Baroness Hale of Richmond, 'Address' in European Court of Human Rights (ed), *Dialogue Between Judges: What Are the Limits to the Evolutive Interpretation of the Convention?* (Strasbourg, Council of Europe Publishing, 2011).

Bates E, *The Evolution of the European Convention on Human Rights: From Its Inception to the Creation of a Permanent Court of Human Rights* (Oxford, Oxford University Press, 2010).

Beitz CR and Goodin RE (eds), *Global Basic Rights* (Oxford, Oxford University Press, 2011).

Bellamy R, 'The Limits of Lord Sumption: Limited Legal Constitutionalism and the Political Form of the ECHR' in NW Barber, Richard Ekins and Paul Yowell (eds), *Lord Sumption and the Limits of the Law* (Oxford, Hart Publishing, 2016).

Benoît-Rohmer F and Klebes H, *Council of Europe Law: Towards a Pan-European Legal Area* (Strasbourg, Council of Europe Publishing, 2005).

Benvenisti E, 'Margin of Appreciation, Consensus, and Universal Standards' (1999) 31 *New York University Journal of International Law and Politics* 843.

Bernhardt R, 'Evolutive Treaty Interpretation, Especially of the European Convention on Human Rights' (1999) 42 *German Yearbook of International Law* 11.

Besson S, 'Whose Constitution(s)? International Law, Constitutionalism and Democracy' in Jeffrey L Dunoff and Joel P Trachtman (eds), *Ruling the World? Constitutionalism, International Law, and Global Governance* (Cambridge, Cambridge University Press, 2009).

—— 'Legal Philosophical Issues of International Adjudication: Getting Over the Amour Impossible between International Law and Adjudication' in Cesare Romano, Karen J Alter and Yuval Shani (eds), *The Oxford Handbook of International Adjudication* (Oxford, Oxford University Press, 2014).

—— 'Justifications' in Daniel Moeckli, Sangeeta Shah and Sandesh Sivakumaran (eds), *International Human Rights Law* (3rd edn, Oxford, Oxford University Press, 2018).

Bjorge E, *The Evolutionary Interpretation of Treaties* (Oxford, Oxford University Press, 2014).

Böckenförde E-W, 'Grundrechtstheorie und Grundrechtsinterpretation' in Ralf Dreier (ed), *Probleme der Verfassungsinterpretation: Dokumentation einer Kontroverse* (Baden-Baden, Nomos, 1976).

Borowski M, 'Formelle Prinzipien und Gewichtsformel' in Matthias Klatt (ed), *Prinzipientheorie und Theorie der Abwägung* (Tübingen, Mohr Siebeck, 2013).

Bossuyt M, 'Should the Strasbourg Court Exercise More Self-restraint' (2007) 28 *Human Rights Law Journal* 321.

Bryde B-O, 'International Democratic Constitutionalism' in Ronald J St Macdonald and Douglas M Johnston (eds), *Towards World Constitutionalism: Issues in the Legal Ordering of the World Community* (Leiden, Martinus Nijhoff, 2005).

Buchanan AE, *The Heart of Human Rights* (Oxford, Oxford University Press, 2014).

Çali B, 'Balancing Human Rights? Methodological Problems with Weights, Scales and Proportions' (2007) 29(1) *Human Rights Quarterly* 251.

—— 'Specialized Rules of Treaty Interpretation: Human Rights' in Duncan B Hollis (ed), *The Oxford Guide to Treaties* (Oxford, Oxford University Press, 2014).

Carozza PG, 'Human Dignity' in Dinah Shelton (ed), *The Oxford Handbook of International Human Rights Law* (Oxford, Oxford University Press, 2013).

Chesterman S, 'Rule of Law' in Rüdiger Wolfrum (ed), *The Max Planck Encyclopedia of Public International Law* (Oxford, Oxford University Press, 2012).

Chirardis V, 'The Limits of Interpretation of the Strasbourg Court and the Principle of Non-regression' in Dean Spielmann (ed), *La Convention européenne des droits de l'homme, un instrument vivant: Mélanges en l'honneur de Christos L. Rozakis, The European Convention on Human Rights, a Living Instrument* (Brussels, Bruylant, 2011).

Cohen J, van Landeghem P, Carpentier N and Deliens L, 'Public Acceptance of Euthanasia in Europe: A Survey Study in 47 Countries' (2014) 59(1) *International Journal of Public Health* 143.

Collected Edition of the 'Travaux Préparatoires' Volume I (The Hague, Martinus Nijhoff, 1975).

Cooke M, 'Contingency and Objectivity in Critical Social Theory: Horkheimer and Habermas' in Giancarlo Marchetti and Sarin Marchetti (eds), *Facts and Values: The Ethics and Metaphysics of Normativity* (New York, Routledge, 2018).

Costa J-P, 'Introductory Remarks' in European Court of Human Rights (ed), *Dialogue Between Judges: What Are the Limits to the Evolutive Interpretation of the Convention?* (Strasbourg, Council of Europe Publishing, 2011).

—— 'On the Legitimacy of the European Court of Human Rights' Judgments' (2011) 7(2) *European Constitutional Law Review* 173.

Cottier T and Hertig M, 'The Prospects of 21st Century Constitutionalism' in Armin von Bogdandy and Rüdiger Wolfrum (eds), *Max Planck Yearbook of United Nations Law* (Vol 7, Leiden, Brill, 2003).

Council of Europe, *Manual on Human Rights and the Environment* (Strasbourg, Council of Europe Publishing, 2012).

Crawford J, 'Sovereignty as a Legal Value' in James Crawford, Martti Koskenniemi and Surabi Ranganathan (eds), *The Cambridge Companion to International Law* (Cambridge, Cambridge University Press, 2015).

Crema L, 'Disappearance and New Sightings of Restrictive Interpretation(s)' (2010) 21(3) *European Journal of International Law* 681.

Desgagné R, 'Integrating Environmental Values into the European Convention on Human Rights' (1995) 89(2) *American Journal of International Law* 263.

Djeffal C, 'Dynamic and Evolutive Interpretation of the ECHR by Domestic Courts? An Inquiry into the Judicial Architecture of Europe' in Helmut P Aust and Georg Nolte (eds), *The Interpretation of International Law by Domestic Courts: Uniformity, Diversity, Convergence* (Oxford, Oxford University Press, 2016).

—— *Static and Evolutive Treaty Interpretation: A Functional Reconstruction* (Cambridge, Cambridge University Press, 2016).

Donald A and Leach P, *Parliaments and the European Court of Human Rights* (Oxford, Oxford University Press, 2016).

Dörr O, 'Interpretation of Treaties' in Oliver Dörr and Kirsten Schmalenbach (eds), *Vienna Convention on the Law of Treaties: A Commentary* (Berlin, Springer, 2012).

Dworkin R, *Taking Rights Seriously* (Cambridge, MA, Harvard University Press, 1978).

—— *Law's Empire* (Cambridge, MA, Belknap Press of Harvard University Press, 1986).

—— *Freedom's Law: The Moral Reading of the American Constitution* (Cambridge, MA, Harvard University Press, 1996).

Dzehtsiarou K, 'European Consensus and the Evolutive Interpretation of the European Convention on Human Rights' (2011) 12(10) *German Law Journal* 1730.

—— *European Consensus and the Legitimacy of the European Court of Human Rights* (Cambridge, Cambridge University Press, 2015).

Eleftheriadis P, 'Constitutional Change through Deliberation' in Ron Levy (ed), *The Cambridge Handbook of Deliberative Constitutionalism* (Cambridge, Cambridge University Press, 2018).

Elias TO, 'The Doctrine of Intertemporal Law' (1980) 74(2) *American Journal of International Law* 285.

Ely JH, *Democracy and Distrust: A Theory of Judicial Review* (Cambridge, MA, Harvard University Press, 1981).

European Court of Human Rights, *Factsheet – End of Life and the ECHR* (Strasbourg, Press Unit of the European Court of Human Rights, 2019).

Finnis J, 'Judicial Law-Making and the "Living" Instrumentalisation of the ECHR' in NW Barber, Richard Ekins and Paul Yowell (eds), *Lord Sumption and the Limits of the Law* (Oxford, Hart Publishing, 2016).

Fitzmaurice M, 'Dynamic (Evolutive) Interpretation of Treaties' (2009) 22 *Hague Yearbook on International Law* 3.

—— 'Interpretation of Human Rights Treaties' in Dinah Shelton (ed), *The Oxford Handbook of International Human Rights Law* (Oxford, Oxford University Press, 2013).

Føllesdal A, 'The Legitimacy of International Human Rights Review: The Case of the European Court of Human Rights' (2009) 40(4) *Journal of Social Philosophy* 595.

—— 'Tracking Justice Democratically' (2017) 31(3) *Social Epistemology* 324.

Føllesdal A, Peters B and Ulfstein G (eds), *Constituting Europe: The European Court of Human Rights in a National, European, and Global Context* (Cambridge, Cambridge University Press, 2013).

Ford CA, 'Judicial Discretion in International Jurisprudence: Article 38(1)(C) and "General Principles of Law"' (1994) 5 *Duke Journal of Comparative and International Law* 35.

Forst R, *The Right to Justification: Elements of a Constructivist Theory of Justice* (Jeffrey Flynn trans, New York, Columbia University Press, 2012).

Fredman S, 'Living Trees or Deadwood: The Interpretive Challenge of the European Convention on Human Rights' in NW Barber, Richard Ekins and Paul Yowell (eds), *Lord Sumption and the Limits of the Law* (Oxford, Hart Publishing, 2016).

Friedman B, 'Dialogue and Judicial Review' (1993) 91(4) *Michigan Law Review* 577.

Frowein JA, 'The European Convention on Human Rights as the Public Order of Europe' in Andrew Clapham (ed), *Collected Courses of the Academy of European Law: The Protection of Human Rights in Europe* (vol 2, Dordrecht, Martinus Nijhoff Publishers, 1991).

Gardbaum S, 'Human Rights and International Constitutionalism' in Jeffrey L Dunoff and Joel P Trachtman (eds), *Ruling the World? Constitutionalism, International Law, and Global Governance* (Cambridge, Cambridge University Press, 2009).

Gardiner RK, *Treaty Interpretation* (Oxford, Oxford University Press, 2010).
—— 'The Vienna Convention Rules on Treaty Interpretation' in Duncan B Hollis (ed), *The Oxford Guide to Treaties* (Oxford, Oxford University Press, 2014).
Gearty CA, 'The European Court of Human Rights and the Protection of Civil Liberties: An Overview' (1993) 52(1) *Cambridge Law Journal* 89.
Gerards J, 'How to Improve the Necessity Test of the European Court of Human Rights' (2013) 11(2) *International Journal of Constitutional Law* 466.
Gerards JH, *General Principles of the European Convention on Human Rights* (Cambridge, Cambridge University Press, 2019).
Glenn HP, *The Cosmopolitan State* (Oxford, Oxford University Press, 2013).
Greenawalt K, *Interpreting the Constitution* (New York, Oxford University Press, 2015).
Greenberg MD and Litman H, 'The Meaning of Original Meaning' (1998) 86 *Georgia Law Journal* 568.
Greer S, '"Balancing" and the European Court of Human Rights: A Contribution to the Habermas-Alexy Debate' (2004) 63(2) *Cambridge Law Journal* 412.
—— *The European Convention on Human Rights: Achievements, Problems and Prospects* (Cambridge, Cambridge University Press, 2008).
—— 'The Interpretation of the European Convention on Human Rights: Universal Principle or Margin of Appreciation' (2010) *UCL Human Rights Review* 1.
Grimm D, 'Constitutional Adjudication and Democracy' in Mads T Andenæs (ed), *Judicial Review in International Perspective* (Vol 2, The Hague, Kluwer Law International, 2000).
—— *Constitutionalism: Past, Present, and Future* (Oxford, Oxford University Press, 2016).
Gutmann A and Scalia A (eds), *A Matter of Interpretation: Federal Courts and the Law* (Princeton, NJ, Princeton University Press, 1997).
Häberle P, 'Zeit und Verfassung' in Ralf Dreier (ed), *Probleme der Verfassungsinterpretation: Dokumentation einer Kontroverse* (Baden-Baden, Nomos, 1976).
Habermas J, *Communication and the Evolution of Society* (Boston, MA, Beacon Press, 1979).
—— *Between Facts and Norms: Contributions to a Discourse Theory of Law and Democracy* (Cambridge, MA, MIT Press, 1996).
Held D, 'Principles of Cosmopolitan Order' in Gillian Brock and Harry Brighouse (eds), *The Political Philosophy of Cosmopolitanism* (Cambridge, Cambridge University Press, 2005).
Helfer L and Slaughter A-M, 'Toward a Theory of Effective Supranational Adjudication' (1997) 107(2) *Yale Law Journal* 273.
Helgesen JE, 'Address' in European Court of Human Rights (ed), *Dialogue Between Judges: What Are the Limits to the Evolutive Interpretation of the Convention?* (Strasbourg, Council of Europe Publishing, 2011).
Hendriks AC, 'End-of-life Decisions. Recent Jurisprudence of the European Court of Human Rights' (2019) 19(4) *ERA Forum* 561.
Hübner Mendes C, *Constitutional Courts and Deliberative Democracy* (Oxford, Oxford University Press, 2013).
Jackson VC, 'Comparative Constitutional Law: Methodologies' in Michel Rosenfeld (ed), *The Oxford Handbook of Comparative Constitutional Law* (Oxford, Oxford University Press, 2012).
Jagland T, 'Deep Security: Building a European Community of Values' (2011) 33(1) *Harvard International Review* 12.
Kavanagh A, 'The Idea of a "Living Constitution"' (2003) 16(1) *Canadian Journal of Law and Jurisprudence* 55.
—— 'Strasbourg, The House of Lords or Elected Politicians: Who Decides About Rights After Re P?' (2009) 72(5) *Modern Law Review* 815.
—— 'What's So Weak About "Weak-form Review"? The Case of the UK Human Rights Act 1998' (2015) 13(4) *International Journal of Constitutional Law* 1008.
Keller H and Stone Sweet A (eds), *A Europe of Rights: The Impact of the ECHR on National Legal Systems* (Oxford, Oxford University Press, 2008).

—— 'Assessing the Impact of the ECHR on National Legal Systems' in Helen Keller and Alec Stone Sweet (eds), *A Europe of Rights: The Impact of the ECHR on National Legal Systems* (Oxford, Oxford University Press, 2008).

Kelsen H, *Pure Theory of Law* (trans Max Knight, Berkeley, CA, University of California Press, 2005 (repr)).

King J, 'Three Wrong Turns in Lord Sumption's Conception of Law and Democracy' in NW Barber, Richard Ekins and Paul Yowell (eds), *Lord Sumption and the Limits of the Law* (Oxford, Hart Publishing, 2016).

Klabbers J, 'Treaties, Object and Purpose' in Oxford Public International Law (ed), *Max Planck Encyclopedia of Public International Law* (Oxford, Oxford University Press, 2008).

Klatt M, 'Robert Alexy's Philosophy of Law as System' in Matthias Klatt (ed), *Institutionalized Reason: The Jurisprudence of Robert Alexy* (Oxford, Oxford University Press, 2012).

—— *Die praktische Konkordanz von Kompetenzen: Entwickelt anhand der Jurisdiktionskonflikte im europäischen Grundrechtsschutz* (Tübingen, Mohr Siebeck, 2014).

—— 'Balancing Competences: How Institutional Cosmopolitanism Can Manage Jurisdictional Conflicts' (2015) 4(2) *Global Constitutionalism* 195.

—— 'The Rule of Dual-Natured Law' in Eveline T Feteris, Harm Kloosterhuis, Jose Plug and Carel Smith (eds), *Legal Argumentation and the Rule of Law* (The Hague, Eleven International Publishing, 2016).

Klatt M and Schmidt J, *Spielräume im öffentlichen Recht: Zur Abwägungslehre der Prinzipientheorie* (Tübingen, Mohr Siebeck, 2010).

—— and —— 'Epistemic Discretion in Constitutional Law' (2012) 10(1) *International Journal of Constitutional Law* 69.

Kleinlein T, *Konstitutionalisierung im Völkerrecht: Konstruktion und Elemente einer idealistischen Völkerrechtslehre* (Heidelberg, Springer, 2012).

Koskenniemi M, *From Apology to Utopia: The Structure of International Legal Argument* (New York, Cambridge University Press, 2009).

Krstić I and Čučković B, 'Procedural Aspects of Article 8 of the ECHR in Environmental Cases – The Greening of Human Rights Law' (2015) LXIII(3) *Belgrade Law Review* 170.

Kumm M, 'Democracy Is Not Enough: Rights, Proportionality and the Point of Judicial Review' (2009) NYU Public Law Research Paper.

—— 'The Cosmopolitan Turn in Constitutionalism: On the Relationship Between Constitutionalism in and Beyond the State' in Jeffrey L Dunoff and Joel P Trachtman (eds), *Ruling the World? Constitutionalism, International Law, and Global Governance* (Cambridge, Cambridge University Press, 2009).

—— 'Rethinking Constitutional Authority: On the Structure and Limits of Constitutional Pluralism' in Matej Avbelj and Jan Komárek (eds), *Constitutional Pluralism in the European Union and Beyond* (Oxford, Hart Publishing, 2012).

Lafont C, 'Philosophical Foundations of Judicial Review' in David Dyzenhaus and M Thorburn (eds), *Philosophical Foundations of Constitutional Law* (Oxford, Oxford University Press, 2016).

Lautenbach G, *The Concept of the Rule of Law and the European Court of Human Rights* (Oxford, Oxford University Press, 2013).

Lester A, 'The European Court of Human Rights After 50 Years' in Jonas Christoffersen and Mikael R Madsen (eds), *The European Court of Human Rights Between Law and Politics* (Oxford, Oxford University Press, 2011).

Letsas G, *A Theory of Interpretation of the European Convention on Human Rights* (Oxford, Oxford University Press, 2009).

—— 'Intentionalism and the Interpretation of the ECHR' in Malgosia Fitzmaurice and OA Elias (eds), *Treaty Interpretation and the Vienna Convention on the Law of Treaties: 30 Years On* (Leiden, Martinus Nijhoff, 2010).

—— 'Strasbourg's Interpretive Ethic: Lessons for the International Lawyer' (2010) 21(3) *European Journal of International Law* 509.

—— 'The ECHR as a Living Instrument: Its Meaning and Legitimacy' in Andreas Føllesdal, Birgit Peters and Geir Ulfstein (eds), *Constituting Europe: The European Court of Human Rights in a national, European, and global context* (Cambridge, Cambridge University Press, 2013).

Linderfalk U, *On the Interpretation of Treaties: The Modern International Law as Expressed in the 1969 Vienna Convention on the Law of Treaties* (Dordrecht, Springer, 2010).

Lord Sumption, 'The Limits of Law' in NW Barber, Richard Ekins and Paul Yowell (eds), *Lord Sumption and the Limits of the Law* (Oxford, Hart Publishing, 2016).

Loughlin M, 'What Is Constitutionalisation?' in Petra Dobner and Martin Loughlin (eds), *The Twilight of Constitutionalism?* (Oxford, Oxford University Press, 2010).

Mac Amhlaigh C, 'Harmonising Global Constitutionalism' (2016) 5(2) *Global Constitutionalism* 173.

MacCormick N, 'Rights in Legislation' in Peter MS Hacker (ed), *Law, Morality, and Society: Essays in Honour of H. L. A. Hart* (Oxford, Clarendon Press, 1977).

MacCormick N and Summers RS, 'Interpretation and Justification' in Neil MacCormick (ed), *Interpreting Statutes: A Comparative Study* (London, Taylor and Francis, 1991).

Madsen MR, 'The Protracted Institutionalization of the Strasbourg Court: From Legal Diplomacy to Integrationalist Jurisprudence' in Jonas Christoffersen and Mikael R Madsen (eds), *The European Court of Human Rights Between Law and Politics* (Oxford, Oxford University Press, 2011).

Mahoney P, 'Judicial Activism and Judicial Self-restraint' (1990) 11(1–2) *Human Rights Law Journal* 57.

Marmor A, *Positive Law and Objective Values* (Oxford, Clarendon Press, 2001).

Mennicken A, *Das Ziel der Gesetzesauslegung: Eine Untersuchung zur subjektiven und objektiven Auslegungstheorie* (Bad Homburg, Verlag Gehlen, 1970).

Morrisson Jr CC, 'Restrictive Interpretation of Sovereignty-Limiting Treaties: The Practice of the European Human Rights Convention System' (1970) 19(3) *International and Comparative Law Quarterly* 361.

Mowbray A, 'The Creativity of the European Court of Human Rights' (2005) 5(1) *Human Rights Law Review* 57.

Oddný Mjöll Arnardóttir and Buyse AC (eds), *Shifting Centres of Gravity in Human Rights Protection: Rethinking Relations Between the ECHR, EU and National Legal Orders* (London, Routledge, 2016).

Peters A, 'Rechtsordnungen und Konstitutionalisierung: Zur Neubestimmung der Verhältnisse' (2010) 65(1) *Zeitschrift für öffentliches Recht* 3.

Post R, 'Theories of Constitutional Interpretation' (1990) 30 *Representations* 13.

Prebensen SC, 'Evolutive Interpretation of the ECHR' in Paul Mahoney, Franz Matscher, Herbert Petzold and Luzius Wildhaber (eds), *Protecting Human Rights: The European Perspective* (Cologne, Heymanns, 2000).

Rainey B, Wicks E and Ovey C, *Jacobs, White and Ovey: The European Convention on Human Rights* (7th edn, Oxford, Oxford University Press, 2017).

Raz J, *Between Authority and Interpretation: On the Theory of Law and Practical Reason* (Oxford, Oxford University Press, 2009).

—— 'Human Rights in the Emerging World Order' (2010) 1(1) *Transnational Legal Theory* 31.

—— *The Morality of Freedom* (Oxford, Clarendon Press, 2010).

Reinhold S, 'Good Faith in International Law' (2013) 2(1) *UCL Journal of Law and Jurisprudence* 40.

Robertson AH, *The Council of Europe: Its Structure, Functions and Achievements* (London, Stevens & Sons, 1961).

Rosenfeld M, 'Introduction' in Michel Rosenfeld (ed), *Constitutionalism, Identity, Difference, and Legitimacy: Theoretical Perspectives* (Durham, NC, Duke University Press, 1994).

Royer A, *The Council of Europe* (Strasbourg, Council of Europe Publishing, 2010).

Sadurski W, *Rights Before Courts: A Study of Constitutional Courts in Postcommunist States of Central and Eastern Europe* (Dordrecht, Springer, 2008).

Scalia A, 'Common-Law Courts in a Civil-Law System: The Role of United States Federal Courts in Interpreting the Constitution and Laws' in Amy Gutmann and Antonin Scalia (eds), *A Matter of Interpretation: Federal Courts and the Law* (Princeton, NJ, Princeton University Press, 1997).

Senden H, *Interpretation of Fundamental Rights in a Multilevel Legal System: An Analysis of the European Court of Human Rights and the Court of Justice of the European Union* (Cambridge, Intersentia, 2011).

Simpson AWB, 'Hersch Lauterpacht and the Genesis of the Age of Human Rights' (2004) 120 *Law Quarterly Review* 49.

Smilov D, 'The Judiciary: The Least Dangerous Branch?' in Michel Rosenfeld (ed), *The Oxford Handbook of Comparative Constitutional Law* (Oxford, Oxford University Press, 2012).

Sonnleitner L, 'The Democratic Legitimacy of Evolutive Interpretation by the European Court of Human Rights' (2019) 33(2) *Temple International & Comparative Law Journal* 279.

Stone Sweet A, 'A Cosmopolitan Legal Order: Constitutional Pluralism and Rights Adjudication in Europe' (2012) 1(1) *Global Constitutionalism* 53.

Stone Sweet A and Keller H, 'The Reception of the ECHR in National Legal Orders' in Helen Keller and Alec Stone Sweet (eds), *A Europe of Rights: The Impact of the ECHR on National Legal Systems* (Oxford, Oxford University Press, 2008).

Stone Sweet A and Mathews J, 'Proportionality, Judicial Review, and Global Constitutionalism' in Giorgio Bongiovanni, Giovanni Sartor and Chiara Valentini (eds), *Reasonableness and Law* (Dordrecht, Springer, 2009).

Stone Sweet A and Shapiro MM, 'Abstract and Concrete Review in the United States' in Martin M Shapiro and Alec Stone Sweet (eds), *On Law, Politics, and Judicialization* (Oxford, Oxford University Press, 2002).

Strauss DA, *The Living Constitution* (Oxford, Oxford University Press, 2010).

Tamanaha BZ, *On the Rule of Law: History, Politics, Theory* (Cambridge, Cambridge University Press, 2010).

Troper M, 'Sovereignty' in Michel Rosenfeld (ed), *The Oxford Handbook of Comparative Constitutional Law* (Oxford, Oxford University Press, 2012).

Tsagourias N, 'Introduction – Constitutionalism: A Theoretical Roadmap' in Nicholas Tsagourias (ed), *Transnational Constitutionalism* (Cambridge, Cambridge University Press, 2007).

Tulkens F, 'Address' in European Court of Human Rights (ed), *Dialogue Between Judges: What Are the Limits to the Evolutive Interpretation of the Convention?* (Strasbourg, Council of Europe Publishing, 2011).

Tushnet M, 'The Possibilities of Comparative Constitutional Law' (1999) 108(6) *Yale Law Journal* 1225.

—— *Advanced Introduction to Comparative Constitutional Law* (Cheltenham, Edward Elgar Publishing, 2014).

Uerpmann R, 'Internationales Verfassungsrecht' (2001) 56(11) *JuristenZeitung* 565.

van der Schyff G, 'The Concept of Democracy as an Element of the European Convention' (2005) 38(3) *Comparative and International Law Journal of Southern Africa* 355.

van der Vyver, Johan D, 'Sovereignty' in Dinah Shelton (ed), *The Oxford Handbook of International Human Rights Law* (Oxford, Oxford University Press, 2013).

Verdross A, *Statisches und dynamisches Naturrecht* (Freiburg im Breisgau, Rombach, 1971).

Waldock H, 'The European Convention for the Protection of Human Rights and Fundamental Freedoms' in Humphrey Waldock (ed), *The British Yearbook of International Law* (vol 34, London, Oxford University Press, 1958).

—— 'The Evolution of Human Rights Concepts and the Application of the European Convention of Human Rights' in Paul Reuter (ed), *Mélanges offerts à Paul Reuter: le droit international: unité et diversité* (Paris, Pedone, 1981).

Waibel M, 'Principles of Treaty Interpretation: Developed for and Applied by National Courts?' in Helmut P Aust and Georg Nolte (eds), *The Interpretation of International Law by Domestic Courts: Uniformity, Diversity, Convergence* (Oxford, Oxford University Press, 2016).

Waldron J, 'A Right-Based Critique of Constitutional Rights' (1993) 13(1) *Oxford Journal of Legal Studies* 18.
—— 'Judicial Review and the Conditions of Democracy' (1998) 6(4) *Journal of Political Philosophy* 335.
—— *Law and Disagreement* (Oxford, Clarendon Press, 2004).
—— 'The Core of the Case against Judicial Review' (2006) 115(6) *Yale Law Journal* 1346.
Walker N, 'The EU and the WTO: Constitutionalism in a New Key' in Gráinne de Búrca and Joanne Scott (eds), *The EU and the WTO: Legal and Constitutional Issues* (Oxford, Hart Publishing, 2003).
Walter C, 'Die Europäische Menschenrechtskonvention als Konstitutionalisierungsprozeß' (1999) 59 *Zeitschrift für ausländisches öffentliches Recht und Völkerrecht* 961.
Weber M, *Wirtschaft und Gesellschaft: Grundriss der verstehenden Soziologie* (5th edn, Tübingen, Mohr-Siebeck, 2009).
White RCA and Ovey C, *Jacobs, White, and Ovey: The European Convention on Human Rights* (5th edn, Oxford, Oxford University Press, 2010).
Wildhaber L, 'Rethinking the European Court of Human Rights' in Jonas Christoffersen and Mikael R Madsen (eds), *The European Court of Human Rights Between Law and Politics* (Oxford, Oxford University Press, 2011).
Wróblewski J, 'Statutory Interpretation in Poland' in Neil MacCormick (ed), *Interpreting Statutes: A Comparative Study* (London, Taylor and Francis, 1991).
—— *Judicial Application of Law* (Dordrecht, Springer, 1992).
Wróblewski J and MacCormick N, 'On Justification and Interpretation' (1994) 53 *ARSP Beiheft* 255.

Index

Lightning Source UK Ltd.
Milton Keynes UK
UKHW020255090422
401309UK00003BA/110

9 781509 946877